ORGANIC GARDENING NOT JUST IN THE NORTHEAST

A HANDS-ON MONTH-BY-MONTH GUIDE

HENRY HOMEYER

BLOCK PRINTS BY JOSH YUNGER

www.bunkerhillpublishing.com
First published in 2011
by Bunker Hill Publishing Inc.
285 River Road, Piermont
New Hampshire 03779, USA

10 9 8 7 6 5 4 3 2 1

Library of Congress Control Number: 2010942805

ISBN 10: 1-59373-090-X
ISBN 13: 978-1-59373-090-1

Published in the United States by Bunker Hill Publishing
Designed by Peter Holm, Sterling Hill Productions
Printed in Canada

IN MEMORIAM

Ruth Anne Homeyer Mitchell
September 9, 1943–July 6, 2009

*Together we discovered daffodils when
I was in kindergarten . . . And you taught
me how to pet bumblebees.*

CONTENTS

PREFACE

For me, gardening is magical. Plant a seed, a bulb, or a rooted twig, and before long you have a tomato, a daffodil, or an apple tree. I started gardening as a toddler more than sixty years ago, and I haven't outgrown the excitement at seeing a leaf emerge from the soil or a flower burst into bloom. Tasting a Sun Gold tomato fresh off the vine or digging a potato gives me great joy. I'd like to share with you what I've learned over the years growing vegetables, flowers, shrubs, and trees in my gardens in Cornish Flat, New Hampshire.

Organic Gardening (Not Just) in the Northeast: A Hands-On, Month-by-Month Guide describes how to start a garden, plant a seed, mulch, pull weeds, and water during a dry spell—that's the same everywhere. Cornish Flat is rated as a USDA Zone 4 area, with temperatures falling to minus 25 or 30 each winter. So when I say that I don't plant my tomatoes outside until early June, you'll need to adjust the date if you live, for example, in Massapequa Park on Long Island, where the last frost is a month earlier. But the bottom line is this: if I can grow something here, you can grow it where you are—unless you happen to live with Santa and Mrs. Claus.

This book was first conceived as a guide to organic gardening in the Northeast. But when my publisher received the manuscript he questioned me: Why only the Northeast? Why wouldn't this work in Nebraska, say, or Maryland? So we changed the title to include the words, "Not Just" before the Northeast. Unless you live in the deep south or west of the Rockies, this book is for you. Just start your plants earlier if you live in warmer parts, and count on picking tomatoes later into the fall. When it comes to timing, your best resource is your neighbor who has gardened the same plot next door for forty years, or the state university extension service. But most of what you read here will apply almost anywhere.

You will encounter the practical—how to grow foot-long carrots—and the less practical—how to grow rice in a five-gallon pail or build a stone igloo as garden art. Organic methods are emphasized throughout the book, from soil improvement to bug control. There is something for everyone, from novice to expert.

This collection of writings is organized by the month. It starts with March, when I start my seedlings indoors. I've included pieces from my weekly newspaper column, from my Vermont Public Radio commentaries, and from the sadly now-defunct *People, Places & Plants* magazine, for which I was the Vermont/New Hampshire editor for ten years. Also included are pieces I wrote for *The New York Times,* a variety of magazines, and some all-new material.

My grandfather, John Lenat (1885–1967), was an organic gardener long before it was fashionable. Grampy grew vegetables for the table and flowers for their beauty, and enjoyed entering them in the competition at the county fair in Worcester, Massachusetts. I learned from him how to make manure tea, pick bugs, and build a compost pile when others were spreading chemical fertilizers and using DDT to kill pests. I grew up with *Organic Gardening* magazine on the kitchen table and just-picked corn and tomatoes as my summer staples. I now grow much of my own food and have learned how to store it for use all year. The winters here are long and cold, but I find something garden-related to do outside nearly every day of the year—which is lucky, as I write a weekly column for newspapers around New England, all year round. I grow hundreds of species of flowers and have a few cut flowers on my table every day from the early snowdrops of March to the fall crocus of November. Sometimes I even cut fresh flowers during the January thaw, such as those cheerful Johnny-jump-ups. And like Grampy, I do bring home a few ribbons from my county fair each year.

This book is based on a lifetime of gardening. As you read how to grow ladyslipper orchids or artichokes, know that I am writing from my own experiences—both the successes and failures. I decided that I would only make minor changes or corrections to my original articles, and add postscripts as needed, particularly for interviews I have done with interesting gardeners.

In addition to working in my own gardens, I also work with my friend and companion, Cindy Heath, to design and install gardens for others in the summer. This allows me to experience different soils, weeds, microclimates, and bugs; I have traveled extensively throughout the United States, interviewing farmers and gardeners, asking questions everywhere I have gone.

I grow organic vegetables for many reasons. I love the flavor of fresh vegetables and I want to eat food that I know is safe to eat. I am a serious cook, a "foodie," and a founding member of our local Slow Food International group. I believe that growing, eating, and cooking with my own food is important. It connects me to the earth, and nourishes my soul as much as my body. I've learned some tricks on how to save the harvest with the least amount of labor, and I'll share them here with you—along with a few recipes.

I've dedicated this book to my sister and soul mate, Ruth Anne Homeyer Mitchell, who had a series of strokes and passed away July 6, 2009, at the age of sixty-five. Ruth Anne was a fabulous gardener, garden designer, and human being. As kids, we picked flowers, ate berries, and spent a lot of our time outdoors and in the garden. She taught me to pet bumblebees without getting stung. As adults we hiked and gardened, shared fabulous meals, and told outrageous stories. I miss her every day.

I'd like to thank Cindy Heath for reading this book in draft and making many good suggestions and corrections. Cindy's fresh set of eyes helped me to polish it. And many thanks to Doris LeVarn, who tracked every comma and semicolon, and put to good use her knowledge of plants and their Latin names. Any mistakes or omissions are mine alone.

Writing a book like this is a bit like gardening: I've written more than five hundred articles about gardening in the past ten years, and I've had to decide which to weed out and which to keep. I'd like to thank the readers of my weekly gardening column for letting me know the titles of the articles they wanted to see here. If your favorite is not here, you might be able be able to find it in the archives section of my Web site, www.Gardening-Guy.com.

I've had many different careers, from school teacher to Peace Corps volunteer and Peace Corps Country Director, to licensed electrical contractor and garden designer. I now make my living writing about gardening and travel, but I have always thought of myself as a "gardening guy." Gardening has been a constant in my life. I believe that gardening is one of the best ways to spend an hour or an afternoon—or a lifetime. I have practical, hands-on knowledge that I'd like to share with you.

So join me. Dig in.

MARCH

Starting Plants from Seed

As an organic gardener and an avid grower of heirloom vegetables, I like starting most of my own seedlings for many reasons. First, I don't want to buy plants that have been surviving on liquid chemical fertilizers all their lives. Also, I can't find all the oddball varieties I want at my local gardening center. I can, however, get them from a good seed catalog or save my own seed. I've never seen Boxcar Willie or Oxheart tomato seedlings for sale at the garden center, but like to grow them—so I start them from seed.

Most garden centers and farm stands sell perfectly nice seedlings. While they are being raised, they are given adequate light and fertilizer, and are sold to you free of insect pests. But many modern hybrids have been developed to do well in situations where they will be given a steady diet of fertilizer—chemical fertilizer, that is. And I don't provide my seedlings with chemical fertilizers. I believe that plants do best when they are not force-fed like those French geese that are raised for pâté de fois gras.

My grandfather taught me not only how to grow tomatoes, he taught me to love a ripe, red tomato picked and eaten the same day. The modern hybrids travel well, have great shelf life, and have all the qualifications needed for success in a modern world—except for that juicy, run-down-your cheek flavor I crave. So I grow many varieties of heirloom tomatoes each year.

If you want to grow your own seedlings, here are a few hints:

1. You will need lots of light. A four-foot, two-tube fluorescent fixture hanging six inches over your seedlings will make the difference between pale, leggy seedlings and robust, vigorous ones.

2. Temperature matters. Keep the room at 60 to 65 degrees during the day and cooler at night. Hot temperatures (over 70) will make plants grow too fast.

3. Don't start too early. Six to eight weeks before the last frost date is good for tomatoes, twelve weeks for peppers and artichokes. You don't need big plants, you need healthy plants. Onions? Sure, start them in March. Leeks, too.

4. Use the biggest plastic six-packs you can find for starting seeds, or make your own soil blocks (see page 225). This will help prevent your plants from getting root-bound.

5. Potting soil has little nourishment for seedlings. Instead of chemical fertilizers, use a diluted organic fertilizer such as a solution of fish and seaweed. There are several good ones that provide the full range of nutrients, not just the nitrogen-phosphorus-potassium (N-P-K) found in chemical fertilizers.

6. Some flowers germinate better if started on top of heat mats. Others, such as larkspur for exam-

ple, only germinate in cold soil. Buy seeds from a catalog that tells you what to do for success, and reread it before you plant.

7. Run your hands over your seedlings each day or two. That will mimic the wind outside, which bends them, stimulating them to develop good strong stalks. And it will feel good to you, too.

It's true that a diet of chemical fertilizers can make seedlings grow fast. But it has also been shown that insects prefer to feed on plants that have been provided with chemical fertilizers, as opposed to those grown organically using manure and compost. Why? Dr. Larry Phelan of Ohio State University told me that insects can sense an imbalance of nitrogen and other ingredients in their tissues, which is common among chemically fed plants. Excess nitrogen (in the form of amino acids) attracts insects the way blood attracts sharks. Nitrogen is one of the key building blocks of protein, so they crave it. Plants have been grown by Mother Nature since before dogs had tails, and she knows how to do it right—naturally. She didn't use chemicals to grow food for those dinosaurs, after all.

If you haven't started seedlings in past years, don't go overboard this year. Try just a few, and accept that while starting seedlings is not rocket science, it does take practice. Me? I've been doing it for decades, and still encounter a few problems some years. But all the extra work is worthwhile when I bite into my first homegrown, organic, heirloom tomato of the season.

Now Is the Time to Start Artichokes, Onions, and Peppers

I'm sick of winter. I love snow and cold and cross-country skiing, but I need sunshine, too, and we've had precious little of it. Starting a few seeds will help me survive the late winter blues.

It's too early for most things, but not for artichokes, onions, and peppers.

Artichokes are wonderful to grow, even if you don't end up with softball-size edibles—and you probably won't. My biggest artichokes have been tennis ball-size. I usually get one good-size artichoke and several smaller ones on side-shoots from each plant. Their gray-green leaves are long and handsome, growing upward from a central point. In warm climates artichokes are perennials. On the island of Iona, in the Inner Hebrides of Scotland, I saw artichokes grown for their flowers. The part we would eat was allowed to continue to develop into gorgeous, purple, thistlelike flowers.

There are two schools of thought about how to grow artichokes. I am of the school that believes they need to be tricked into thinking that they are in their second year of growth during the first year. That makes them produce artichokes sooner in the summer, and more reliably. But I know one grower who just starts them early in February and does well anyway, so who knows?

Here is how I trick my (not so very smart) artichokes: First, I start seeds in late February or early March. When they have true leaves that are three inches long, I transplant them into four-inch pots. Then, a couple of weeks later, I move them to a cold space for two weeks to make them think they've gone through a winter. They must be kept cooler than 50 degrees, but above freezing. I do this in a cold basement under lights, but a garage might work, too. Then I move them back upstairs where the temperature stays in the sixties, but drops down a bit at night (which is good). I plant them outdoors after June 1. I give them a generous dose of organic fertilizer, plenty of compost, and keep their soil moist all summer. I'm careful to pick my artichokes before the flowers start to open, or they'll be tough.

Onions can be grown from seed, sets, or from purchased seedlings. Starting from seed is best, but you need to get started early in the growing season if you're going to do this. Sets are those little bulbs that are for sale by the pound at garden centers each spring. They work, but I don't think they're as vigorous as those started from seedlings.

Onion seeds are tiny and hard to plant individually. I don't start them in plastic six-packs, but rather those plastic containers that are like the six-packs but that have no divisions. I plant onion seeds in a 50-50 mix of commercial potting soil and high-grade compost. I sprinkle seeds on the surface, water them, and then cover them with just a thin layer of potting soil that I put in a sieve or colander and shake over the surface. That gives a fine covering, but doesn't bury the seeds deeply. Sometimes I sprinkle agricultural vermiculite instead of potting soil on the surface, as it holds water well and is very finely textured.

Like most vegetables, onions need lots of light when grown indoors. I set up four-foot, two-tube fluorescent fixtures over them. I hang the fixtures from lightweight chain that I get at the hardware store, about six inches above the tips of the plants, and raise the lights as they grow. In order to get strong, stout onion plants I give them a haircut when they are about six inches tall, taking off a couple of inches. Then, every few weeks, I repeat the process. It's a good idea to water them once a week with a dilute solution of fish-and-seaweed fertilizer. For the less ambitious, onion plants are available in bunches of fifty from seed companies, ready to go in the ground.

Light frost is not a problem for onions, so I try to get mine outside and in the ground in four to six weeks before last frost, spaced four inches apart in rows a foot apart or more. Closer spacing will yield smaller onions. Good soil with lots of organic matter is best, so I work in lots of compost. Onions do not tolerate weeds, so you must keep them well weeded. Their root systems are shallow; be careful not to disturb them when weeding. It's important to keep onions well watered, too, if you want good production.

Peppers are notoriously slow growing, so I like to start them in early to mid-March. I use an electric heat mat to keep the soil warm—I want them to think they're in Arizona. Our climate really isn't great for peppers. They do best with minimal water and hot temperatures, so they are good candidates for growing in a greenhouse if you have one. Even a simple tunnel made of plastic pipe and plastic sheeting will help them along. My favorite is Hungarian Wax, a mildly spicy yellow pepper. For sweet peppers, Ace is probably the best.

Come April, I'll plant lots more seeds, but for now starting even a few plants will help my attitude.

Pruning Apple Trees

It's easy to take apples for granted. They're always available at the grocery store, even by the checkout of your local gas station. They're red, shiny, and sweet—every day of the year. But if you are trying to grow your own apples, your trees need some care about now. Many gardeners put off pruning the way children avoid cleaning their rooms. And their trees, like the rooms, just get messier with time, and tougher to deal with. It's time to prune.

If you haven't pruned in recent years, there's much work to do. And you should know that pruning this year won't increase production right away. Fruit load is determined by early June for the following year. But by pruning now, you can make your tree more vigorous and shape it so that it's more likely to produce good fruit in future years. Experts say that you can cut off 20 to 25 percent of the branches of a tree without doing it any harm.

First, stand back and take a good look at the tree. Your job will be to get rid of the clutter and to open up spaces so that light can reach all the leaves. And you should try to make your tree pleasing to the eye, as apple trees can be lovely sculpture if pruned well.

You will need a good tri-cut pruning saw with a pointed tip to get in tight places. A bow saw will not do. And sharp pruners, not dull things that you used on roots, or to cut fencing. Bypass pruners, good ones that work like scissors, are a worthy investment. You will need them every year, once you decide that pruning is actually fun.

It's important to know where to make your cuts. Don't cut flush to the trunk or larger branch, but leave intact the swollen area that bulges out where a branch begins. This is known as the branch collar and is the site where healing takes place. Don't remove it, but don't leave long stubs, either. A three-inch stub will have to rot away until it falls off at the branch collar, where bark will then grow over the wound. But that could take years, and meanwhile it's an avenue for disease or insects to enter the tree.

Begin with the easy stuff: Cut out all the deadwood. Dead branches have dry, flaky bark. If scratched with a fingernail, deadwood shows no layer of green beneath the surface. No decisions about how much to cut: All deadwood must go.

Next, take out any branch that is touching a neighbor. Branches that touch will rub each other raw in brisk breezes, and open up sites for infection. Remove the newcomer, or just leave the healthier of the two.

Continue pruning by removing branches that are headed toward the center of the tree, as they can only clutter it up, and have no future. Useful branches should be heading away from the tree, reaching out to get sunlight.

When two branches are growing parallel to each other, it is best to remove one. One will be shaded out, and is not likely to produce fruit. Pruning is not like amputating a person's limbs, so you need not agonize over which branch to cut. Just pick one, and do it.

Branches that shoot straight up—often called water sprouts—are not likely to bear fruit and can clutter up the interior of a tree. These pencillike sprouts on fruit trees are a stress response. In summer, photosynthesis stops when temperatures are too high; the stomata (the pores on the underneath side of leaves) shut down to minimize water loss. The interior of the tree, shaded by the outer canopy, stays cooler, and photosynthesis continues. Water sprouts grow to provide the tree with a way to continue producing food by photosynthesis in hot times.

You can remove most water sprouts now, but it's a good thing to leave a few. It will reduce the number of new sprouts that appear each summer, and these vertical branches can be trained. Bend a few to 45-degree angles, and tie them in place or attach a weight to bend them down. Remove the weights or strings by midsummer, and they will stay in place at the angle you set.

Fruit generally is produced on branches growing at about a 45-degree angle to the vertical. Short "fruit spurs" (twigs about two to three inches long) grow on these branches, blooming and producing fruit. But don't count on getting apples from every fruit spur—some, mysteriously, only produce leaves. And fruit is only produced on spurs that are two years old or older.

Apple scab, a fungal disease that makes apples small and deformed, with patches of brown leathery skin, can be greatly reduced by cleaning up around your apple trees early in the spring. The spores overwinter in last year's apples, either on the ground or on the tree. While you are pruning, remove any of last year's apples still on the tree, knocking them off with a bamboo pole if you can't easily reach them. Then rake up any around the tree and get rid of them, and any leaves, far from the tree.

To avoid spreading diseases from tree to tree, sterilize your pruners and saw after you finish working on each tree. Make up a one-quart spray bottle with a solution of 10 percent chlorine bleach, and spray your tools before starting work on another.

One more suggestion: Wear eye protection of some sort while pruning—even sunglasses will help to keep you from getting the proverbial poke in the eye with a sharp stick.

Gardeners often ask me what to spray on their apples trees, or how to fertilize them. I do neither. Pruning and cleaning up are all I do, and both promote healthier trees. The apples may not be perfect, but then again, neither am I. Meanwhile, it's time to get outside and give your trees a good tune-up.

Sharpening Pruners

Dull pruning tools are like dull kitchen knives: They'll do the job, but not very well. For years I've wanted to learn how to sharpen my shears, clippers, scissors, and pruners, but it's largely a lost art, and until recently I'd never met anyone who knew how to do it. I made do with what I had—or bought new ones. But then I met Sukie Kindwall, a self-described "tool nerd," who conducts sharpening workshops at trade shows and gardening conferences, and she agreed to give me a private class. I traveled to Conway, Massachusetts (population: 1,990 people and 550 dogs) to meet with her.

Kindwall works for OESCO, Inc. (www.oescoinc.com), formerly known as Orchard Equipment and Supply Company, a company that caters to groundskeeping professionals, but sells retail to anyone who craves good tools. Their showroom has every type of pruning saw, grafting knife, hedge clipper, pruner, and lopper one could want—and more.

I brought with me a selection of dull and, I'm ashamed to admit, somewhat rusty tools. The first thing Kindwall did was to clean off the rust and gunk that had accumulated on my pruners. She explained that WD-40 or kerosene would work, but she prefers something called Sap-X. She put some on, let it set for thirty seconds, then scrubbed the blades—first with coarse steel wool and then, after reapplying the solvent, with a green kitchen scrubbie. Hardened sap and rust disappeared, allowing the pruners to open and close more freely. Cleaning also removes gunk that would clog up the file.

Kindwall explained that most of us can get by with a couple of diamond-embedded files, one coarse, one fine. The best sharpeners for hardened steel tools are made using synthetic monocrystalline diamonds embedded in nickel; she recommends files embedded with diamonds such as those made by DMT. We used a coarse-surfaced, tapered file, $4\frac{1}{2}$ inches long, that folds up nicely in its blue plastic handle. Fine files are better for scissors and knives that are kept very sharp.

We wanted to restore the sharp bevel on the cutting edge of my bypass pruners. It is important to sharpen a bevel at the proper angle—the angle set when it was manufactured. To sharpen the bevel evenly and to follow the proper angle, start by taking a magic marker and coloring the bevel on the cutting edge of the blade. If you are doing the job correctly, your file strokes should remove the magic marker coloring evenly across the full width of the bevel as you work on it. If only a small portion of the blade turns shiny, you need to change the angle of your file slightly.

Grasp the pruner in your left hand (if you are right-handed), holding onto the handle that extends to the cutting blade. Steady it by bracing your wrist against your hip or by placing the pruner on the edge of a table. Working under a bright light helps, because it will help you to see the shiny edge that develops as you sharpen.

Start sharpening as near to the throat of the pruners (where the two handles join) as you can. Place the narrow tip of the file at the throat, and push the file away from you, sliding it down the length of the beveled edge. With practice you will be able to use the full length of the file as you run it down the blade.

You need to apply a little pressure as you sharpen, but not much. Sharpening will feel awkward at first, but gets easier as you do it. Watch the magic marker pattern on the bevel, trying to adjust the angle of your file so that the shiny, sharpened, portion includes the entire bevel.

Asked for a final bit of advice, Kindwall suggested sharpening off-season, or on a rainy day—a time when you're not in a hurry. Sharpening takes time, especially if you've waited until your tool is dull. You shouldn't rush. "But," she said, "you're not going to ruin your tool learning to sharpen it. You're going to get better at it. High-quality tools are not cheap, so why not learn to sharpen them?"

Hedge clippers and scissors have bevels on each blade, so require more work to sharpen than bypass pruners, but the same principles apply. Loppers are sharpened like pruners. Good pruners have replaceable blades, too, so if you've been cutting fencing or roots with your pruners and have badly nicked them, you can buy a new blade. A replacement blade for a pair of Felco pruners (which cost $40 or more new) only cost about $10. Changing a blade requires an adjustable wrench and a pair of pliers (or an adjustable wrench, and a screwdriver or Allen wrench), some common sense, and less than five minutes of work.

Daunted by the idea of sharpening? Look in the Yellow Pages under "Sharpening Services" and you should be able to find someone to do it for you—and maybe even show you how to do it yourself next time.

Starting a Garden from Scratch

During World War II, Americans started Victory Gardens, growing up to 40 percent of their fresh produce. After the war, Americans switched to supermarket food made possible by cheap fuel, an interstate highway system, and mechanized farming. We entered the age of industrial agriculture. Now statisticians say the average distance traveled by each food item we eat is 1,500 miles. It doesn't have to be so. We can grow better food that costs less if we grow it ourselves. And a sun-warmed tomato from your garden tastes better than one that traveled from California on a truck.

If you're not yet a gardener, here's what you should do: Start small. New gardeners often get discouraged because they start with a big plot, and the weeds get ahead of them. If you are willing to give up a piece of your lawn ten feet by twelve feet (roughly the size of the parking spot for your car), you can grow a significant amount of good food and put a dent in your grocery bill. And I have timed it: You can do so in fifteen minutes a day. You can grow food that is organic, food that is tasty, food that is healthy.

First, choose a spot that has full sun—which means six to eight hours of sun per day—and as far away from any trees as possible. Tree roots can compete with your plants for water and nutrients.

The first year of gardening will require the most investment—both in terms of the money you spend to get started, and the time spent preparing the plot. You will need some tools. At a minimum you will need a spade, a garden fork, a garden rake (the kind with short tines), a hand tool for weeding, and a watering can or hose. You will need to buy some compost and a bag of organic fertilizer. You will need to buy a few plants from your local farm stand or garden center, and some seeds. The second year you will just have to buy the plants, and perhaps a few more seeds, though most packets have more than enough for several years of small gardens, and most seeds last three years or more.

I recommend getting your soil tested by your state university extension service. A soil test will tell you what minerals your soil has, what minerals the soil needs, and the percentage of organic matter in the soil. You are striving for 4 to 8 percent organic matter for a vegetable garden—the higher, the better. Also get your soil tested for lead and heavy metals, especially if the plot is near a house built before 1978 that may have been painted with lead paint. You might have to move to a different site if the lead levels are too high, or use a raised bed and purchased soil.

The hard part of starting a new garden in the lawn is getting rid of the sod. No, you don't want to rent a rototiller to make it disappear. Chopping up the grass does not get rid of it. Even a scrap of root is enough to start a new grass plant. So you must dig it all out. Starting when the lawn dries out, you can slice through the sod with a shovel and cut it into one-foot squares. Pry out each square with a garden fork or weeding tool, shake off any topsoil attached to the roots, and save the sod for your compost pile.

I like a tidy garden, so when I make a garden in the lawn I want the edges parallel and the corners square. You can do this by using string, stakes, a measuring tape, and a carpenter's framing square. If the sides are equal (and the diagonals are, too), your garden is a nice rectangle.

You can build boxes to contain the soil and your plants, though that is an added investment in time and money. Gardeners Supply Company (www.gardeners.com or 802-660-3500) sells a variety of things for making those sorts of raised beds. Or you can just make a garden that consists of two mounded, raised beds of soil with a walkway down the middle.

To make mounded, raised beds, first loosen the soil. Use a garden fork, plunging it in and working it back and forth to loosen the soil. Then rake the soil into beds. Start by raking the soil away from the edges of the lawn, creating a six-inch perimeter around the edge of the garden. This will create a moat to keep the grass from creeping in. Then create a walkway up the middle of the garden, raking soil toward each of the two beds. Your two beds should be about thirty inches wide and six inches higher than the walkway.

Because lawns generally are on pretty crummy soil you will need to add compost. Lots of compost. I recommend buying a good grade of composted cow manure such as MOO DOO, which is made in Middlebury, Vermont. MOO DOO comes in thirty-quart bags, and you will need four to five bags of it for each of your two beds. If you buy another brand, check it out before you use it. It should smell good—like soil, not rotten eggs—and it should have no recognizable chunks of bark or other matter in it.

Dump it on top of the beds and mix it into the top few inches of soil. When you are done, you are almost ready to plant.

The last addition to the soil is some bagged organic fertilizer. Pro-Gro, made in Bradford, Vermont (by North Country Organics, www.norganics.com), is excellent, but any fertilizer marked "organic" is fine. Unlike chemical fertilizer, which only has nitrogen, phosphorus, and potassium, plus lots of filler, organic fertilizers are made from a variety of natural ingredients such as seaweed, oyster shells, compost, peanut hulls, and alfalfa meal. These ingredients provide the three basic minerals, plus a dozen more—the micronutrients. You will probably have to buy a twenty-five-pound bag, which is more than you need your first year, but you will need some every year at planting time. You're investing in your soil and your garden. Sprinkle about six cups of it on each bed and stir it into the top three inches with a hand tool. Organic fertilizer slowly releases its goodness over the course of the summer.

Mulching the garden is a big time saver. Put down six pages of newspapers covered with a layer of grass clippings, leaves, or straw. That will keep most weeds from bothering you. Do this in the walkways, too. Mulch helps conserve water, too. Mulch after your plants are up and a good-size, and leave a little space around them so that short rain showers can wet the soil easily.

In one of these little gardens I planted the following: Two tomato plants, some carrots and onions, two broccoli plants, three peppers, a teepee of pole beans, one zucchini, six Swiss chard plants, and a cucumber on a small trellis. We also got eight heads of lettuce early in the summer that grew around the tomatoes. For a start, for most things, it is easier to buy plants than to start seeds. Wait until frost is no longer a threat before planting.

So have at it. Start small, visit the garden daily. Pull a weed, water when the soil is dry, and pick your beans and zucchini before they get too big! It's as easy as that. And if you prefer to grow flowers, you can. It's your garden, and you can plant whatever you want.

Listening to the Garden Spirits

If you stop to think about it, planting a seed and getting a flower or a vegetable really is magical. Hidden inside each seed is all the information needed to create a plant—something beautiful, useful, or both. Being a gardener means working with life forces that we can't fully understand.

A book that challenged my thinking is *The Findhorn Garden: Pioneering a New Vision of Humanity and Nature in Cooperation* by The Findhorn Community (Findhorn Press, 1975). I already knew a little about Findhorn, as I had visited a garden that was run on the principles of the Findhorn gardens when working on an organic croft on Mull, in the Hebrides of Scotland.

A key tenet of the Findhorn Gardens is that there are spirits connected with a higher being that affect how our gardens grow. The founders of the original Findhorn garden in Northern Scotland knew next to nothing about gardening. They started a garden in a trailer park that had horrible soil and a difficult climate. Yet, by listening to the "devas" or angels or spirits, they were able to grow plants well. Even within their community not everyone was able to communicate with the devas, only a few who apparently got very specific advice from them. According to what I saw in the Hebrides and what I read, the Findhorn gardens are most remarkable in the results they get.

Many of the practices described in the book are common sense for organic gardeners. First, the Findhorn gardeners "refrain from using things which destroy life"—even when their crops were threatened. They also recognize that improving the soil improves "life force," and produces better, stronger, more productive plants. They use animal manures, compost, and wood ashes to improve the soil, but also believe that the devas worked with them, adding energy to their crops. In their second year of gardening they got forty-pound red cabbages!

Another way of increasing the total positive energy of their gardens, they maintain, is to grow many different varieties and species of vegetables, flowers, and fruits. This also makes sense to me. Early in the season beneficial insects sometimes feed on the nectar of flowers, for example, and then later in the season they eat insects.

Growing the right plant in the right place is important for the Findhorn gardeners. A gardener might ask the devas whether to plant tomatoes or lettuce or carrots in a particular part of the garden, and plant according to the answer given.

I pay attention to my plants and my garden, but I have never heard a peep out of a deva or a garden spirit. But I don't discount them. And I know there are many ways to communicate with the spirit world, something I learned while living in rural Africa as a Peace Corps volunteer. I know that my science degree doesn't give me answers to many of life's mysteries.

After reading the book, I called Jim Linn of Canaan, New Hampshire, an instructor in dowsing techniques, to see if he ever used his dowsing pendulum to make decisions in the garden. He said he did, and offered to teach me how to do so.

So I made a pendulum, and went to see him. He explained that the dowsing instrument interfaces with a higher power. Questions need to be answered with a simple yes or no. For example, "Can I plant corn here and be successful?" or "Do I need to add more compost?" I watched Jim ask questions to a gently swinging pendulum, and then watched it start to change direction on its own, answering the questions. Jim warned me that, "You gotta go with your answers." And, he said, "You don't always get the answers you want."

So I learned to work with a pendulum. Jim explained that it takes practice: The more you have worked with a pendulum, the more pronounced the movement of it becomes. Last summer he successfully dowsed a well two thousand miles away by using his pendulum and a map—a fairly complicated and difficult procedure.

If you would like to learn how to work with a pendulum to connect with the garden spirits, or the energy of the natural world and information that flows though living things, you might want to attend the American Society of Dowsers annual convention that happens in Vermont each summer. For more information go to www.doswers.org

I also talked to Eliza Bergeson, a kinesiologist practicing in Cornish Flat, as I understood that kinesiology and dowsing both depend on interacting with energy fields. Eliza explained that, "We live in a sea of energy made up of all the information that ever was. If you know how, you can access the information. It's like tuning the knob on a radio to get a specific frequency. The information is there for you to use."

Surely I will never understand how the energy of living things flows through plants and animals. But I do accept that there is mystery in the garden, and that I should be open to all theories of how that happens. And I hope I will be listening if a deva speaks to me.

Spring in the Garden

I don't know about you, but mud season is my least favorite time of year. Day after day of gray, raw weather gets me down, and March is a month that usually has plenty of gray days. I'm a gardening guy, and what I really love to do is work outside in my gardens. Unfortunately, it's still too early to do much outside— even on one of those warm, sunny days. The snow has melted on some of my flower beds, and I'd love to start cleaning them up, but I know better.

Right now there is still frost in the ground at my house, even though the top few inches of soil have thawed. I try not to walk on the lawn or in garden beds until the soil has completely thawed and drained. Walking on wet soil compacts it, driving out air spaces needed by roots, and ruining soil structure. Roots grow best in fluffy, well-aerated soils, so I try to control my urge to work in the garden this early.

Later this spring I'll clean up the flower beds by raking off dead leaves, twigs, and the remains of last summer's flowers. If I'm working when the soil is still a little wet, I'll lay down a couple of six-inch-wide boards, each about five feet long, and walk on them. That distributes my weight more evenly, so I'll do less damage.

One outdoor task I'll do now is sticking labels in the ground to remind me next fall where I need to plant more bulbs. This is the time to observe where the snow melts first, and where there are no bulb plants poking up their little green noses.

I plant dozens of bulbs each fall, and I'm rewarded each spring with hundreds—nay, thousands—of blossoms, starting now with those dainty white snowdrops. The season progresses though the whole list of bulb plants: Deep purple scilla that seem to frown as their blossoms look down at the ground from their short stems; their cheerful upward-looking cousins called glory-of-the-snow *(Chionodoxa luciliae)* that are blue, with little white eyes that seem to stare right at me.

Then come crocus, in a range of colors, from yellow and white to shades of blue and purple; little ones, and big ones ready to entertain the early bumblebees that crawl right inside. And of course, before long, there will be the daffodils—classic big-trumpeted King Alfreds, clumps of little yellow Tete-a-Tetes, and later those fragrant pheasant-eye daffodils with short, bright trumpets. And assuming my dogs discourage the deer, there will eventually be tulips in all colors and shapes.

I can't wait for spring to arrive—but I guess I'll have to. Meanwhile, I think I'll go pick some snowdrops.

Growing Rice: You Can Do It

I wouldn't call myself a rice farmer, but I did grow some paddy rice one summer. I attended a workshop in Westminster, Vermont held by rice farmers Takeshi and Linda Akaogi. I left with two small rice plants—each like a one-inch blade of grass—which they had started and tended in their greenhouse. I grew one, and gave the other to a gardening friend. My plant developed about fifty stalks and gave me about three quarters of a cup of rough rice before de-hulling.

Some basics about growing rice: Paddy rice grows in standing water. The type of rice I grew comes from the northern, colder part of Japan and is a variety called Hayayuki. Takeshi and Linda start the rice season in early April, soaking rice grains in 50-degree water for seven days, changing the water every day or two. Then they plant the grains in plastic trays filled with potting soil. For two weeks they treat them as one would any vegetable seedling, then they add more water so that a little standing water covers the soil surface.

Rice is not frost hardy, but the Akaogis planted their rice in paddies on May 7 last year. They have a series of rice paddies that are fed with warm water they preheat in a pool that is lined with a rubber liner. The sun warms the black material, heats the water, and they drain it by gravity into the paddies as needed.

So how did I grow mine? They said I should plant it in a five-gallon pail with ordinary garden soil, leaving an inch and a half of space at the top. I decided to add a little bagged organic fertilizer ($\frac{1}{4}$ cup of Pro-Gro) along with one to two quarts of composted cow manure.

Since I only had one plant, I babied it as I am wont to do with rare or special plants. I filled my bucket of soil with water as hot as I could get from the tap, which warmed my cold spring soil. As it absorbed the water, I added more. Finally, when it would absorb no more water, I placed it in the afternoon sun right next to the front door of the house.

I carefully inserted the rice plant into the soil, settled it in with my fingers, and added a little more water so that it would think it was sitting in an Asian rice paddy. I kept an eye on the plant, and as it grew, I added water to keep the lower part of the stem in water.

I planted my rice seedling on May 12, but we often have frost until the first week of June, which is why I placed the bucket where I did. The stone foundation of the house absorbs the heat of the sun and radiates it back out. Even so, on cold nights I carried the bucket inside. In early June I brought the bucket down to my vegetable garden where it would get sun all day.

Rice does something that farmers call "tillering." That means that as a plant grows bigger it sends up lots of shoots from the same roots, forming a clump. This is highly desirable when planting grains, as it multiplies the number of stalks that you get from each seed planted. By the end of the summer I had more than fifty stalks with seeds on them.

About 90 percent of all rice in the world is harvested by hand, so I went with the time-honored technique. Not all the grains were ripe, but when 70 percent of the leaves had turned a golden yellow-brown I harvested—with much ceremony and a pair of ordinary kitchen shears. I allowed the grain to dry for two to three weeks, then used my hands to pull the grains (which were still covered with their hulls) off the stems. I stored them in a closed container until I decided that I was hungry for home-grown organic rice.

Threshing, or removing the outer hull, is generally done by machine. Not having one, I just spread out the rice I had on the kitchen counter. I used my grandmother's wooden rolling pin, rolling it back and forth over the rice. I could hear crunching, but much of the rice still had hulls. I then put it in a stone mortar, and gently worked it over with a pestle. Then I spread out the rice and debris, and used my breath to blow away the chaff from the rice. I was left with a little under a quarter cup of homegrown rice.

To learn more about growing rice go to www.novaft.org/ resources/nofa-notes and click on "Summer 2008" for an article about the Akaogi rice farm. Other sites on rice production include http://ricelab.plbr.cornell.edu/new/ or www.plant sciences.ucdavis.edu/uccerice/main.htm

I will never become a rice farmer, but enjoyed seeing what goes into growing one the of the world's major food crops. You might like to try it, too. Now is the time to learn more and order some seeds.

APRIL

Growing Giant Carrots

April is a good time to plant carrots, or at least to prepare a bed for planting them soon.

Everybody likes carrots, but they're, well, pretty ordinary. Not much to exclaim about. But last year at the Tunbridge World's Fair in Tunbridge, Vermont, people stopped and stared at Joey Klein's carrots. Little kids pointed to them and called out to their siblings. "Hey, you gotta come see these carrots." Joey's carrots were eighteen inches long.

Joey Klein is an organic farmer who lives and works in Plainfield, Vermont, on the banks of the Winooski River. He has a rich, sandy soil that was deposited by the river eons ago. And he has been nurturing it with compost and manures for more than thirty years. So it's not surprising that he can grow pretty good carrots. But with a little work, you too can grow carrots like his. Well, maybe only a foot long, but long enough to draw attention. Here are his suggestions:

1. Work on the soil. Add lots of compost to your soil and mound up raised beds that stand six inches or so above the walkways. Joey recommends adding some gypsum to the soil if you have clay, as it will loosen it up. Cultivate deeply, and remove all the rocks you can.

2. Carrots need lots of water, right from the beginning. Raised beds dry out faster, so you will need to water regularly in dry years. Carrots need at least one inch of water per week. Keep a rain gauge, and add water as needed.

3. Spacing is important. Joey plants three rows fifteen inches apart in each wide bed. He thins to one inch in early June, then thins to two inches about six weeks later. Carrots will compete with each other for water and nutrients, just as weeds do.

4. Don't let the weeds beat out your carrots. Joey likes to use a weed torch to burn off weeds after planting, but before the carrots germinate. Then he uses a scuffle hoe (see July article on hoes for more information) to eliminate the next crop of weeds between the rows of carrots. But, he warns, be careful not to weed deeply, as that will bring up new weed seeds. And there is no alternative to hand weeding, to get weeds that cozy right up to your carrots.

5. Add some fertilizer after the carrots get established. Joey top-dresses the carrots with an organic bagged fertilizer after the second weeding.

6. Occasional light cultivation with a scuffle hoe rips up the top roots, encouraging roots to go

down. This also keeps the soil surface loose, allowing rain to go down deep.

7. Buy carrot seeds for long carrots if that's what you want. Joey buys pelletized Sugarsnax 54 from Johnny's Select Seed. "They look so good, and they taste good, too," according to Joey.

Joey attributes much of his success to the way he has tended the soil. He is pretty fanatical about farming organically, and is one of the founding members of the Northeast Organic Farmer's Association of Vermont. That's a long way from the North Shore of Long Island where he grew up. Joey went to college in Vermont, and while in college he went to both Mexico and Norway where he lived and worked with farmers. He fell in love with working the soil, and he's been a farmer ever since he graduated in 1970.

"The exciting thing is that we harvest the sunshine," Joey said recently. "We turn it into broccoli and carrots, and they get consumed and turned into good human health, which is what I find so satisfying. But the real question is how do you keep the land productive after taking all that food out?"

For Joey, the answer is simple: Keep building the soil. He grows cover crops—things like oats, peas, and barley—and mows them down and turns them in. These crops produce organic matter, feed the microorganisms, and keep the soil loose and friable.

Joey and his wife, Betsy, bought Littlewood Farm more than twenty years ago, and they raised their two boys, Jake and Abe, to appreciate the importance of growing their food organically. Joey would love to see one of them take over the farm eventually. In the meantime, he wonders about the sustainability question in human terms: "Is there enough here to employ another family member?" Just as he doesn't want to wear out the soil, he doesn't want to wear himself out, either. For a farmer, that's always an issue.

If you want to see some of Joey Klein's carrots, visit the Tunbridge World's Fair. It's always the third weekend in September. It's a great, old-time fair, with everything from ox pulling to a demolition derby, and some of the most impressive vegetable competitions anywhere. My money is betting on Joey to get the blue ribbon for carrots again this year.

Making Good Compost

Good compost works like a magic wand for your plants. Scientists have calculated its fertilizer value and found that it is more effective than adding the same amount of nitrogen, phosphorus, and potassium with chemicals. It improves plant health, but no one is quite sure why. We do know that it enriches the soil, making it come alive—literally. Compost is full of beneficial bacteria, fungi, and other organisms that work symbiotically with your plants.

Like most gardeners, I make some compost from slimy salad, and bread turned blue. I make it from leaves and weeds from garden beds, and sod from the lawn when I expand my gardens. But I also buy it by the dump truck-load from a local dairy farmer. If you buy some, always ask your farmer for hot-composted manure, or aged manure, not fresh. And although there are advertisements in the garden magazines that promise you "rich dark compost in just weeks," don't believe them. Making good compost takes time.

To efficiently break down organic matter—whether using your kitchen waste or the byproducts of a cow—takes the proper ratio of carbon and nitrogen, and adequate moisture and oxygen. The microorganisms that produce compost need about thirty parts carbon for every one of nitrogen. But all you really need to know is this: You need a little fresh manure or green material (grass clippings are great) to mix in with lots of dry, brown material like hay or dry leaves. That will help to get a compost pile "cooking," or heating up as it breaks down the material.

If your compost pile doesn't heat up, check to see if it's too moist or too dry. A handful of the materials should feel as moist as a wrung-out sponge. Squeeze it, and no water should drip out. If it feels dry, turn it once, watering each layer. Too wet? You probably have it sitting in a low spot where water collects and wicks up into your compost pile. Move it onto a layer of brush that will keep it out of water and allow it to drain during rainy periods.

When I was working on an organic farm in Scotland in 2006, I helped produce compost using agricultural waste—dry bracken fern that had been mowed down earlier in the summer, mixed with fresh green leaves and grass. To increase air flow through the pile I added a chimney to one pile, a four-inch pipe drilled full of finger-size holes. I stood it up in the middle, and added material around it. As the pile heated up, hot air was sucked through the holes and up the chimney. Thus fresh air was drawn in through the pile, accelerating the process. (To learn how you can take a working vacation on an organic farm overseas, go to www.wwoof.org).

Many gardeners buy bins to contain compost, but you don't have to. I live out in the country and up until recently I just threw everything into piles and let it all break down in three years or so. Last year I built a four-sided wooden bin from pallets because my young corgi, Daphne, is a rascal. She loves digging in the compost, looking for edibles and getting as dirty as possible. So now I use a bin for food garbage, and put weeds, sod, and leaves in piles elsewhere.

To make a low-cost compost bin, start by procuring four wooden pallets. Stand up the pallets (forming a rectangle) by tying their corners together with building wire or with nylon rope. I use plastic-sheathed 14-2 building wire which contains three strands of 14-gauge wire. (12-2 wire also works, but is a little stiffer.) Staple landscape fabric or chicken wire on the inside of the bin to keep garbage from falling through the gaps between the boards, but allowing air to circulate. Place four inches of cut branches in the bottom, to provide for drainage and to help with air circulation. Voila!

If you live in the city, a plastic bin is good. It keeps out skunks, raccoons, and curious dogs. Rotating bins are, in principle, better than the plain stationary ones, but cost much more. Not only that, but most gardeners I've known who bought them lost their enthusiasm for them after a while, and stopped doing the daily whirl. I say, "Save your money."

A working compost pile shouldn't be very smelly, though some ingredients can be, when first added. To minimize odors, keep a supply of grass clippings, straw, or leaves to toss on the pile after you add your kitchen scraps. Your compost won't break down materials during the winter months, but your bin will hold it until spring.

What should you put in your compost pile? Any plant material, except weeds with seeds or flowers. Goat, sheep, rabbit, and llama manure is great. Cow and horse manures have viable seeds, so make sure your compost gets hot if you use some. Seashells of any kind are great. Pulverize shells first if you want them to break down in your lifetime.

And what should you keep out of the compost? Roots of aggressive weeds like Japanese knotweed or goutweed. No plant material that is diseased, or that might harbor insect pests. No weeds that have already bloomed—some can produce seeds even after being pulled. No cat or dog manure, as they may carry diseases. No meat, fat, cheese, or grease.

Whatever method you choose to make your compost, just remember, it ain't rocket science, and every bucket of it that you make is one less you'll need to buy.

Planning the Vegetable Garden

I'm an optimist by nature. A cautious optimist, however. In 2009 we got hammered by bad weather (cold and rainy) and bad luck (late blight that came early and killed tomatoes and potatoes). Even those normally overly enthusiastic zucchinis were less than bountiful. And the next year? I hoped for lots of sun and great harvests of everything—with no blight. But just to hedge my bets a little, I modified my plans a little for 2010.

First, I planted more leafy greens. Greens do well in wet weather, and need less sun. After all, they aren't producing fruits, tubers, or seeds, all high in solar energy costs. Kale freezes extremely well and I am happy to eat it every week all winter. So I planted a few extra including my standby Winterbor and another variety, Ripbor. Both did well.

When I was in Jamaica for my niece's destination wedding I was introduced to a cooked green called calaloo. Lovely stuff. Yummy stuff. Chefs down there prepare it with onion, garlic, tomato, thyme, and Scotch bonnet peppers. I found it—quite by chance—when thumbing through a Johnny's Seed catalog—one of the advantages of a real, not virtual catalog (www.johnnyseeds .com). It was listed as "red-leaf vegetable amaranth." The catalog shows a variegated purple and green leaf. I've grown other kinds of amaranth as decoratives—they can have nice flowers. It's a hot weather crop, so I waited to direct seed until mid-July.

Another green, this one from the Fedco catalog (www.fedco seeds.com), comes with an almost unpronounceable name: piracicaba. It was described as a non-heading broccoli that sounded interesting. I ordered seeds and started eight plants in the house in April. It germinated easily and, once in the garden, it produced plants as large as broccoli, but more quickly. It is a very satisfactory vegetable—it produces florets similar to the side shoots of broccoli, but the leaves and stems are edible and tender, too.

Lastly, I grew an Asian green, called Happy Rich. Ready to eat in fifty-five days, the Johnny's catalog says, "Large plants produce jumbo-size florets that resemble mini heads of broccoli, and have an excellent sweet broccoli flavor. Produces ample amounts of side shoots." Sounded good to me, and it produced lots of edible leaves, stems, and florets.

Rutabagas do well in rainy summers, and are as tasty and useful as potatoes—with no chance of getting late blight. They look like turnips, but without any bitterness. I use them in stews all winter long. You can start them now indoors, or later directly in the garden.

Celeriac did well for me in 2009—it needs consistently moist soil, so our rainy summer kept it happy. If you want an alternative to celery, try it. It makes a nice tuber that tastes like celery in a cooked dish and it keeps all winter. I have given up growing celery—too tough, too prone to insects and diseases. Celeriac is not usually found in garden centers, so you will probably need to start some from seed. Start some now—it takes 100 days from seed.

What about our tomatoes? Well, if the blight is in the air and the weather cold and rainy, we may see it again. Start your own plants from seed or buy plants from local growers who start their own—some big-box stores brought in diseased plants from the South in 2009, and may again. Some of the new hybrids are perhaps more resistant to the blight, though none in the Johnny's catalog was listed as "late blight-resistant". Most growers I know had good luck with Sun Gold, an orange cherry tomato that has superb flavor.

In 2009 I started some Super Bush tomato seeds that I got from Renee's Seeds (www.reneesgarden.com) that were developed for growing in containers. I planted a seedling in a self-watering five-gallon planter and gave it to a friend in a retirement community. She had great luck with hers on a sunny balcony—fifty nice tomatoes, and no blight. There is no guarantee that tomatoes in planters will avoid late blight—the spores are airborne—but they are less likely to get soil-borne fungi, as there should be little or no splash-up (which transmits early blight, for example).

This word of warning: Potatoes can overwinter late blight because they contain living tissue. If you had late blight on your tomatoes (and/or potatoes) and you see volunteer potatoes coming up this spring, be sure to pull them and dispose of them immediately. And do not start potatoes from last year's crop or from grocery store potatoes. Buy certified disease-free seed potatoes.

My last pick for new plants this year is the tomatillo, which I plan to use for making salsa verde, a Mexican delicacy not sold in Cornish Flat. Tomatillos produce fruits that look like cherry tomatoes but are covered with a paperlike covering, which is removed before cooking. Unlike tomatoes, they are not tasty raw, but great when cooked and blended with onion, hot peppers, lime juice, and fresh cilantro.

So get busy. Buy your seeds, set up your lights, and start planting. I have, and it sure is fun to get my hands dirty on a rainy day.

Day-Neutral Strawberries

If you want to eat strawberries all summer long, now is the time to order your plants. Most strawberries produce their fruit when the days are longest—in June. However, by planting a type of strawberry known as day-neutral or everbearing you can spread the harvest out all summer long and get a nice fall crop, too. And you don't have to make strawberry jam in June, just when the weather is perfect for gardening.

Unlike conventional berries, day-neutral berries will produce the first year. You should have some by August and more in September. The second year (and after) they produce a few berries every week all summer, with a good crop in the fall.

Strawberry plants are not long-lived, so you will need to replant your berry patch every three to four years.

All strawberries like rich, well drained soil. If you have a heavy clay, that means adding a ton of compost—literally. Apply six to eight inches of compost, and work it into the soil with a garden fork or rototiller. For average soil, work in three to four inches of compost to start the bed. A bed for twenty-five plants should be three and a half feet wide (accommodating a double row of plants) and fifteen to twenty feet long. Day-neutral strawberries need less space than June-bearing strawberries because each plant tends to stay in a nice clump. That means you do not have to fuss with the runners or shoots sent out by June-bearing varieties—pruning them off, rooting them, etc. Day-neutrals are the lazy gardener's best berry.

In addition to the compost, work in five to eight pounds of slow-release organic fertilizer for a twenty-five-plant bed. Other good additives are dried kelp, granite dust, rock phosphate, and green sand. These provide a rich mixture of minerals that may not be present in your soil, and help to energize your plants.

Because strawberries need good drainage, they grow well in raised beds. By adding compost and mounding up extra dirt from the walkways next to the bed you can raise the level of the bed about six inches.

To plant, make a little mound of soil for each bare-root plant, and arrange the roots over it. The crown, or growing point for the leaves, should be right at ground level. Cover the roots with rich soil, and pat down well.

All strawberries hate weeds. Grasses and weeds love strawberries, and want to cuddle right up to them. But if they take over your strawberry patch, you won't get much production. The key is to prepare your strawberry patch well: Get out all grasses and weeds before you plant, and then mulch like crazy. The easiest way to prevent a recurrence of weeds is to spread thick layers of newspaper (six pages at least) between the plants, and cover with wood chips. Wood chips are often free for the asking from the guys who clear brush under power lines.

The most common day-neutral strawberry, Tristar, can be purchased from Johnny's Select Seed of Maine (www.johnny seeds.com or 877-564-6697). Also available from Miller Nurseries, www.millernurseries.com or 800-836-9630).

Day-neutral strawberries are not the biggest berries you've ever eaten. They range in size from the diameter of a dime to that of a quarter. No fifty-cent pieces. But they are easy to grow, and tasty too!

Planting Bare-Root Roses

"You can make growing roses as hard or as easy as you want. If you want a hybrid tea rose shaped like a tulip, that's the hardest rose to grow in northern New England. If you want an old-fashioned garden rose that will give a thousand blossoms in the spring, that's the easiest. Everything in between is just a variation." That's according to Mike Lowe, a rose expert in Nashua, New Hampshire.

Mike Lowe knows roses. He has been growing them for more than forty years, and has been in the business for over twenty-five years. His English uncle was a famous rose grower. But more importantly, he grows four thousand roses around his home and on a nearby lot, including a thousand different varieties. He has tried more roses than I can imagine. He breeds them, he propagates them, he studies them. One of his creations, Autumn Sunset, is now being propagated by others, and more than twenty thousand of its descendants are sold every year.

April is a good time to buy and plant bare-root roses, according to Mike, as they need to be shipped, received, and planted while dormant. One advantage to buying bare-root roses is that you can choose among hundreds, even thousands of varieties offered through catalogs or online.

Mike had just received a shipment of bare-root roses the day I was visiting, so I helped him get them ready for planting. His driveway was lined with large plastic tubs full of water, and we immersed each rose in water. He keeps plant completely submersed for twenty-four hours before planting.

Preparing the soil for a rose is crucial to success. Mike suggests preparing a hole twenty-four inches deep and thirty-six inches wide, and filling it completely with a good soil mix made from equal parts of sandy loam and compost. He said digging an even deeper hole and putting a couple of inches of pea stone in the bottom for drainage is better if you are planting in heavy clay. But don't despair if you don't have the energy to recreate The Big Dig, it won't kill your rose. Mike is, after all, a rose fanatic.

To promote good roots and lots of blossoms, Mike mixes in a heaping cup of super triple phosphate (0-44-0) to provide phosphorous. Since I am an organic grower, I substitute rock phosphate for the super phosphate, mixing in more because it is less concentrated.

Roses like a soil that is neutral or just slightly acidic, one with a pH of 6.5 to 7.0. I recommend getting your soil tested and adding ground limestone as needed. Mike adds a three-inch square of sheetrock (gypsum wallboard) directly below each rose he plants. He said this adds calcium, and sweetens the soil. He gets scraps free from his local building supply company.

Most serious gardeners have a few special tricks. In addition to planting a chunk of sheetrock in the hole, Mike also puts two or three large nails in the soil for iron. Although I've never read about either technique, I tried it with the roses I bought from him, though it is impossible to know if it really helped.

Although old-fashioned roses are grown on their own roots, many of the fancy new roses are grafted onto hardier rootstock. When planting own-root roses, Mike plants the rose at the depth it was grown. (You will see a difference in color and texture in the above- and below-ground portions). He told me that grafted roses should be planted with the graft (which looks like a scar) below ground level. The colder the climate, the deeper it should be planted. An inch below the surface is good for Zone 5, two inches for Zone 4, three inches for Zone 3.

Mike recommends providing protection from the wind when planting a bare-root rose. He said that until the roots get established a rose is in danger of dehydrating. He uses rose cones (Styrofoam buckets made for protecting roses in winter), but said you can cut the bottom out of a cheap Styrofoam cooler and place it over your new rose instead. The top should be open to prevent overheating on a sunny day.

Mike does not recommend adding any nitrogen at planting time, but does fertilize his established roses once a month with a liquid organic fertilizer until August, when he stops fertilizing. Any fish-based liquid fertilizer should do.

Roses need lots of water, about twice what we normally get. Mike has soaker hoses throughout all his rose beds so that he can deliver water to the roots without wetting the leaves. Mildew—a fungus—attacks wet leaves more readily than dry leaves. Roses need to get watered any time there has been a week-long drought; give each rose plant five gallons of water, the equivalent of an inch of rain.

Another trick I learned from Mike Lowe pertains to raised beds made using lumber sides. Normally the winter's cold would spread laterally into a raised bed, damaging the roots of roses or other perennial plants. He solved the problem by insulating the insides of his raised beds with an inch of Styrofoam. He said he uses that technique whenever creating beds more than eight inches tall, and on stone retaining walls.

Although Mike Lowe is a consummate rose grower, it is reassuring to know that he is fallible, too. He told me that his wife, Irene, loves a rose called Distant Drums; it is allegedly hardy to Zone 5, but has died in his Zone 5 garden four times. So he bought it again the year I visited him, saying he will grow it as an annual if need be. Now that's true love.

Rototilling—Good or Bad?

With apologies to Shakespeare, To rototill or not to rototill, *that* is the question. And not one with an absolute answer. More to the point is the question, when does it make sense?

Starting a new vegetable garden or large flower bed? Unless you are starting with dark, rich soil that was deposited on the banks of a river, or built up by decades of barnyard animals, you probably should consider renting a rototiller to work in organic matter. That's right: Rent, not buy. Rototilling is not something you need to do every year. Here's why:

Rototilling does a good job of making weeds "disappear" each spring. But perennial weeds like dandelions, quack grass, and many others don't stay hidden long. Chopping up their roots and burying them doesn't kill them. They will sprout soon—every last piece. One root can yield many weeds after rototilling. Not only that, weed seeds won't germinate if they are buried deep in the soil. Generally, only weeds near the surface germinate. Rototilling brings up seeds that have been waiting their chance.

Organic matter can oxidize and break down in the soil—much as wood oxidizes in your stove, only much slower. Aerating soil by rototilling accelerates that process—and can ruin soil structure if the soil is too wet. Good soil structure develops over time. Microbes and earthworms are living in your soil. They produce organic substances—waxes and resins—that help small soil particles to join together, creating a light, fluffy soil that holds together but allows water and air to penetrate it. Rototilling disturbs that structure. Notice what happens after rototilling: The first hard rain deflates that fluffy soil like a birthday balloon a week after the party.

But rototilling is not all bad. If you want to start a new vegetable garden, you will need to add compost, aged manure, or even old leaves. Stirring them into the soil is tough work. You can do it with a garden fork and a shovel, but a rototiller can help decrease the work.

If you are starting a garden in a lawn or field, you need to remove the sod before you rototill. There are a motorized machines called sod-lifters that can be rented to help you remove the sod. Those I've used were heavy, awkward machines that worked best on flat places. But they can save a lot of backbreaking work if you want to prepare a new twenty-by-twenty-foot garden. The machine moves along, cutting an eighteen-inch swath, slicing under the sod. You can then cut it into manageable-size pieces and haul it away to use it somewhere else, or add it to the compost pile.

Most new gardens need lots of organic matter. Get your soil tested, and ask for the test that indicates the percentage of organic matter. You are striving for 4 to 8 percent, but might be starting with only 1 to 2 percent organic matter. Spread a thick layer of organic matter over the new garden, and rototill it in. Most dairies now sell aged manure or better yet, hot-composted barn scrapings. Hot composting kills weed and grass seeds that are viable in fresh manure, and even in some aged manure. Buy it by the truckload, and work it in.

There are many sizes and brands of rototillers. For the heavy work of preparing new beds, a full-size rear-tine rototiller is probably best. Ask at the rental center how to adjust the tooth that determines how deep the machine will go. If you have compacted, heavy soil, do one pass with the blades only four to six inches deep. Then do it again at full depth.

Do not rototill if your soil is wet. How do you know if your soil too wet for rototilling? Take a handful of soil and squeeze it into a ball. Open your hand. Unless you can fragment the ball of soil with the tap of a finger, don't rototill. For soils dominated by clay, or during rainy times, that may not happen until long past planting time. Think garden fork instead of rototiller.

Instead of rototilling this spring, think about building up wide, raised beds in your vegetable garden. Loosen soil with a garden fork, and rake soil into thirty-inch-wide raised beds. Use soil from the walkways to build up the beds, and add compost. You can leave them in place for years, adding compost each year.

One last bit of advice: Before you pull the rope on that rented rototiller, make sure it is clean. You don't want any diseases, eggs of pests, or roots of perennial weeds to go from someone else's garden to yours. Hose down the blades and undercarriage of the rototiller on the road or in your driveway, not in the garden. Pull off roots that may be entwined on the blades. It's a five-minute operation that can save you years of grief.

Organic Seeds: Worth the Money?

I have a confession to make: Despite being fully committed to being an organic gardener and one who tries to eat only organic food, I have not always bought exclusively organic seeds for planting. I would not buy treated seeds—you know, those beans or corn seeds that are pink with poison to keep the seeds from rotting in wet soil. But other seeds? In the past I have purchased both organic and conventional seeds. I've done some thinking about this, talked to seed producers, and have decided that from here on in, I will try very hard to buy *only* organic seeds.

Why did I buy conventional seeds in the past? First, some of my favorite varieties are not available as organic seed. Giving up certain vegetable varieties will be tough. But organic seeds are becoming mainstream, and seed companies like High Mowing Seeds and Seeds of Change are fully organic, with lots of varieties I've never even tried. And many companies like Johnny's Select Seeds and Fedco have extensive listings of organic seed in addition to their conventionally-grown seeds.

Other excuses? Price. Convenience. Organic seed is more expensive. But not much more. Pennies more. I just need to stop being a skinflint. As my friend Fred Brossy, an organic farmer and seed producer in Idaho (who I worked for in the summer of 2003) said to me recently, "Cowboy up. Just do it." And, although it is convenient to pop into my local garden center or hardware store and grab an extra packet of lettuce seeds when I need them, I'll just plan better. Honest. High Mowing now has seed racks in our local food coops, which is very handy.

Since I use no chemical fertilizers there are some major advantages for me when I buy organic seeds. Tom Stearns, the owner of High Mowing Seeds in Wolcott, Vermont pointed out that plant varieties that have been selected and bred using chemical fertilizers can be different than those that have been raised using lower inputs of soluble nitrogen. "Imagine plants grown for fifty successive generations next to drip lines that provide chemical fertilizers. Those plants don't have to develop big, aggressive root systems to find their nutrition," Tom said. Plants developed and bred under low-input conditions need to have better root systems in order to produce well.

Stearns also pointed out that an unintended benefit of a bigger root system is that it will benefit plants during dry summers. Extra root hairs and roots that plunge deeper into your soil will be able to keep plants alive and well while you go to the beach for a hot dry week in August.

Organic gardeners do not have the same arsenal of fungicides and chemical weapons against pests that conventional gardeners do, so organic seed companies need to select for varieties resistant to diseases. They want organic growers to be successful, and to come back to buy their seeds the following year.

Organic seed producers are now not just growing the heirloom plants of past years, they are working with research scientists at places like the University of New Hampshire (UNH), Cornell, and Oregon State University to develop tasty, disease resistant varieties of vegetables including hybrids. Dr. Brent Loy at UNH, for example, developed a hybrid yellow-orange slicing tomato called the Sunkist that is, allegedly, as tasty as an heirloom. Stearns' crew blind taste-tested forty different yellow slicers last summer, and all agreed that Sunkist was the winner. When I called Dr. Loy he said that he believes it will prove to have good resistance to tomato diseases, though it is still too new to know for sure.

As Dan Sandweiss of Seeds of Change said to me, "As we become more conscious of the footprint we leave on the environment, it only makes sense to grow organically—starting with the seed." I agree. Each packet of seeds we buy is a declaration of our beliefs, and I'm committed to organics.

On Gardening and Grampies

If I make it to heaven, I know there will be homegrown tomatoes there. And asparagus all year round, and different colors of lettuce, peppers, and potatoes. But to hedge my bets, I grow all these things—even if I can't have them all year.

I learned to grow things from my late grandfather, John Lenat. Grampy came over from Germany about a hundred years ago. He was a tailor and could make a nice three-piece suit to measure using a treadle Singer. But Grampy's real passion was gardening—and sharing the fruits of his garden with others.

He spoke several languages with a German accent, and held on to his old-world belief that all a gardener needs is a good compost pile and a little manure. That's right, my grandfather was an organic gardener before the term even existed.

We made manure tea, diluting hen manure in a wooden rain barrel for use on his tomatoes. We picked bugs and drowned them in soapy water—or he just squished them with his fingers. His compost pile was rich in earthworms that doubled as fishing worms when it got too hot to garden. Today, in this age of genetically modified organisms, chemical fertilizers, and pesticides, I still use his methods—and they work just fine.

Grampy loved fresh vegetables. Tomatoes, hot from the August sun. Cucumbers right from the garden. I can still see him at the porcelain sink in the summer kitchen, rinsing off radishes and cukes. He'd slice them with a slim, black-handled pocket knife that he kept razor sharp, shake a little salt on them, and pop them in his mouth—just five minutes after he'd picked them.

I learned more than just gardening from Grampy. He was generous of spirit—and with his vegetables. He had a regular vegetable route: He drove around town each week in the summer delivering succulent red tomatoes and crisp heads of lettuce that he gave away. We went to the A&P in his red-and-white Nash Rambler, Grampy sitting on a thick cushion so he could see over the steering wheel. He delivered his homegrown tomatoes to the checkout clerks. He remembered everyone, and made each feel important.

If he were alive today, Grampy would be 121. I can't imagine him in a twenty-first-century grocery store buying tomatoes in a cello four-pack. He wouldn't understand why people would want to buy vegetables that had traveled 1,500 miles, the average distance an American vegetable travels today to reach the grocery store.

If, through some miracle, Grampy came back to visit and needed to buy vegetables, he'd visit farm stands and farmers markets. He knew that local food is good food. He understood that there is no "better life through chemicals" when it comes to food. Back in his day, DDT was thought to be the answer for any wayward bug that appeared in the garden, but he didn't buy that idea.

I spent a week or two with Grampy every summer, from 1952, when I was six, to 1967, the year he died. Just the two of us. His wife had died, and I suppose my parents had initially sent me to cheer him up. We both had fun, and I kept on coming.

My visits with Grampy were wonderful. He never criticized me. He told lots of bad jokes. ("Do you want to go get a haircut?"

Yes, I'd say. He'd respond, "No, you better get them *all* cut."). He taught me to fish. He understood that kids don't like to weed. He let me learn to love gardening at my own pace.

Now I'm a Grampy. My grandson George is not quite three, but when he comes to visit me this summer, we'll go down to the garden. I'll show him earthworms in the compost pile and we'll look for toads. I'll let him have his own corner of the garden for toy trucks. He already loves cherry tomatoes, so we'll eat some off the bush—and maybe I'll tell him a few corny jokes.

Postscript: As of publication, George is seven, and has a sister, Casey Jean-Marie, who is almost four. Both are avid gardeners—and connoisseurs of carrots, potatoes, and tomatoes. I'm a lucky Grampy.

MAY

Dandelions

I try real hard to eat just locally grown, organic food. I cheat, of course, when it comes to the local part. I eat chocolate and ginger and drink coffee and the occasional bottle of French red. But I plant a big vegetable garden each year, and I freeze, can, and dehydrate much of our garden's bounty. I support the local farmers market, buying our chicken, beef, and pork from farmers who use no hormones or chemicals, and who let their animals outdoors to bask in the sun. I love fresh fiddleheads, and consider them a spring treat. But dandelions? I never found them palatable—until recently.

I was having breakfast with a bunch of guys the other day. My friend Rev Wightman said that he and his wife, Nancy, had just finished off the last of their frozen dandelions. Frozen dandelions? I thought maybe I'd misunderstood. To me, dandelions have tasted bitter and nasty—until now.

I like the concept of having a lawn that's chemical-free. A lawn so pristine that I can eat anything growing in it. So I have, on occasion, harvested and eaten dandelions from my lawn, but never really enjoyed them. I asked my friend if he'd show me how to harvest dandelions and explain how to prepare them. He did. I had them for dinner, and they were exquisite. Delicious.

The key to enjoying dandelions is picking them young, before they bloom, and knowing just how to harvest them. Rev has an old table knife that he uses to slice through the taproot about an inch below the surface of the soil. He pulls up the dandelion, being careful not to let any dirt get onto the leaves. He uses his knife to scrape off any dirt from the crown of the dandelion, which is bulbous and white, and grows just below the surface of the soil. He cuts off the rest of the taproot, and picks out any bits of grass from the cluster of green leaves. Finally, he shakes off any soil that eluded his touch.

Rev left me with a basket of dandelion greens that I immediately rinsed, and cooked within the hour. I steamed them until tender and served them with a sprinkle of cider vinegar. And the great part is, I can go out and do it again tomorrow—not because I think it's healthy, or to prove a point, but because the flavor of those fresh organic greens is absolutely fabulous. And since I've never used herbicides, fungicides or insecticides on my lawn, I know that whatever grows there is safe to eat. If your lawn is chemical free, dandelions should be tasty until they bloom. Bon appétit!

Postscript: Rev Wightman passed away December 20, 2008. I think of him every time I harvest dandelion greens.

Hardening Off Seedlings and Planting the Vegetable Garden

It's mid-May, and despite many hot days, I predict more frost here in my cold, Zone 4 garden. I have spinach, peas, radicchio, onions, and shallots outdoors in the garden, and I don't worry about them. But some plants that shrug off temperatures in the low twenties in the fall—Brussels sprouts, broccoli, and kale—are not ready for hard frosts yet. Young plants—like young people—are not as tough as old ones. And it's important to get seedlings ready for life outdoors before they go in the ground.

Hardening off is a process that is not taken seriously enough by many gardeners. Young plants can be sunburned, wind-burned, or damaged by cold temperatures. Having been raised in a greenhouse or on a windowsill, plants have leaves that are not as tough as they would be if they had been grown outside; they are tender and easily damaged. So you must introduce your plants to the outdoors the way you would introduce a Danish lad to the equatorial sun. If you do not harden off your plants, they might not thrive for a few weeks.

On nice days I take my seedlings for a walk. Not far, mind you, but out into the direct sunshine for a few hours. Morning sun is the gentlest of the day, so I start the hardening off process on a north-facing deck that gets no afternoon sun, and that has some protection from stiff breezes. If rain is forecast, I leave them inside as a hard rain can easily beat down plants that have not developed strong stems indoors. Later they get afternoon sun, and finally all day sun.

So when should you plant tomatoes and other frost sensitive plants? Ask your neighbors, and then plant a little later. I know that my plants catch up to those planted earlier. And after weeks—nay, months—of coddling my tomatoes and peppers, I don't want to shock them in cold soil or take a chance with a late frost.

If your plants are a bit long and leggy, as is often the case for those started indoors, give them as much direct sunshine now as you can. Come planting time, tomatoes and broccoli can be planted deeply so that weak stems are buried and turned into extra roots. I often plant tall tomatoes sideways with just the top leaves showing—after I pinch off the lower leaves.

That urge to plant need not be ignored until all chance of

frost is past. Frost-hardy plants can be planted by seed weeks before your tomatoes. Those tough guys include beets, carrots, chard, greens, lettuce, onions (seedlings or sets), peas, potatoes (chunks), radishes, rutabagas, and spinach.

All the vine crops (cukes, zucchini, and winter squashes) are quite frost sensitive, so I don't plant them outside until early June. I like to plant vine crops indoors a month before last frost in three- to four-inch pots so that they have several leaves when planted. That makes them less susceptible to defoliation by striped cucumber beetles, which are common in my garden. Beans are also quite easily frost damaged so I hold off on planting seeds until June.

If your beets and chard are up and growing, you can thin them now. The "seeds" you planted are actually seed capsules (think of them like apples with several seeds inside each capsule). So no matter how carefully you spaced out your beets and chard, they will need thinning. And they compete with each other just as much as they do with weeds. Some folks wait until their greens are big enough to eat before thinning, but I find thinning early produces larger beets. Johnny's Seeds has just started to offer beets with just a single seed in each capsule, Moneta. I haven't grown it, but will.

My perennial vegetables are up: Asparagus, rhubarb, and two less common greens: sorrel and Good King Henry. Sorrel has a lemonlike flavor; I favor using it in salads, as the leaves are thin and don't amount to much when cooked. Good King Henry is made of tougher stuff and can be steamed or sautéed.

I really want to get my teeth into vine-ripened tomatoes as soon as possible but I generally don't plant tomatoes outdoors until June 10, ten days after most gardeners have planted theirs—although this year I may plant a wee bit earlier. I can always cover them up if Jack Frost looms on the horizon.

Spring planting is a dance of sorts, lugging seedlings in and out of the house, or covering and uncovering. I'm ready for summer!

Fertilizers: Chemical versus Organic

As you get ready to plant your garden this year, think about giving up your dependence on oil. That's right, oil. You may not think that you are supporting the petrochemical industry as you plant your tomatoes, but if you are using chemical fertilizers, you are.

A bag of 10-10-10, the standard fertilizer for many gardeners, is made using very energy-intensive manufacturing methods to heat, compress, and cool gases to turn nitrogen from the air into the nitrogen in fertilizer. The basic feedstock for making nitrogen fertilizer is natural gas. Each fifty-pound bag of 10-10-10 uses the energy equivalent of about a gallon and a half of fuel oil. Given that there are tens of millions of gardeners in America, the petrochemical cost of fertilizer used by home gardeners is significant.

Aside from the environmental aspects of using chemical fertilizers, there are the practical reasons for avoiding them. Chemical fertilizers only provide three of the seventeen chemical elements needed by plants. They provide nitrogen, phosphorus, and potassium, but not the micronutrients needed by plants. Much of what you buy is inert filler—usually pellets of lime that are much too large for use by plants, but which help in the dispersal of the fertilizer. Unlike compost and organic fertilizers, chemical fertilizer doesn't contain magnesium, manganese, zinc, copper, and the other elements needed in small quantities.

Most chemical fertilizers are largely water soluble. A rainy spell can wash away the ingredients you just bought and worked into your soil. Organic fertilizers are now readily available in bags for use like chemical fertilizers. But organic fertilizers typically have only one quarter of their nitrogen available in a water-soluble form. Most of the nitrogen in organic fertilizers needs to be broken down over time by soil microorganisms. This allows plants to take up nitrogen slowly over the course of a summer, rather than in a big burst in spring.

The phosphate in a chemical fertilizer generally comes from rock phosphate that has been processed in a factory with sulfuric or nitric acid to convert it to a soluble form. The phosphate in organic fertilizers is finely ground rock. Over time that rock phosphate is dissolved with the help of acid rain or by organic acids produced by soil fungi. This slow release helps to prevent phosphate from leaching into water sources, which can be a problem where chemical fertilizers are used.

Mother Nature has always nurtured the soil and our plants through natural symbiotic processes—plants and animals benefit from each other and are interdependent. Plants produce foods that are eaten by animals—from the birds and mice to you and me. In nature, animals distribute seeds and add their manure to the soil. Each year leaves fall and annual plants die, leaving organic matter that earthworms munch on and fungi digest. And so on, until farmers and gardeners disrupt the cycle with their machinery, chemical fertilizers, and pesticides. People have also introduced (either intentionally or inadvertently) insects and plants from other countries that have become pests—which often has led to chemical "solutions."

Organic gardeners disrupt the cycle of nature, too, of course, but we are less intrusive. Mother Nature would not have selected tomatoes or zinnias for our gardens, but we need or want them. The very act of gardening is a disruption of nature, but properly done it is a benefit, not a liability—for us, or for the environment.

The mainstay for organic gardeners is compost, or composted manure. Compost is not high in nitrogen—perhaps one or two percent—but it has many advantages over chemical fertilizers. First, compost helps to develop better quality soil. It helps to build that light, fluffy, dark-colored soil that we all want. It helps clay soils to drain better, and sandy soils to retain water better. No chemical fertilizer can make that claim.

As the organic matter in compost ages and is processed by

microorganisms, it can turn into humus, a stable carbon product that can serve to hold onto minerals and water for use by our plants. And there is no petroleum used in making or transporting compost. Even if we buy composted manure from our local farmers, it is traveling ten miles instead of hundreds of miles from a chemical plant.

There are benefits to using fertilizers, of course: They're easy to apply and can provide needed ingredients just when we need them. Plants use up minerals from the soil, so they need to be replaced. Composting the plants at the end of the season recycles some ingredients, but other minerals are removed from the soil—including those we eat.

Instead of using soluble chemical fertilizers for a quick fix, think about using a foliar fertilizer (one sprayed on leaves) made from fish and seaweed extract. During extended rainy periods, plants don't take up water and minerals from the soil the way they do in sunny times. Are your tomatoes looking yellow? Spraying with a foliar fertilizer can deliver nitrogen and other needed nutrients directly.

You may not think that buying a bag of chemical fertilizer will affect global warming, but it does. If we each take a small step toward reducing energy consumption, we can make a difference. As the Chinese philosopher Lao Tzu said, the longest journey begins with a single step.

Organic Lawns

Contrary to what you've been told, you don't have to weed and feed your lawn three or four times a summer. You can have a nice lawn without chemicals. As the summer heats up, lawns that are kept short and "fed" with chemicals get stressed, and often go brown and dormant—especially if watering bans are imposed. Here are some nontoxic ways to have a nice lawn.

First, start by cranking up the deck on your lawnmower as high as it will go. It won't look like the turf at Fenway Park, but get over it. Mere mortals can't have midsummer lawns that short, not unless you want to be constantly watering and applying chemicals. You'd have to quit your day job and tend the turf constantly.

Any lawn survives stress better if allowed to grow taller. Instead of setting blades at 2 inches, raise the deck to $3\frac{1}{2}$ inches. This provides each grass plant with much more surface area, allowing it to capture more sunshine. The more photosynthesis, the more food produced for root growth. Deeper root systems allow the plants to survive droughts and heat better.

An organic lawn has beneficial soil organisms that share nutrients with grass plants. They also help to keep the soil soft and pleasant to walk on. Chemical fertilizers, herbicides, moss killers, grub killers, and fungicides applied to the lawn also kill beneficial organisms. This creates hard-packed soil, and grass plants become dependent on another chemical "fix" from you.

Thatch, an accumulation of dead grass, is a good indication that your soil does not have enough beneficial microbes in it. A healthy lawn benefits from grass clippings because the little critters digest them, incorporating the organic matter. Lawn services that chemically weed-n-feed usually catch the lawn clippings when they mow and take them away to prevent build up of thatch.

According to Paul Sachs, organic lawn expert (and manufacturer of Pro-Gro and other organic fertilizers), a healthy organic lawn will resist most pests and diseases without the application of pesticides.

Paul recommends a simple test to determine if your lawn is compacted and in need of help. Get a screwdriver with a six-inch shaft, and try to insert it into your lawn. You should be able to push it in, using moderate force, up to the hilt. If you can't, your lawn is compacted and needs help.

One way to improve your lawn is with applications of well-made, well-cured compost. A teaspoon of good compost has literally millions of microorganisms. Spreading half an inch of compost on the lawn will introduce beneficial microorganisms and provide them with nutrients. Earthworms are Mother Nature's rototillers and will magically appear and work on the soil if you add some compost.

If your lawn fails the screwdriver test and you wish to take drastic action, the next step is to rent a core-aerator. This is an engine-powered machine that will punch little holes in the lawn to loosen up compacted soils and allow compost or fertilizer to get down to the roots of the grass. In small areas, you can aerate with a garden fork. Applying compost after aerating will jump-start the recovery process.

A note on compost: You will probably have to buy some if you wish to apply it all over your lawn, and not all compost is created equal. A finished compost is not stinky or sticky. If you're buying it by the bag, buy one bag and open it in the parking lot of the store. You shouldn't be able to identify undigested organic matter like wood chips in it. And it should smell nice, like freshly plowed soil, not sour or stinky. If it passes those tests, buy all you need. Or visit your local dairy farm to see if they sell composted or aged barn scrapings by the truckload.

When I was growing up, clover was in every lawn. Now it's excluded from most seed mixes because the herbicides used in weed-n-feed products kill it. Clover is a nitrogen-fixer, so it will help your lawn by introducing free fertilizer—nitrogen taken from the air. Scuff up your lawn with a rake, sprinkle on some clover seed, and keep it moist until it grows. Ask for white clover.

Old habits die hard. If you're accustomed to fertilizing your lawn with chemicals, try an organic fertilizer this summer instead. But the most important change to make may be your attitude. Practice saying to yourself, "If it's green, and I can mow it, it's a lawn." I've never heard of a child or a pet getting sick from dandelions or crabgrass. Unfortunately, I can't say the same about lawn chemicals.

Planting Trees and Shrubs for Birds

Over the years I've planted plenty of trees and shrubs to provide berries for birds. Some we share, others are just for them. Birds need more than berries, of course. They need safe places to nest. They need shelter from the harsh winter winds. And they need food every month of the year—and not just the food we supply in feeders. If you take the family to Disney World at Christmas, what will the birds eat while you are gone? It's important not to make our feathered friends dependent on us. Feeders can provide dessert, but their main courses should be based on plants growing in our landscape.

Birds are like teenagers: They like fatty, high-calorie foods. If there were a "pepperoni tree," birds would be there every day. When the robins return each spring there are no worms available to eat, so they eat what they can find—including staghorn sumac berries. The sumac berries have virtually no fat, so they've been ignored by birds all winter; birds prefer seeds that are relatively high in fat. But robins, crows, red-winged blackbirds and others will eat those sumac berries if that is all there is. Since sumacs spread by root and are hard to control I do not recommend planting them. There are plenty by the roadside.

Here are some bird-friendly plants you may wish to consider:

Elderberries *(Sambucus canadensis)*. Some forty species of birds eat elderberries, according to my bird/plant Bible, *Trees, Shrubs, and Vines for Attracting Birds* by Richard M. DeGraaf (UPNE, 2002). It grows best in wet areas, and can spread by root, though I've never found it invasive. Each cane only lives a few years, but the bushes replenish themselves freely. The early summer blossoms are spectacular white, flat-topped cymes (flowers resembling Queen Anne's lace) that are fragrant and lovely. In the fall the dark berries are good for jelly, juice—and the birds. There are ornamental varieties with dark purple or chartreuse leaves, but the ordinary varieties are hardiest, most vigorous, and best for the birds.

Grapes (*Vitis* spp.): All birds love grapes, whether domestic or wild. Not only do some forty species of birds eat them, many use the flaky bark in their nests. Ordinary Concord grapes are very hardy, as are many of the newly introduced varieties. Prune them hard early in the spring for best grape production, and to keep them under control.

Crabapples (*Malus* spp.): All are beautiful to our eyes, but not all are appealing to birds. Varieties that birds like to eat include Snowdrift, Sugar Time, Indian Magic, Sargent, Red Jewel, Prairie Fire, and Golden Rainbow. If you buy a crabapple from a family-owned and operated nursery, you can ask for a variety loved by birds—information is not always available at big-box stores. Ruby-throated hummingbirds will nest in crabapples— another good reason to have one.

Shadbush, also called serviceberry (*Amelanchier* spp.) is one of several early-blooming roadside trees that birds love. Some forty species eat the berries, which are much like blueberries. I had these shrubs for years before I ever got to eat a berry—the birds ate them all, a day or two before I considered them ripe! An understory tree, this will do well in part shade. I keep them pruned to shrub size, since some will grow to twenty to thirty feet if left alone.

Pagoda dogwood *(Cornus alternifolia)*: Lovely in form, this native dogwood lives in part shade, and produces berries loved by birds in mid- to late summer.

Evergreens: White pine, eastern hemlock, balsam fir, and all the spruces are very important bird plants. Many species eat their seeds, but even more use them as safe places to rest and nest. They are important since they hold their foliage all winter,

blocking cold winds and allowing birds to conserve their heat—
and thus their food needs. And if you have an evergreen near a
birdfeeder, they are used and appreciated by our silly chickadees
that only take one seed at a time, then dash off to eat it somewhere else.

Whatever you plant for the birds, be sure to water regularly
all summer, particularly in the hot days of August. Dehydration
is the most common cause of plant failure in the first two years
after planting.

I recently learned from Paul Franklin of Riverview Farm in
Plainfield, New Hampshire that blueberries that ripen late in the
fall have fewer bird problems than earlier varieties—so he grows
only those, and doesn't net them. He grows just three varieties:
Elliot, Darrow, and Late Blue. But don't forget what you were
taught in kindergarten: Sharing is good!

Compost Tea

For many gardeners, soaking fresh manure in a bucket or barrel
of water has been an easy way to extract nutrients, an organic
alternative to soluble chemical fertilizers. My grandfather did
this when I was a boy, using hen manure to make tea for his
tomatoes.

Now there is a high-tech "compost tea" that only vaguely
resembles the solution Grampy made sixty years ago. For the
past decade or so farmers and gardeners have been brewing this
compost tea in containers as small as a gallon or as big as five
hundred gallons, injecting air into a solution of compost, earth-
worm castings, molasses, and naturally occurring minerals. The
goal is to grow beneficial microorganisms that can be sprayed on
plants, particularly the leaf surfaces.

The scientific theory behind all this has largely been developed
by Dr. Elaine Ingham, formerly of Oregon State University, and

now an independent research scientist (her Web site is www
.soilfoodweb.com). The theory is that plants can benefit from
this foliar spray because it supplies a healthy dose of beneficial
microorganisms that create a living biofilm on leaf surfaces.

It may sound strange to be introducing bacteria and fungi to
your plants, especially since these critters are often associated
with disease. But good microorganisms offer two benefits to
plants. First, many share minerals with their hosts. They live
on leaf surfaces, benefiting from excess sugars produced by the
plant, while releasing and sharing minerals to plants. Many
microorganisms can ingest minerals during the tea-brewing
process and share them with plants while living on leaves.

Secondly, beneficial microorganisms on the leaves and fruit
claim the sites where harmful bacteria or fungi might attach
themselves—if they had the opportunity. Apple scab has a harder
time getting its foot in the door, for example, because the apart-
ment is already rented. There is no room at the inn.

Mark Fulford of Monroe, Maine is a fruit and vegetable farmer
who had a great crop of apples in 2002, despite the drought
which plagued others. He attributed his success to spraying
compost tea, which provided the minerals needed by the fruit—
especially since fewer minerals were being transported up from
the ground during the drought.

And although most people think you can't grow apples commercially without spraying toxic chemicals, Mark does it. Touring
his orchard at harvest time, it was obvious that apple scab, the
bane of organic gardeners, was not a problem. He reduces scab
by timely spraying with a dilute solution of hydrogen peroxide,
followed by four sprayings of his special compost tea.

It is widely understood that a good healthy soil full of bacteria,
fungi, and other microorganisms is important for the development of healthy plants, and that microorganisms nourish plants
in symbiotic relationships. The proponents of aerobic compost
believe that the same is true for the leaf surfaces.

Opponents of compost tea worry that growing bacteria and spraying them on vegetables or fruit is a recipe for disaster. They say that some forms of *Escherichia coli* bacteria are highly toxic to humans, and they fear that bacteria in the tea could be dangerous.

Compost tea advocates disagree. They point out that *E. coli* is a bacterium that lives in the guts of mammals, an environment where there is little oxygen and no light. Compost tea is made by mixing the ingredients in a bucket or vat while pumping in air. A day of tumbling in a tea brewer bubbling with air will kill *E. coli* bacteria, they believe, and no reports have shown otherwise.

Here's what Mark Fulford puts in his twelve-gallon compost tea brewer: Water, good finished compost, and fresh worm castings from his worm bin. Then he adds dried kelp powder, naturally produced humic acid, and minerals—including colloidal phosphate, Azomite, and granite dust. He puts in an Ontario greenstone with very high paramagnetic strength to help energize the system. Lastly, he adds molasses, which is food for the rapidly expanding numbers of bacteria and fungi.

Once Mark hits the switch, the compressor starts up, and the solution becomes a roiling stew of air, water, minerals, and microorganisms. His tea will brew for eighteen to twenty hours before it is ready to spray on the trees. During that time aerobic microorganisms will reproduce, feeding on the molasses and changing the minerals into a form usable by his plants.

Mark uses different types of compost to achieve different ends. For perennials and trees, he uses a compost largely made from leaves and wood chips—to insure that there are plenty of fungi. For vegetables, he uses one made from annual plants. He sometimes gets his compost tested at Dr. Ingham's lab to see what the bacterial/fungal ratio is.

There are plenty of inexpensive tea brewers for the home gardener. I have a K.I.S. (which stands for "Keep It Simple") brewer that I bought for about $75. It allows me to brew tea in a five-gallon bucket. And although K.I.S. sells compost tea bags all set to go, I use my own compost and minerals. It is hard to know for sure what compost tea really accomplishes, of course, as there are so many variables in the garden. But it's one more tool for the organic gardener, and time will tell us if it's worth the effort.

Primroses

I recognize that many Americans unwind by watching some television—the news, or perhaps a sitcom or a ballgame. I don't have a television connected to the outside world (though I can watch a rented movie if I want), and have no problem with the concept of watching television. But I grew up in a household with no television, and have never gotten into the habit. I have an Adirondack chair set up under an ancient apple tree where I can unwind on a spring or summer day—and do my viewing. It faces a rocky ledge, some woods, and my primrose garden. I can sit and watch the primroses longer than I can sit still watching television.

Primroses are, to my way of thinking, some of the most satis-factory of all flowers. They are bright and cheerful, bloom over a long period of time, spread nicely, and come in an amazing array of colors and sizes. There are many good ones to look for.

Among the earliest of my primroses are the drumstick prim-roses *(Primula denticulata)*. Like most primroses, these have a basal rosette of light-green leaves. The flowers appear on four-to eight-inch stalks, each blossom a globe-shaped mass of florets that stand proudly, despite early spring chill and rain. They come in a variety of colors—white, rose, magenta, and lavender. Each plant may present two to three flowering stems once it reaches maturity. As with many flowers, drumstick primrose flowers increase in size and number as the plants get older.

The common cowslip *(P. veris)* is also early blooming, but this one is yellow. Each stem holds half a dozen small yellow and green flowers—each an inch long. In England it is a wildflower, and I've seen masses of them by the roadside there. Most primroses tend to spread by seeds and will increase in number rapidly if growing conditions are right, but here in Cornish Flat I have not had my cowslips seeding in and multiplying.

A bright magenta primrose, *P. kisoana* (it has no common name) is the most amazing spreading primrose that I have ever encountered. I have it growing in two locations: First, in dry shade with morning sun; second, under an aging apple tree where the soil is lightly moist and any sun is filtered through its leaves. In both cases, a small clump will send out roots and soon cover the ground with fuzzy leaves over an area two feet square. In a few years mine spread to fill in any free spaces in both growing areas, but never pushed out other, more delicate plants, so I don't consider it a thug. I dig clumps every year to give away, and the spaces are soon filled.

Like most primroses, *P. kisoana* does best in rich soil and in spots that are not baked in bright afternoon sunshine. It may just be coincidence, but three of the best primrose gardens I have seen have been under old apple trees. Other plants that do well in my primrose garden include astilbe, hosta, turtlehead (*Chelone* spp.) and many native wildflowers like wild bleeding heart, Dutchman's breeches, and baneberry (*Actea* spp.).

Japanese primroses (*P. japonica*), also known as candelabra primroses, bloom later than most, and may be the most dramatic. Each rosette of leaves sends up a stalk that has tiered layers of blossoms radiating out from the stalk like spokes on a wheel that is parallel to the ground. They come in the usual colors—white, pink, deep pink. Tall plants, their flower stems can reach two feet.

One of the most endearing qualities of the candelabra primroses is their willingness to spread by seed if soil conditions are right: Moist (but not soggy) rich soil in shady areas. From an original planting of a half a dozen plants or so ten years ago I now have many dozen. I even find young plants that have popped up in the lawn, which transplant nicely to new locations. Their leaves have that distinctive light-green color and each new plant grows as a rosette.

Of course, if your garden is covered with landscape fabric and bark mulch, the seeds will be kept from the soil and your plants will not spread. No weeds, but no volunteer plants either. Everything is a trade off.

I have tried a few of many other types of primroses, some of which succeed, some don't. *P. vialii* is the most unusual one I have tried, but it is rated as a Zone 5 plant (only hardy to 20 below), and I lost mine after a couple of years both times I tried it. It reminded me of a dunce cap on a stem, the top a deep red, the bottom wider and pink. I did not recognize it as a primrose when I first saw it. I've read they can grow to twenty-four inches tall, though mine were half that.

The polyantha primroses *(P. x polyantha)* are hybrids that come in a wide variety of colors, producing large quantities of single or double blossoms on low plants with short stems. Breeders come up with new varieties every year, some of which are amazingly beautiful. I can't keep track of them.

One last note: The common yellow-flowered garden plant called evening primrose *(Oenothera missouriensis)* is not a primrose at all. It's a full-sun perennial that is so vigorous I consider it a thug.

So if you have twenty-seven channels of television and nothing to watch, plant primroses. Pull up a chair and relax. It works for me.

Weeding 101

As the Bible says, "To every thing there is a season . . . a time to plant and . . . a time to weed." Okay, I'm paraphrasing Ecclesiastes 3 a little bit, because, as far as I know, the Bible says nothing directly about weeding. But this is a good time to get started on your weeding program. 'Tis the season.

Everybody has weeds, and most gardeners are both self-conscious and apologetic about theirs. But they shouldn't be: Weeds are omnipresent, inevitable, and persistent. Good gardener or bad, weeds show up about now to keep us humble—and they will take over any garden that is left alone.

There are two basic types: Annual weeds that are sprouting in my garden even as I type this, and perennial weeds that live from year to year—things like dandelions and thistles and many creeping grasses. Good gardeners try very hard to pull the perennial weeds, though frankly many gardeners waste considerable time by pulling perennial weeds ineffectively. They pull weeds but leave part of the root in the ground. If you don't get every scrap of root out, perennial weeds will be back to plague you.

What should you do? First, get rid of the annual weeds because they're so easy. They're babies now, just producing their first leaves. Use a sharp hoe to cut their stems at ground level (slicing off the leaves) and the weeds will die. I like the stirrup hoe because it can slice off weeds without disturbing the soil. Some garden centers sell them, and they are available from Johnny's Selected Seeds of Maine (www.johnnyseeds.com or 877- 564-6697).

Each fall I cover my vegetable garden with leaves that I sucked up with my lawn mower and caught in a bagger. Earlier this spring I raked the leaves off the raised beds and into the walkways, allowing the soil to dry out and warm up. This also allowed weed seeds to germinate. That's good. I want them to germinate now—so I can kill them before they compete with my lettuce and tomatoes later on.

Weed seeds are everywhere. Some are tiny and arrived on breezes last summer or fall. Some floated downhill in rivulets created by rains. Some seeds have been lurking in the soil for a long time—years, even decades. The seeds in the soil are collectively called the seed bank. Seeds in the bank will wait until they are near the surface of the soil—brought up by a rototiller or a hoe—to germinate. Many have photo-triggers that keep them dormant until they are near the soil surface and sense light.

Perennial weeds are tough to eradicate, and a few impossible. Goutweed, creeping Charlie (ground ivy), witch grass, and horsetail (*Equisetum*) are very persistent—even if you try herbicides, which I don't recommend.

So how can you eradicate them? First, try digging them out (even though Japanese knotweed has roots that can go down eight feet into the earth, and goutweed roots can survive five years without any sunshine). Reducing a weed's root mass and minimizing the amount of sunshine it gets can help to reduce its vigor. Covering persistent weeds with landscape fabric and mulch to block out the sun will help considerably if you have the patience to cover the soil and then wait for a year or more.

A garden fork is a good weeding tool—for a first step. Loosen the soil with a rocking motion and roots are easier to loosen and extract. But pulling big weeds by hand is not realistic. You need something that can get under the roots, something to lift them out while you pull with the other hand. The best tool I've found is the CobraHead weeder (www.cobrahead.com or 866-962-6272). Shaped like a tine out of an old cultivator, it acts like a steel finger, loosening roots or teasing out long grass roots without breaking them off.

Whatever weeding tool you choose, weed when the soil is moist. Dry soil, particularly dry soil with a preponderance of clay, makes getting all the roots out very difficult. Sandy soil? Piece of cake—weed anytime.

Good gardeners recognize weeds and try hard to prevent them from flowering. Even if you have no time for extracting weeds, snap off flowers or seed heads before the seeds get dispersed. Some big clumps of weeds (purple loosestrife for one) can literally produce millions of seeds, or so I have read. And each one can wait for its chance to grow in your garden!

My late sister, Ruth Anne Mitchell, a great gardener, often said, "The weeds always win." She said that because weed seeds can wait practically forever before germinating, and gardeners have kids, dogs, jobs, and the occasional crisis. We aren't always attentive to weeds. Turn your back on them, and they're back in your garden. My recommendation? Pull weeds every day for a few minutes. Make it a habit, like brushing your teeth. If you do, you might just beat those weeds. Let me know if you win.

JUNE

Growing Green Beans

I love beans. I love planting them and watching them race up a pole. I love eating them fresh off the vine and freezing them for winter use, or drying the seeds for making baked beans on a snowy day. June is a good time to plant some in Cornish Flat—frost is gone for good, or at least until September.

Beans are legumes, a family of vegetables that has the ability to cooperate with soil bacteria to extract inert nitrogen from the atmosphere and transform it into a form usable by plants. Beans have roots with little nodules where the bacteria do their magic. Native Americans used to grow beans with corn, knowing that the beans offered the corn something essential, even if they didn't call it nitrogen.

If you are growing beans for the first time, buy some soil inoculant to introduce *Rhizobium* bacteria to your soil. It may be in the soil, but it might not, and without it the beans do not fix nitrogen. Each packet contains more inoculant than you will need, but I have read that it does not last from year to year, so use it up or share it with a friend. If I forget to apply it at planting time, I sprinkle some on the soil surface and water it in, which should do the trick.

Plant beans about an inch deep and two to three inches apart. Thin bush beans to six inches apart once they are up. Plant pole beans around a pole, five to six per pole, thinning to three or four plants. Beans need full sun, and about an inch of water per week—either from Mother Nature, or from your hose. Mulching around the beans helps to retain moisture and suppress weeds.

Green beans taste pretty much the same whether they're pole beans or bush beans. The main difference is the way they grow. A pole bean seed produces a vine that grows about six to eight feet long. The vines climb upward by spiraling around whatever they can find. If you provide a sturdy vertical support or teepee and you keep the plants well picked, pole beans will usually produce for six to eight weeks. As soon as the little plants break through the soil surface, they'll be looking for something to climb. So, for best results, put up your bean tower or trellis at the same time you plant your beans.

A bush bean seed will grow into a sturdy little two-foot tall plant. Each plant will produce for three to four weeks if you pick the mature beans every day or two. To extend your harvest of bush beans, sow a second crop a few weeks after planting the first beans. Once the plants stop producing, pull them out, put them in the compost pile, and replant the area with a late summer or fall crop such as lettuce or spinach.

Bean plants are susceptible to a number of fungal diseases. For this reason, you may have better luck with pole beans than bush beans if we have a wet summer. As a general precaution, try to keep bean foliage as dry as possible and avoid touching it when wet with rain or dew. Good air circulation around the plants helps keep fungal problems in check, so avoid overcrowding.

The classic pole bean is Kentucky Wonder. It is a great producer and has been around for many decades. My favorite pole bean is called Kwintus, available only from The Cook's Garden (www. cooksgarden.com or 800-457-9703). I like it because the beans are good eating even when they get big, and it freezes well. Most beans get tough and mealy when allowed to get big—which happens fast.

Jacob's Cattle is a popular bush bean grown for drying. The seeds are white with maroon speckles. It takes ninety days to produce the crop, and all the beans get ripe at once, which is handy for a storage bean—you can process them all at once. Royal Burgundy is a snap bean that only takes fifty-five days from germination to harvest. It is stringless, which is nice, and is a good cultivar for northern regions. I haven't grown it, but plan to.

Beans are a healthy food. If eaten with rice or tortillas, they provide a complete protein, which is important for vegetarians. According to the Idaho Bean Commission, a half cup of dry beans provides six to seven grams of protein and 25 to 30 percent of your daily fiber needs.

When I was a boy, if I was too lively, my mother would remark that I was, "full of beans," though I never really understood what that meant—I just knew she wanted me to calm down. And I loved the story of "Jack and the Beanstalk." A few years ago the Cornish General Store had "Mexican jumping beans" for sale— beans with bugs inside that would make them jiggle, and little boys giggle. And we all know what else beans do that make little boys giggle. So put some in, stand back, and watch them scamper up a pole or develop into lush green bushes.

Watering 101

Finally, on June 6, we got three quarters of an inch of rain—the first significant rainfall in over five weeks. I work in gardens besides my own, and this makes me appreciate my own soil—and how well it holds onto water during a drought. I've also come to realize that many people don't really know how to properly water a garden. It's not rocket science, but it's easy to do a bad job of it during a drought. Here are a few tips.

Dry soil has a very hard time accepting moisture, particularly if it comes all in a ten-second blast from a hose. Dry soil tends to shed water, not absorb it. You can build little walls of soil around your broccoli or tomatoes to catch water and encourage it to slowly seep in. Otherwise it tends to run off and away from your thirsty plants. I like to use a watering wand, going down a row, then turning around and watering everything again.

An essential tool is the watering wand. Dramm is a brand that I like, as the holes in the rosette are such that I can deliver a lot of water without producing a sharp spray that might injure small plants or erode the soil. It has a thirty-inch handle so I can direct water under leaves without bending over.

Sprinklers for the garden are good—but the simpler the better. My favorite is a brass frog that spews water out if its back. Rotating and flip-flopping sprinklers are good, too, if you don't mind being a target as they change their spray pattern. Timers are available to control sprinklers—the simpler the better. Some can be programmed to water on any imaginable schedule, but if your microwave is still blinking at you since the power went out last winter, they are not for you.

You also need to buy a rain gauge, or put out tin cans to catch rain water so you will know how much fell while you were away. I recently bought a basic one for $3.29 and it serves me well. Yes, you can spend more, but I think the basic one is fine. Vegetable gardens, in general, need an inch of rain a week—either from Mother Nature or from your hose.

Learn how your soil handles water: Take a hand tool or your finger and poke the soil after you think you've done a good job watering. You might be surprised to find dry soil an inch below a wet surface. Of course it also depends on the type of soil.

Sprinklers are good in dry times—they don't get bored with the job and leave to pull weeds or answer the phone, the way we do.

Next, you need to know that soils have different abilities to hold water. Clay soil is the best for water retention because the particles of clay are microscopically small, and water molecules attach themselves to each particle. Lots of particles means lots of water retained.

Sandy soil is the worst: Think of it as a wire basket full of golf balls. Turn on the hose, and water runs right through it. Add compost and organic matter to sandy soil and it's like adding bits of sponge to the basket of golf balls. Water will still run through it, but some will be retained.

A good loam is what we strive for: Some clay to hold water, some sand for drainage, lots of organic matter to support life in the soil and to hold onto water. Adding compost to any soil improves it in many ways—including its ability to retain or drain water.

Gravity and the presence of rock ledge affect the water-retaining abilities of your soil, too. A hilly site will lose its water much faster than a flat site, as gravity pulls it downhill. On the flat, ledge near the soil surface can act like the bottom of a bathtub, holding water. On a hillside, a layer of ledge near the soil surface can help to drain water downhill on its rocky surface, just as a paved parking lot might.

If you mulch your flower beds, a light rain or a sprinkle with a hose may not even penetrate the mulch. Bark mulch is probably the worst culprit: It takes a lot of water to soak and penetrate two to three inches of bark mulch. And yes, it will stay moist for a long time, but that doesn't do much for your peony that has a root going down a foot or more in the soil. For that reason, I leave a mulch-free zone right around each plant.

My soil, having been treated to compost every year for decades, weathers drought very well. Even so, I hope that we get good gentle rains every week all summer. If not? My frog and I are ready.

Annual Flowers for Color All Summer Long

Reclining in an easy chair on a recent raw and rainy day, I imagined myself a bumblebee. I meandered from flower to flower, taking in the colors and scents and textures of annual flowers, starting with A (alyssum) and ending with Z (zinnias). I wasn't a good or careful bumblebee who only visited flowers of one kind: I was a bumblebee tourist, seeing everything my mind could imagine—and all were in bloom at once. Then, returning to reality, I got out of my chair and planted yet another flat of annual flowers.

Annual flowers are wonderful. Perennials are great, too, but most have a relatively short performance. Annuals are born to flower: Many start early and keep on blooming all summer. I like starting annuals by seed in six-packs, even when it's warm enough that I could plant them directly in the ground. Flowers can easily get lost or misidentified as weeds when planted by seed directly in the soil, especially things I haven't tried before, or if I just want a few. Last year, for example, I started some Bells of Ireland by seed, and they were great cut flowers, but this year I don't remember what the seedlings look like. I do remember they are slow to germinate—all the easier to lose them among the weeds.

I love zinnias. They come in such a profusion of colors, and range in size from diminutive to giant. I love the lime-green ones such as Envy and Benary's Giant Lime because they look so great mixed in with other flowers—in a vase, or in a flowerbed. Zinnias come as singles, such as the Profusion series, which are short (twelve inches), and doubles such as Sunbow (twenty-four to thirty inches) and Oklahoma (thirty to forty inches). Now, if someone would develop zinnias with as many fragrances as there are colors, my bumblebee alter ego would be in heaven. And the more you cut these flowers, the more they branch and rebloom.

Marigolds, like zinnias, are considered old-fashioned flowers, and some sophisticates turn up their noses at them. Not me. I love their special aroma (which is said by some to repel certain insect pests) and their cheery faces. They range in size from eight to thirty-six inches tall. Plant the tall ones deep, covering the lower part of their stems so they will develop bigger, stronger roots. Marigolds take hot, dry weather without complaint, and don't need rich soil. From seed to flower is about two months, so buy six-packs if you didn't start some indoors in two months before your last frost date.

Near my front door there is a large pot that contains an Angel's Trumpet (*Datura* spp.). This is a plant I pay attention to every day. It produces white, lilylike blossoms all summer long. In bud, the flowers are spirals of creamy yellow; in bloom, they are trumpets looking up at me, throat open, nine inches long, with velvety-textured blossoms. Their beauty stops me in my tracks sometimes, even when I'm carrying in two bags of groceries. Because it has many large leaves, it transpires—sweats—like a drunken sailor sleeping in the sun, so it is best planted in soil that stays moist, or in a self-watering container. I got my container from Gardener's Supply Company (www.gardeners .com or 888-833-1412).

Annual blooming vines are wonderful, too. Over the entry arch to my garden I grow scarlet runner beans, and usually purple hyacinth beans. Both are very fast to reach the sky—perhaps they were the inspiration for the story of "Jack and the Beanstalk"— and produce bright flowers and edible beans. Plant them now, and by midsummer you'll be amazed at their beauty. I plant the beans about six inches apart (or thin them to six inches). Plant them near a climbing rose and they'll climb the climber.

Nasturtiums are vines that don't climb. They sprawl. Plant in full sun, perhaps in a bed of daffodils. The daffies need sunshine to recharge their bulbs until the foliage dies away, and the "nasties" will fill in and hide the dying foliage. But don't fertilize your daffodils now, if you have nasturtiums growing there, as nasturtiums won't flower much if you give them fertilizer. They like lean soil.

I grow some of my favorite annuals not for their flowers, but for their leaves. These beauties are always in bloom—which is to say, their leaves are a treat to look at. I love their bright colors and shiny surfaces. Here are some good ones:

Perilla *(Perilla frutescens)*: This is a terrific bicolored plant—leaves are green on the top side, purple underneath—but the leaves curl a bit so you can see both colors. It gets to be very bushy and can reach three to five feet tall. It self-sows exuberantly, so pinch off the flowers (which are not at all showy) if you don't want it come back next year. The Magellanica cultivar is taller, and has foliage in shades of hot pink, deep plum, and vibrant green.

Persian Shield *(Strobilanthes dyerianus)*: This plant just shimmers with silver and pink overtones on dark purple leaves. It loves hot weather, and gets big. One plant can spread over a three-foot circle and stand three to four feet tall.

Coleus *(Coleus* spp): Long used as a colorful foliage plant for shady nooks, in the 1990s breeders developed new strains that do well in full sun. Colors range from deep crimson to brilliant chartreuse and golden sunset orange. Some plants have three or more colors on a single leaf. They like rich, moist soil and need to be two feet apart if planted in the ground.

Licorice plant *(Helichrysum petiolare)*: I buy some of this every summer because I love the silvery leaves, because it mixes so well with bright colored flowers in planters, and because it takes abuse. It rarely complains if I let it dry out in a pot. It flows over the edge of pots and weaves it way through other plants. It's also exceptional in flower arrangements. There are also chartreuse and variegated lemon-lime varieties.

So even though annuals are disposable plants—they die when frost comes—I have to have them. I grow them in the vegetable garden, and in pots to fill in drab corners of the flower garden after perennials have finished blooming. Most are great cut flowers—and the bumblebees love them.

Growing Ladyslipper Orchids

Flowers have always made a big impression on me. I remember coming across a clump of pink ladyslipper orchids while we lived in Hingham, Massachusetts—even though I must have only been about two years old at the time. My sister, my mother and I were walking in a pine woods when we came upon some. I suppose our mother must have explained they were rare and delicate plants, and probably forbade me from touching or picking them. So I guess that's why I've always wanted to grow some. Now I have.

First, you should know that I did not dig up a clump of ladyslippers from the woods and bring it home. That rarely works, and is illegal in most states. I bought a potted clump of showy ladyslippers *(Cypripedium reginae)* from Cady's Falls Nursery (www.cadysfallsnursery.com or 802-888-5559) in Morrisville, Vermont, last summer. I held my breath all spring, waiting to see if they would bloom. They did, and it was worth the effort and the wait.

Ladyslippers have the reputation for being difficult to grow, and some are. In the wild, their miniscule seeds generally cannot develop into plants without the presence of special soil fungi to nurture them until their second year when they develop green leaves. In return, the ladyslippers exude carbohydrates from their roots, feeding the fungi for years as payback. It is that symbiotic relationship that has led people to believe that all ladyslippers must have the special fungi in the soil in order to get them to grow and survive. Not true. Once established, most ladyslippers are like other plants. They have requirements for sunlight, soil moisture, and soil acidity (pH) that must be met, and if so, they will thrive.

Don and Lela Avery of Cady's Falls Nursery sell fifteen kinds of ladyslippers, including the showy ladyslipper and two kinds of yellow ladyslipper (*C. parviflorum*), all three native to New England. In the wild I've seen lots of pink ladyslippers (*C. acaule*) on Cape Cod in the National Seashore near Provincetown and on Prince Edward Island. Don Avery does not recommend trying to introduce the pink ladyslipper as it is the most difficult to grow. He says they will come and go according to their own whims, and although you can introduce them to your woods, they might not stay around.

Pink ladyslippers do best with a pH of 4.0 to 6.0. Since the pH scale is logarithmic, not linear, a pH of 6.0 is ten times as acidic as a pH of 7, a 5.0 is one hundred times more acidic, and 4.0 is a thousand times more acidic. Even with adding sulfur, peat moss, and pine needles, I can't imagine getting my soil to a pH in the 4.0 to 5.0 range without removing all the soil in a bed and bringing in a big scoop of acidic soil.

Showy ladyslippers, on the other hand, like a pH of 6.8 to 7.5—and the soil in the bed I'm growing them in was about pH 7.0 before I added any amendments. I added lots of compost and some ground oyster shells to keep the pH slightly sweet over the years. Ground oyster shells are available from feed and grain dealers who sell it to feed to chickens.

Showy ladyslipper orchids never want to be in soil that dries out completely, and mine is perfect—it is almost always lightly moist. They will grow in light shade to full sun (if kept moist). In the wild, they often grow in fens, or areas where water is present (and moving slowly through it) and with a limestone-based substrate.

Don Avery recommends top-dressing the soil around showy ladyslippers with some compost every year—they like very rich soil—but no fertilizers. He also warns against adding any wood ashes, which can be fatal if applied in large doses. A little agricultural limestone at planting time is fine, he told me. In general, ladyslippers want loose, aerated soil, not compacted dry soil. If your showy ladyslippers do well for you, you can divide them like hostas early in the spring or in the fall to get more plants.

The soil in which the yellow ladyslippers do best is slightly acidic to neutral (6.5 to 7.0) and contains some organic humus. But they need less organic matter than the showy ladyslippers, and will grow in ordinary forest soil, according to Don. Yellow ladyslippers do best in medium to light shade. They finish blooming just as the showy ladyslippers are pushing up their buds in late May to mid-June.

Buying a clump of ladyslipper orchids from a reputable nursery like Cady's Falls is a moderate investment—as much as buying a small tree, perhaps—but worth every penny of it. They are magnificent. They might bloom for just a week or two, depending on the weather, but will bring me joy each day when they do—and months of anticipation as I look forward to their show again next year.

Dealing with Insect Pests without Chemicals

Even though I'm an organic gardener, I understand why others use chemicals. There are so many bad bugs, and they want to eat up our cucumbers, our roses, our lilies, our tomatoes. The natural reaction is to want to "nuke 'em." Unfortunately, many home gardeners take this one step beyond the fantasy.

Years ago I lost a lot of cucumber plants to the striped cucumber beetle. I'd plant, and once my cukes were up and proudly carrying two little leaves, the beetles would come at night and eat them. I suppose those tender leaves were as appealing to them as fresh asparagus is to me. So I'd replant, and they'd do it again. And again. Some years I got a very late start, and very few pickles.

Now, after I've planted my cucumbers, I cover the hills with row covers—two good brands are Reemay and Agribon. Row covers keep the striped cucumber beetles off, and I only have to plant once. It is a lightweight spun fabric, sort of like those squares of "anti-cling" material you might use in the clothes dryer. It breathes, allows moisture and sunshine to pass through—but not bugs. It is available at most garden centers. I remove it once the plants are flowering so that pollinators can get to them.

Another trick I've learned is to start my cukes and squash in the house and transplant them into garden beds when they have half a dozen good-size leaves. That way even if the beetles get to them, they will survive.

Tent caterpillars are out and active in June. These critters build sticky web tents, and spend all day inside watching videos (or sleeping) and getting hungry. At night, after you and the birds have gone to bed, they come out and eat the leaves of your fruit trees and other plants. In a week they can strip the foliage off a tree. Now is the time to act, but not by spraying.

I look for tents early in the season, and try to eliminate them. My preferred attack is with a bucket of soapy water and a rag. I wet the rag, surround the messy mass, pull it off, and drop it into the bucket. Or if the tent is in a small crotch in a tree, I might use loppers to cut out the branch and drop the mess into the bucket. I don't use chemical sprays—they would kill good bugs along with the bad.

The good news is that trees are very resilient, and will survive a lot of abuse. Even if tent caterpillars defoliate your favorite apple tree, it should survive and even produce another set of leaves later in the summer. Dormant buds will produce leaves after the caterpillars have gone. There is also a biological control called DiPel that is effective. You spray it on the affected plant, the caterpillars ingest it and die. It is made from a bacterium that is not harmful to anything but the bad boys.

Oriental and Asiatic lilies are under attack in many places

now, too. If you see bright red beetles with black legs and antennae on your lilies, you have trouble. Their larvae are actually worse pests. These quarter-inch long critters are disgusting and have huge appetites. They are plump greenish yellow, orange or brown grubs, and carry their own feces on their backs to deter birds—and gardeners. But you can pick them off and drop in soapy water, just as you do with Japanese beetles. You may wish to wear gloves, however. They do not attack daylilies, fortunately.

Although European parasitic wasps that attack these lily leaf grubs have been imported and tested successfully, they won't be widely available for quite some time. In the meantime, keep a sharp eye out, and pick off the grubs and beetles. I've found that hand-picking is not effective once the beetles are well established in a neighborhood, and have given up growing lilies for the present.

The Japanese beetle can be repelled instead of killed. I generally have few of these, and just hand-pick. But one summer they arrived in larger numbers, and went for my young plum tree and my grapes. I picked them off, then applied a repellent, which really helped.

Although garlic sprays such as Garlic Barrier provide some relief, I prefer a foliar fish fertilizer as a repellent. A concentrated solution of rotten fish guts will disgust any self-respecting Japanese beetle. A teaspoon in a gallon of water is recommended for fertilizing, but I make it stronger (a tablespoon/gallon or more) for use as a repellent. It also provides some minerals to my plants. The fish oils penetrate leaves, leaving a residual smell that only bad bugs care about. You won't notice the smell after a few days. A word to the wise, however: Wear rubber gloves when you make up your fish solution. Otherwise your hands may be stinky, even after washing them.

I avoid all pesticides, even botanical pesticides like rotenone, sabadilla, neem oil, and pyrethrin. The botanicals are approved for organic gardeners, but that doesn't make them safe. I won't use them as they can be toxic to us, or to fish and beneficial insects. If a spray kills insects on contact it can't be good for me, my pets, or my grandchildren.

Resisting the urge to spray chemicals really does pay off. One summer I got a lot of mail about tomato hornworms, but I only had three of them—and each was parasitized by the larvae of braconid wasps that sucked them dry. I didn't need to spray. So cuss the bad bugs furiously if you need to, but keep away from the poisons. Instead of "nuking" the so-and-sos, think physical combat. Go one on one.

Gardening with Kids

My two grandkids, George and Casey Jean-Marie, are going to be great gardeners. George, who is six, won his first blue ribbon at the Cornish Fair when he was four. Casey, who is three, loves to plant things and watch them grow. And I love being in the garden with them.

My Grampy taught me to love the garden because he loved it so. He never asked me to weed. Kids don't like to weed. We—I mean they—love to look at bugs and flowers and all living things. I still remember vividly the day sixty years ago when Grampy found a nest of bunnies in a pile of hay in the garden.

I think it's important for kids to have a little piece of soil that they call their own. It doesn't have to be large—in fact it shouldn't be. A nice size for a child's garden is the child's height in one direction and "wing" span in the other.

Kids often want to grow things like watermelons or giant pumpkins in their first gardens, but a small garden is not big enough for either of those. And, quite frankly, watermelons don't do well in this climate anyway. Children need guidance when choosing plants to grow. With George, the choices are easy: He loves cherry tomatoes and carrots, so that's what we grow. And I buy purple carrot seeds to make his carrots even more special.

A child's garden can also include flowers. Educational experts say young children don't do well with delayed gratification. So why not go to the local garden center with your child and buy a four-pack of blooming flowers? Teach your loved one to gently place it in rich soil and water it tenderly. Bingo. Day one, blooming flowers. Oh boy!

Siblings compete. We try to teach them to play nicely and to share. But in the garden it's unnecessary. Each child can have a garden space—and brothers and sisters beware! Hands off the plants!

Success is important. I could, I suppose, teach my grandchildren the consequences of not watering or what happens if the weeds take over. But George and Casey live more than half an hour away, so they can't come every day to water or check for weeds. So I do it. I want their gardens to be successful.

And, of course, our gardens are organic. Children are highly vulnerable to chemical exposure. If you plant potatoes or roses and the beetles arrive, pick 'em off. There is no reason to spray for anything.

An Appreciation: Tasha Tudor (1915–2008)

Tasha Tudor, one of America's favorite children's book illustrators and writers—and a great gardener—died peacefully at home in on June 18, 2008 at the age of ninety-two. She sold her first book, *Pumpkin Moonshine,* in 1938 by going to New York and walking from publishing house to publishing house with her book under her arm until she finally sold it, after many rejections, to the New York office of Oxford University Press. Since that time she has illustrated about one hundred books, including classics like *Little Women* and *The Secret Garden,* and written several of her own books, including *Corgiville Fair* and *Corgiville Christmas*, which came out in 2002—when she was eighty-six. I was one of just a handful of journalists who interviewed her in her later years—and I visited her twice.

Mrs. Tudor dressed and lived as if she were living in the 1830s, making her own clothes (similar to those of that period), growing vegetables, and until the mid-1990s, milking her own Nubian goats. She loved to go barefoot in warm weather, wearing shoes only when entertaining guests or traveling. She lived in a little house far off the beaten track in Marlboro, Vermont. Her house, built by her son, Seth, was modeled on a New Hampshire farmhouse built in 1740; it was so small that when I visited her I had to duck to get through the doorways.

Mrs. Tudor told me that, in general, she hated politicians and journalists. I managed to wheedle my way into her good graces by bringing her homemade cookies and unusual plants. I'd read that she loved clematis and primroses, so I brought some of each and presented her with varieties she did not have. After she decided I was all right, she admitted, with a wry smile, that she lined her bird cage with newspapers showing the faces of politicians—face up. A very proper lady, she did not say what she did with pictures of journalists, but I think we got the same treatment.

An excellent cook who believed in the goodness of butter and cream, Mrs. Tudor had made a pineapple upside down cake in my honor. She loaded it with heaping spoonfuls of fresh cream she had whipped up just before my arrival, telling me she didn't believe in the evils of cholesterol. Once, when she was tired of waiting for a stone mason to show up to build a retaining wall behind her house, she put up a "Wanted" poster for him at the local post office. She offered a homemade pie as the reward for bringing him. The mason turned up the next day, claimed the pie, and began the work.

Gardening was a passion for Mrs. Tudor, and she did some every day all spring, summer, and fall. She also had a small glass greenhouse in which she grew tropical plants like Angel's

Trumpet and a huge peach-blossomed *Brugmansia*. She told me she first fell in love with plants at the age of five, while she and her well-connected family were visiting Alexander Graham Bell, who grew a fragrant yellow rose known as Father Hugo's rose *(Rosa hugonis)*. She grew that rose most of her life.

Mrs. Tudor was quite formal in some ways, but progressive, too. She used her mother's last name, not her father's or her husband's. She expected to be mentioned in writing as Mrs. Tudor not Tasha, and insisted on calling me Mr. Homeyer, even when I protested that I preferred being called by my first name.

Mrs. Tudor believed that soil quality is a key to success. Soil pH is very important, she told me. When trying a new, untested variety she always bought at least three plants and tried them in different places on her property to see how much sun they needed and where they did best.

Mrs. Tudor was an organic gardener, and for many years her goats provided her with top-notch fertilizer. In her later years she gave up the goats, but she got composted manure every year to apply to her vegetable and flower beds. But when asked what a new gardener needs most, she didn't talk about soil improvements. "Patience," she said. "It takes twelve years to make a garden. Everything takes time that's worthwhile."

During our first visit she lamented that she wanted to plant two of her favorite crabapples varieties, but she hadn't been able to find either one. The first I found at E.C. Brown's nursery in Thetford, Vermont, and she had her son take her there the very next day. She generally traveled with her pet rooster, Chickahominy, but no one at E. C. Brown's remembers him being there that day. Maybe he was feeling tired—her corgi, Meggie, loved to chase him. She told me that Chickahominy "likes to go motoring" and that for his ceaseless efforts controlling cutworms, he was "getting a PhD in entomology."

The other variety of crabapple she wanted was out of commercial production, so Wayne Mezitt of Weston Nurseries in

Hopkinton, Massachusetts grew one especially for her—grafting a scion of a variety called White Weeper onto rootstock. She had purchased the same variety of crabapple some forty years before at Weston Nurseries, and was still remembered there—I spoke to the guy who waited on her back then. She made an impression wherever she went. Wayne and I visited her in 2005 and presented the special young crabapple to her.

Mrs. Tudor loved birds of all kinds, and was fond of snakes. She once had a garter snake that she would bring in the house, and it would occasionally nap with her. Her pet rooster, Chickahominy, also spent much time with her in the house. She explained that he was box trained, and that if he missed the box, he would bring her a Kleenex to clean it up. Chickahominy was a ladies' man, according to Mrs. Tudor. "He's like an eighteenth century gentlemen," she said. "He goes for women with well-turned ankles."

Mrs. Tudor stayed fit and trim throughout her life. When I saw her in 2005, she said that she could still fit into her wedding dress and chin herself on a bar—at age ninety!

In a small greenhouse attached to her home Mrs. Tudor had a huge peach-blossomed *Brugmansia*, which was blooming impressively when we visited her. She gave Mr. Mezitt a cutting of it and told him her secret for starting cuttings. In the spring she cut the growing tips of a willow and boiled up a handful of cuttings in a quart of water. After it cooled, she used the liquid to start cuttings.

The Tudor family hopes to continue the legacy of Mrs. Tudor by starting a nonprofit museum to house many of her artifacts and artwork. You may learn more by visiting the Web site www .tashatudormuseum.org. The family also has a Web site (www .tashatudorandfamily.com) with photos of Mrs. Tudor and articles for sale.

Near the end of my second visit with Mrs. Tudor, I asked her to what she attributed her energy, good health and long life. Without a moment's hesitation she said, "Goat's milk and gardening." Then, with a straight face but a twinkle in her eye she added, "And choosing the right parents." Mrs. Tudor grew huge expanses of forget-me-nots that bloomed in waves beneath her crabapples, which I think was appropriate: She marched to her own drummer, and will not be soon forgotten.

JULY

Scarecrows: They're Not Just for Crows Anymore

Back when I was a kid in the 1950s, scarecrows were functional. They were designed to deter crows from stealing newly sprouted corn. A flock of hungry crows could make serious inroads into our family's plans for feasting on those tiny delectable ears of Golden Bantam come August. If a scarecrow could keep crows out of the field for a week, then the corn was too well-rooted for crows to yank, and it was judged a success.

Now scarecrows have become garden art and they have gone high tech. No longer are they simple overalls and a red-checked flannel shirt blowing in the breeze, with an old straw hat on top of a pole. They are built to last, and they are often built with materials Grampy never knew.

When I met Sister Margaret, one of my favorite scarecrows, she had been appearing in Randolph, Vermont for five years. Each year she strikes a new pose, and although her denim jumper is getting faded, she hasn't lost her full-figured look that tricked me into thinking that she was real. A basket in one hand, she appears to be catching her breath before harvesting some mesclun, perhaps, or sampling a fresh Red Core Chantenay carrot. Last year she was bent over weeding all summer, a three-dimensional nonmigrant laborer.

Given the work in creating a lifelike scarecrow, it's important that the materials last through rain and sun, wind and weather. The key to longevity, I've learned, is to stuff the innards with material that won't absorb water. Styrofoam, woven-plastic grain sacks, Reemay (spun synthetic row cover), plastic grocery bags, and a good steel fence post are the basics.

After meeting Sister Margaret, poking her, and talking to her maker, I made my own. From the ragbag I extracted an old house dress, a turtleneck, and a pair of corduroy pants with a ripped seat. In the barn I found an old sun hat and a pair of tatty garden gloves. In the closet I found a beloved pair of worn-out sneakers I couldn't bear to throw away.

I started with a six-foot steel fence post. I slipped one leg of the corduroys over the post, set the post in the ground, bunched up the waist and tied the pants to the post.

Next I cut a seventeen-inch-long piece of one-by-four lumber for the shoulders, and rounded the corners for a natural look. I sent a sheetrock screw though a predrilled hole in the metal post into the wood, holding the shoulder "bones" in place.

To create a scarecrow that causes double takes, one must create a natural pose, and a body with curves. Crows can be tricked with a shirt on a stick, but not the human eye. I slipped an old life jacket over the shoulders to fill up the torso, then put on the turtle neck. Not bad. A chunk of Styrofoam under the turtleneck filled out the bosom nicely, and I tied on another piece below the waist to give her hips and a bottom. She was almost ready for her dress.

But first the legs needed some work. I rolled up two woven plastic grain sacks, and slid one up each pant leg to give them substance. I tucked the sacking into the tennis shoes, and arranged the legs in a natural, though slightly pigeon-toed stance, with one knee slightly bent. On went the dress.

Next I made a head consisting of plastic bags inside a pillow case. Anything fluffy and nonabsorbent can be used for stuffing.

Not much of a tailor, I managed to sew on two buttons for eyes. Big buttons are best. For a nose I bunched up the pillowcase and added a few stitches to keep it place. The mouth is a red hair clip, which looks okay from a distance, though a red magic marker can be used for lips by those with some artistic skill. The neck I filled with scraps of row cover, which is lightweight, fluffy, and doesn't hold water. I topped the head with the traditional straw hat.

The arms of the turtleneck I also filled with pieces of grain sack. I then tucked the ends into stretchy garden gloves that I had stuffed with row cover. One hand I attached to a garden fork producing a nice bend in the elbow when I stuck the fork into the ground.

I finally settled on Mary Lou as the name for my new garden companion. Building her only took me an hour, and it has provided me with both starts and grins. Even weeks after creating her I jump slightly, particularly at dusk, when I turn my head and see her in the distance as I come around from behind the barn.

Mary Lou moves a little some days. Perhaps the wind helps her arm or hat to find a new position. Or maybe the little people of the garden enjoy playing tricks on me, just as Mary Lou and I have tricked the crows.

Biennial Flowers

Biennial flowers are often misunderstood. People often ask me what they did wrong—their nice purple foxgloves that were so splendid last year are gone. Here's what I tell them: They did nothing wrong. By definition, biennials die after blooming.

Flowers like purple foxgloves *(Digitalis purpurea)*, rose campion *(Lychnis coronaria)*, and hollyhocks *(Alcea rosea)* grow from a seed their first year, generally producing a low rosette of leaves. You need to learn to recognize those leaves so you won't pull them out. In their second year biennials send up a flower stalk, bloom, toss their seeds on the ground, and (generally) die. And those foxgloves? If you aren't too obsessive about weeding and don't have three inches of bark mulch that prevent seeds from settling into the soil, chances are that in two years you'll have some more foxgloves. It's a two-year cycle.

Part of the confusion is that biennials often come back year after year because they produce lots of seeds, some of which start new plants in the vicinity of the mother plant. Not only that, not all biennials die after blooming. I have some hollyhock plants that come back every year, even though they are technically biennials.

One theory is that if you pick the flowers before they've had a chance to throw seeds, they live another year to try to produce progeny. The late Dave Talbot, plantsman extraordinaire, once told me that there are some strains of hollyhocks that are perennials, not biennials—even though they are the same species as the biennials.

One of my favorite biennials is the purple foxglove. These plants are tall and stately, with up to fifty blossoms on a strong stem reaching thirty-six inches on occasion (though more often just twenty-four inches). The flowers are pink and purple with little spots and dots. The name foxglove actually comes from its German name, which means gloves for little folk (fairies)—and makes more sense than gloves for foxes.

I don't pick all my foxgloves for cut flowers because I want some to go to seed. I'll wiggle the stem of a foxglove that is done blooming and if it rattles, I know it's ready to drop seeds. I cut a stem and shake out the seeds over places where I would like some plants in two years—either in a flower bed, at the edge of the woods, or even in a corner of the vegetable garden. Foxgloves do fine in part shade. Of the hundreds of seeds that I simply sprinkle on the ground, just a few will grow.

Rose campion is another of my favorite biennials. It has gray leaves and intense magenta flowers that are about an inch across, each with four or five petals. I like the contrast between leaf and blossom, and the way the flowers stand up nicely on their own, rarely flopping in a rainstorm. They stand about eighteen to twenty-four inches tall. And they have a mind of their own, popping up wherever they please, often threading their flower stems through other perennials. They are only occasionally seen for sale at plant nurseries. Perhaps if we all ask for them, more growers will start them from seed.

And then there are those majestic hollyhocks. They produce a flower spike that may reach six feet tall, adorned with two- to three-inch-wide flowers in a range of pinks, whites, and reds— and even a deep purple. The blossoms open in sequence over a period of several weeks. Mine are clearly happy here. The seedlings pop up everywhere, including in the vegetable garden. The small ones pull easily, so I put some in pots and share them as gifts. Everyone likes a free flower.

The problem with hollyhocks is that they take up much more space than the other biennials I've mentioned. A mature hollyhock needs a two-foot circle of garden space, though my volunteers often get much less space. I have learned to weed some out when they are small if there is no space for them. And often the leaves turn brown with rust, a fungal disease, late in the season.

Only recently did I learn that forget-me-nots (*Myosotis sylvatica*) are considered by most (but not all) experts to be biennials. These tiny blue (or occasionally pink or white) flowers on wispy stems and with small leaves pop up all over my property, from the sunny banks of the brook to full shade in a dry location. I let them do their thing, then weed them out, but still I have literally hundreds of plants each year. They don't bother other plants, accentuating the beauty of tulips when they bloom in masses around them.

There are countless books about perennials, and magazines at the grocery store checkout that tout reviews of "the hottest new annuals!" But those poor biennials? They're largely ignored. Do your part, and get some. Just remember that they need to be planted two years in a row if you want to have biennial flowers every year. They'll do the rest.

July Chores in the Vegetable Garden

Recently I've been working like crazy in our vegetable garden. Beavers look lazy by comparison, but soon I'll be able to slow down and take time for swimming or just plain goofing off. I find that by getting my garden relatively weed-free and mulched early, I have much less to do later and I get better production from our vegetables.

A first thinning of carrots and beets should be done by early July—an inch apart is fine. If they're too close, they compete with each other just the way they compete with weeds. Beet greens are edible and tasty, so eat your thinnings. Both carrots and beets will need another thinning a month after the first one. Carrots like a side dressing of organic fertilizer by mid-July.

There haven't been many potato bugs this year, but I regularly look for them. If you see holes in the leaves, there must be something eating them and you need to go after the culprits—with your fingers. Pick anything on your potatoes, such as striped beetles and yellowish larvae, and drop them into a jar of soapy water. Keep the jar in the garden and look anytime you go to the garden. Look under leaves for the orange masses of eggs, too, and scrape them off with a fingernail. And if you haven't hilled your potatoes, you better get to work: Potatoes grow above the seed potato you planted and need plenty of soil if you want to have lots of spuds.

Midsummer is a great time to plant vegetable seeds for a fall harvest. For starters, seeds that would take a week or more to germinate in the spring pop up out of the ground in no time. I planted some broccoli seeds on a Saturday afternoon and their little green leaves were up and smiling at me by Wednesday morning. Last year I planted broccoli seeds on July 27 and we ate broccoli heads in October and side shoots even after Thanksgiving.

The length of time from germination to harvest varies considerably from variety to variety, and should be written on the seed packet or in the catalog. It's important to pay attention to those numbers when planting in midsummer, because some varieties take much longer than others. I recently bought some carrot seeds marked "fifty-four days to harvest." That means that I could start harvesting those carrots in mid-September. I avoided another carrot variety, one that I really like, because it's labeled "seventy-two days to harvest"—almost three weeks longer. Yes, even a seventy-two-day carrot planted now would produce carrots, but they wouldn't be as big when I harvested them.

I try to plant lettuce by seed every three weeks all summer long to have plenty into the fall. Sometimes I plant the seeds thickly, then lift a clump of seedlings from the soil when the leaves are an inch or two in size. I separate the seedlings to replant six inches apart. Done at dusk and with a good watering afterwards, the lettuce babies barely know what happened.

Seed beds and new seedlings must be watered every day. The heat of summer is much more potent than that of April, so the soil dries out more quickly. All your veggies will appreciate a good watering in dry times. If you see any wilting, water!

Herbs like basil and cilantro need to be pinched to keep them bushy and to keep them from going to seed. Once they flower and form seeds, the greens are tougher and are not as tasty. Parsley doesn't bloom until its second year.

Don't let all those chores sound daunting. Go out every day, and you'll easily keep on top of them—and have time for a snooze in a hammock, too.

Perennial Fruits and Vegetables

Tired of tilling the soil and planting veggies every year? You may wish to look at some of the plants that require less work on an annual basis than standard vegetable crops. Think about some perennial veggies and small fruits. Asparagus and rhubarb produce lots of food while coming back as reliably as weeds every year— whether you do much for them or not.

If you are considering adding landscape plants to your yard, try thinking outside the box: Instead of choosing traditional shrubs like barberries or rhododendrons, what about blue-berries, elderberries, or raspberries? Or plant strawberries to border a sunny bed instead of annual flowers. And if you worry about birds "stealing" your harvest, please remember that these are the same birds you probably feed all winter!

A successful garden depends on many factors, chief among them adequate sunshine, good soil, and appropriate amounts of water. Most perennial fruits and vegetables require at least six hours of sunshine a day to succeed and produce fruit. The more sun, the more fruit.

A soil test performed by your state extension service is a good investment. You need to know if you have adequate organic matter, minerals and if the pH (a measure of acidity) is appropriate for what you want to grow. Almost any soil can benefit from a generous helping of compost.

Perennial fruits and vegetables need about an inch of water per week—either from Mother Nature or from your hose. Traveling a lot? Forgetful? Think about an automatic timer and a drip system. Watering wands are great if you have to limit water use—you can deliver the water directly to the plants, not to the walkways—or weeds! The soil should be well drained, but retain moisture after watering.

If you have crummy soil—heavy clay, or very sandy—you may wish to grow your plants in raised beds so that you can build the soil needed. A 50-50 mix of compost and topsoil is, in general, a good mix. Perennial plants tend to have deeper root systems than annuals like lettuce and tomatoes, so go with boxes eight inches deep or more.

One of the easiest ways to keep down weeds and hold in moisture is with mulch. You can use chipped wood products, leaves, or grass clippings, too. Natural mulches break down, adding organic material to the soil.

Here are a few tips on some of my favorite perennial fruits and vegetables:

Asparagus: Modern cultivars in the "Jersey" series produce all-male plants, which produce much higher yields than older varieties (Washington series). Plant roots six inches deep after improving the soil in a sixteen-inch-diameter circle. Stir in two inches of compost or rotted manure to the soil, and a cup of organic fertilizer. Spread out the roots and cover with just two inches of soil; after the seedlings grow, keep adding soil until the holes are filled. Weeds are terrible enemies of asparagus, so mulch and weed carefully to keep them at bay. Then wait; you don't get to pick for three years. Well . . . you can have a few spears in year two, but don't get greedy!

Blueberries: The keys to success are to have the proper pH or level of acidity, and to keep the weeds down. Blueberries need very acidic soil, so test yours, and then add garden sulfur or acidic fertilizer to bring the soil to a pH of 4.0–5.5. This is best done the fall before planting and repeated yearly right after blooming. Holly-Tone and Pro-Holly are two brands of organic acidic fertilizer. Birds seem less interested in stripping your plants in the fall than in summer. Fall varieties don't generally need to be netted to keep off the birds. Three good fall-bearing varieties are Elliot, Darrow, and Late Blue. Blueberries are hardy to minus 30 degrees F.

Kiwis: This climbing vine can be trellised on a fence or wall with support. In spring the Arctic Beauty variety sports tri-colored leaves, in pink, white, and green. Plant in rich soil amended with compost; keep the soil lightly moist. Northern gardeners can grow this plant because it survives temperatures down to minus 40 degrees F. I've never tried them yet, but under-stand they do well—but with much smaller fruit than what you buy at the grocery store.

Rhubarb: Grown for its stalks, rhubarb can be grown with less sunshine than the berry plants as it is not making fruits, which require lots of energy. Four hours of sunshine is sufficient. Add a bucket of compost and a cup of organic fertilizer with each plant. Plant it where the soil stays lightly moist for best results.

Raspberries and blackberries: If you like to eat these berries, they are a must for your landscape. Berries don't travel well, and are expensive to buy. Because the plants tend to multiply and spread by root, these are good plants to grow in a wood-sided raised bed that will contain them. Plant in full sun in rich soil amended with compost and organic fertilizer. Hardy to minus 30 F.

Strawberries: Day-neutral strawberries are the way to go. Read more in the April chapter.

Gardening is always a combination of work and fun. If you want to minimize the work and still harvest some food, at least some of these plants should be in your garden. And remember: Good soil is the key to success. Take some extra time to work in compost and get rid of the weeds, and you'll do just fine.

Hoes

I like to use my grandfather's garden tools. Nowadays many gardeners rototill the weeds in the walkways of the garden. I know some gardeners who are so good with a string trimmer that they can slice off the weeds in the garden with high-speed precision, but I like the old ways better. I believe there are still many uses for an old fashioned hoe—and a few of the newer varieties of hoes that have spawned like minnows in a pond over the past twenty years or so.

Most gardeners have at least one hoe, but no one hoe is best for all tasks. There are two basic types of hoes—those that work by pulling, and those that work by pushing. Hoes can be used for weeding, to hill up potatoes or make raised beds, and to make furrows for planting.

Walkways constantly sprout little weeds and if you don't apply mulch to them, you will need to hoe them regularly. Of the hoes that work by pulling, a good one is the "trapezoid hoe" from Johnny's Select Seeds. It comes razor sharp, and has a replaceable blade. It is a relatively lightweight tool, and works well for gardeners of all sizes. One can drag it across the soil surface or draw it along just beneath the surface.

My friend Scott Stokoe of the Dartmouth College Organic Farm in Hanover, New Hampshire, taught me that you can reduce back pain and fatigue by using your hoe properly. Instead of leaning forward and dragging a hoe, stand up straight and grasp the handle with your thumbs pointing up, not down. Move your body—not just your arms—to move the hoe. He advised me not to reach too far with a hoe, and to weed a wide bed first from one side, then from the other.

The scuffle hoe, also known as the stirrup hoe, also from Johnny's Seeds, is another style I like. This is a five-inch-wide stirrup-shaped blade with both leading and trailing edges sharp, allowing one to cut either by pulling or pushing. It is excellent for weeding walkways quickly, but harder to use in a bed where plants are close together. It cuts cleanly through hard packed soil just below the surface once you get the hang of it.

The standard old fashioned hoe such as my grandfather's is a multi-use hoe. You can cut weeds by drawing it towards yourself, though this type of hoe can also be used to hack at large weeds. It can be used to build a raised bed, or to hill potatoes.

A pointed or triangular hoe can be useful, too. A pointed hoe can be used to create a furrow for planting corn, beans, or any large seed. As you pull it towards you, the dirt slides out of the furrow, much as a snowplow pushes snow. If you want to cut off weeds with a scuffing action, the sides of it will do so even though they are not designed to be sharpened.

Every hoe will please some gardeners. If possible, visit your friends and try some different hoes before buying a new one. Or go to a yard sale—if you're lucky, you'll find one like the hoe my Grampy used.

Mulching 101

Mulch is the gardener's friend. Properly applied, mulch can keep down weeds, diminish needs for water, and make the garden look like something out of a glossy garden magazine.

There are many kinds of mulch, and different parts of the garden need different types of mulch. Let's start in the vegetable garden: I wait until the soil has warmed up nicely and I pull out—or slice off with a hoe—any existing weeds. Then I spread out layers of newspaper over the soil—one section, or six sheets per layer. In the old days newsprint had heavy metals in the ink, but nowadays inks are all soy-based, even the colored sections. If you are still worried about the possibility of chemicals getting into your garden, soak your newspapers overnight in a recycling bin, and pour the water out on your driveway. That should rid your papers of soluble chemicals.

I leave a little space around the plants so that light rain showers will get the roots wet. Then I put down mulch hay on top of the papers to keep them from blowing around, and to make the garden look nice. The newspapers keep sunshine from getting to weed seeds, so most won't germinate. And the paper acts as a barrier for those that try to start up anyway. By the end of the summer the newspapers—which are really just a modified wood product—will have broken down and/or been eaten by your earthworms. Flattened-out cardboard boxes work well as mulch, too.

Mulch hay is an inexpensive product I can buy from my local farmer. It's animal feed that has been rained on, so cows won't eat it. It does contain grass seeds, so some gardeners avoid it. They buy straw, which is a byproduct of threshing wheat or other grains. Straw should have no seeds, but it costs five times as much. I find the newspapers keep the hay seeds out of the soil, so I buy hay, not straw. Grass clippings from the lawn are also good mulch.

In the walkways I generally put down the same paper and hay, but another technique is to use landscaping fabric. I get the industrial-strength stuff that feels like cloth, not the cheap, see-through fabric that is sold at most garden centers. You might be able to buy some of the good stuff at your local garden center—many of them buy it in bulk to put down in the yards where they set out trees or perennials. They may agree to cut some off a roll for you. You'll also need some of the special "earth staples" that are sold at garden centers—they are three inches long and an inch wide. Push them through the fabric and into the soil to keep the fabric in place.

Black plastic is favored by some gardeners, but I don't like it. Yes, it's cheap and it's easy to put it down in your pumpkin patch, for example, but it degrades in sunlight and you have to dispose of it—more petrochemicals for the landfill. In low spots it holds water and breeds mosquitoes. And it's ugly. Not for me, thanks.

In the perennial gardens, landscape fabric can be used if covered with wood chips or bark mulch. But be aware that the holes you cut for new perennial plants will not be adequate forever. In a few years you will have to go around your plants with scissors to make bigger openings.

Bark mulch and wood chips are sold by the bag at the big-box stores. Beware: Most of those bags have "colorant" added to make them a different color. Some are just shredded lumber salvaged from construction sites. I don't want colored wood in my yard—anywhere. The dyes may have chemicals that may affect my soil's health. Read the bags carefully, as many do not advertise what is in the bag in a way that is easy to find.

Better garden centers and some landscapers sell ground bark from lumber yards—the real stuff. I have a fellow locally who gets some "double ground" bark that is really fine and has no big lumps. Around my blueberry bushes I use wood chips that I get free—electric companies have crews that shred brush and branches near their wires, and are glad to have a place to dump it.

Besides keeping down the weeds, mulch minimizes evaporation from the soil surface—and that's important in midsummer. On the other hand, a light shower might not get to the soil, particularly through a thick layer of bark mulch. You never need more than two inches of bark mulch.

Lastly, beware of the trend to create volcanoes of mulch around your trees. Bark mulch holds moisture and probably harbors wood-eating fungi, too. Trees are very sensitive to damage near the base. If the bark rots, you can lose the important cambium layer below—and kill the tree after a few years. Always leave a four-inch space between the tree and the mulch. A ring of mulch around your trees can save them from string trimmers and runaway lawn mowers, too.

So even though I don't aspire to Martha Stewart–like grounds, I use mulch to save work and help my plants. I recommend that you do some mulching, too.

On a Fad Diet of Rock Dust, How the Garden Does Grow

For years I had been hearing about the virtues of gardening with rock powders. Finally I gave in, acquiring some finely ground granite from a company that engraves tombstones. I scratched the stuff in around my peppers. Although it was August, the plants were small and appeared to be sulking. By mid-September I needed stakes to keep them from tipping over from the weight of the fruit—a first in my twenty years of growing peppers in chilly New Hampshire.

Joanna Campe, down the road from me in Northampton, Massachusetts has been folding rock powders into her garden soil since the mid-1980s, when she came across the work of an engineer turned farmer and writer, John D. Hamaker, who argued that rock dust could mimic the action of soil-enhancing glaciers.

"If we imitate how the earth forms soils, we need to give our gardens more than just the three elements found in chemical fertilizers," Ms. Campe said, suggesting plants need close to ninety minerals.

Like Mr. Hamaker, Ms. Campe believes that over the millenniums the soil has been depleted, leaving the food chain deficient in important trace minerals. For centuries people in the remote Hunza Valley of Pakistan farmed soil irrigated by "glacial milk," routinely living to be one hundred. Other factors were of course at play, but rock powder enthusiasts theorize that the health and longevity of the Hunza people were related to the plant-borne minerals in their diet.

I was intrigued. So after my pepper explosion, the following spring I added granite powders to half of my potato plot, following Mr. Hamaker's recommendation of about fourteen pounds of rock dust per hundred square feet of garden bed.

At the beginning of the growing season, the potatoes with rock powders grew like sprinters leaving the starting block. They were six to eight inches tall when the others had reached two to three inches.

The action of the powders was a bit mysterious. Rocks contain no nitrogen, the fuel for fast green growth and one of the three components of chemical fertilizers. Although they may contain some phosphorus or potassium, my soil tested more than adequate for both, so they were not correcting a deficiency.

Dr. John M. Duxbury, a professor of soil science at Cornell University, pointed out that common soil treatments like limestone and phosphorus started out as rocks—as did soil in general. But he was not convinced that rock powders raised the quality of soil already treated with fertilizer. "In the tropics we use rock phosphate because it is cheaper," he said.

Research in the tropics by Dr. Ward Chesworth, an emeritus professor of land resource science at the University of Guelph in Ontario, found that rock powders did indeed improve the productivity of soil deficient in minerals because glaciers never got that far. But even in New Hampshire, he suggested, soil could lack trace minerals, because farmers have been "making tea with the same bag for ten thousand years."

Though there are few field trials to prove the rock powder case, anecdotal evidence abounds. After using rock powders at her nursery in Claremont, New Hampshire for ten years, Susan Lawrence said her hostas became more disease-resistant and winter-hardy, and better bloomers, too.

That leaves gardeners like me experimentally dusting their plots with ground granite, basalt, or other rocks. Luckily, these powders (also called rock fines and rock flour) are inexpensive— often free—from quarries and rock-crushing plants. For more information, visit Ms. Campe's Web site, www.remineralize.org.

Last fall, with winter breathing down my neck, I harvested my potatoes without stopping to compare the weight of those grown with and without rock powder. This year, I treated the whole garden. And who knows? Maybe that extra dash of minerals will help me, like the Hunza farmers, live to be a hundred.

Postscript: Since that article appeared in *The New York Times* in 2004, I have tried a number of different rock powders, and I believe they help plants, even though I cannot prove it. One experiment I did was with radishes in small pots—with rock powders, or without them. There was no obvious difference as they grew, so I put the pots outside under an overhang and forgot about them. Only weeks later did I notice that some radishes had died of drought, while the others, clearly marked "rock powder," were alive and healthy. The only rock powder that is available commercially is Azomite, a manmade mixture of fine rock powders from Utah that is for sale from Fedco Seeds and Johnny's Seeds. Azomite is certified for use by organic farmers.

The Berrymeister, Lewis Hill

Lewis Hill, who passed away in 2008, had a lifelong love affair with berries. As a boy in the 1930s he would sometimes sneak into the family garden, pick two leaves of lettuce, and use them as the "bread" for a red-raspberry sandwich. Lewis and his wife, Nancy, lived on a farm they called Berry Hill, in Greensboro, Vermont, for many years and they had all the berries anyone could wish for.

The fruits of the genus *Ribes*, which include gooseberries, currants, jostaberries, and worcesterberries were among the Hills' favorites. He told the story of how, on a visit to New York City, he admitted over dinner that his favorite pie was made from gooseberries. A hush, apparently, fell over the room: He and Nancy were the only ones present who had ever tasted one.

Gooseberries *(Ribes hirtellum)* are easy to grow, and very tasty not only in pies, but straight off the bush. They can be as small as a pea or as big as a small plum, and range in color from green to lavender to deep red. They have a nice crunch, and taste something like a cross between a kiwi and a grape. They grow on bushes that rarely exceed five feet in height or diameter.

Although Europeans and Canadians treat gooseberries and currants as gourmet fruits, they are little-grown in the United

States. Members of the *Ribes* family can serve as alternate hosts for white pine blister rust, a fatal disease of some pines, so they are banned in parts of the United States. And although the USDA lifted its ban on growing gooseberries and currants decades ago, some people still fear to grow them.

Everyone in New England, according to Lewis Hill, knows that currants and gooseberries are liable to kill pine trees, even though that is not necessarily true. "On the first day of kindergarten, children learn how to pile up blocks. On the second day, they learn that gooseberries kill pine trees," he said. But, he pointed out, there are adequate numbers of wild currants and gooseberries in many woods to carry the disease, so banning them serves no purpose.

Lewis Hill told me that during the Depression of the 1930s unemployed laborers were hired to go through the woods pulling up and burning wild currant and gooseberry bushes. Sometimes they would even enter farmyards and destroy domestic *Ribes* plants. The memory of the "Ribes police" still affects attitudes toward the plants in New England, despite the fact that many rust-resistant cultivars are available. Check with your local agricultural extension service or USDA office before ordering any.

Sea buckthorn *(Hippophae rhamnoides)* was another berry grown by Lewis Hill. No relation to the invasive glossy buckthorn *(Rhamnus frangula)*, it is originally from Siberia, and is hardy to minus 50 degrees Fahrenheit. Lewis explained that they never harvest the berries until after several frosts, but that the cold has, if anything, a beneficial effect. "Ripening so late means the birds have gone south," he said. "If they learned about them, they might stick around."

The berries are small, bright orange, and have a unique flavor something like an orange or a passionfruit, though they are too tart to eat off the bush. Lewis and Nancy cut the heavily laden branches in the late fall, bringing them indoors to strip off the berries. They cooked the berries, mashed them, strained the juice, and bottled it hot, and froze it. They added sugar and used it like orange juice, or mixed it with orange juice.

The sea buckthorn is dioecious—there are male and female plants—and one must purchase a male plant for every eight or ten females. One could start them from seed, but it would be several years before a plant would be old enough to bear fruit, and male plants never do. It's easy to start females (or males) from hardwood cuttings in the early spring. It is a vigorous grower in full sun, and grows to be six to ten feet tall. One word of caution: Lewis told me that he had seen seedlings popping up at the edge of the woods, so it may have a tendency to wander. I have seen that the roots send up suckers near my plants, which I control by mowing.

Another favorite berry of Lewis Hill was the elderberry. He claimed that the elderberry juice helped to prevent arthritis. Elderberry *(Sambucus canadensis)* bushes are native to the United States, turning up uninvited in wet, brushy locations. Elderberries will spread by root suckers, and get to be eight to twelve feet tall, depending on the variety. They produce clusters of white flowers in June, and masses of quarter-inch-diameter black fruit in September. It is hardy in Zones 4 to 9.

To obtain unusual berries, Lewis recommended Raintree Nursery (800-391-8892), Whitman Farms (503-585-8728), or One Green World (877-353-4028).

Lewis Hill grew and sold plants for nearly sixty years on a farm that had been in the family for two hundred years. Although he never had the chance to pursue a higher education, he and Nancy wrote sixteen books on gardening, including *The Flower Gardener's Bible*, their last book. His *Fruits and Berries for the Home Garden* (Storey Books, 1992) is a good resource for anyone interested in berries. His books are full of good advice and Yankee humor, and are written by a plantsman who knew his berries—and just about anything else that grows.

AUGUST

Garden Follies

Gardens are not just for plants. For the past two or three centuries, a few eccentric gardeners in England and Ireland have included something they call garden follies. These are buildings made just for fun and are not intended to provide shelter. A few are huge, but most are quite small.

I remember the first time I saw a garden folly. I was walking through a park in Dublin, Ireland, when I saw a small pond with an island in it. On the island was a perfectly formed three-story mansion, but only big enough to be inhabited by gnomes or leprechauns—perhaps eight feet across and three or four feet tall.

For years I harbored a secret desire to build my very own garden folly. Finally last fall I got my inspiration while hiking in rural southwest France. I happened upon a fascinating structure: A small abandoned hut made entirely of stones. It used no masonry, no wood—not even rafters to support the roof. Clearly, it was extremely old, yet there was no sign of deterioration. Its cone-shaped roof was made of small stones, none bigger than a loaf of bread. I studied it, photographed it, and decided that I would like to try to build something like it when I got home.

So I did. I built a small stone igloo like the roof of that French hut. My folly is just four feet in diameter and about two feet tall, with a one-foot-tall doorway that is about seven inches wide. The doorway allows my grandkids to peer inside, but not to get in there. It is sturdy, too—I tried standing on the roof, and nothing wiggled or fell.

Before building an igloo, I recommend making a model of an igloo using dominoes (or building blocks) so that you get a feeling for what is entailed. First, trace a small plate on paper to make a perfect circle. Place eight dominoes inside that circle. The next layers should use seven, then six, then five dominoes—and so forth. Each joint, or meeting of two dominoes, should be covered by a domino of the next layer. This ties the structure together, particularly when using stones which are rough-surfaced and irregular.

Each layer of dominoes is smaller than the one below it, so the dominoes overhang the layer below it a little, and the opening is a bit smaller. You will find that the dominoes do not fit properly if you do not let them overhang enough, or have them overhang too much.

Outdoors I began the project by placing the iron rim of an old wooden wagon wheel on the lawn to define a perfect circle four feet in diameter. I dug out all the sod inside the rim, creating a nice round hole. I dug down twelve inches, removed all the soil, and replaced the soil with fine gravel. I did this because soil tends to freeze and thaw in winter, moving any structure sitting on it. The gravel provides good drainage, minimizing any heaving of the soil. I placed flat stones on top of the gravel, making the floor.

Once finished, an igloo is a very stable structure because

the force of gravity pushes the stones together, not apart. But the stones need to be placed carefully. Each layer must be just slightly smaller in diameter than the layers below it. Think of it sort of like a structure made by stacking donuts of decreasing size, each donut made of several small stones. It is important that each stone overlaps the stones below, sitting on at least two stones. Never stack two stones of the same size, one on top of the other.

To create the doorway to the igloo, I just left a gap in each layer until I'd reached the appropriate height, then I spanned the opening with a long stone which served as a lintel. When the igloo was nearly completed I placed a large flat stone on top of the small opening at the top, finishing the project. And as I had done many times during construction, I wiggled and pushed the stone to make sure it was securely seated. Small flat stones are great for reducing wiggle: I just slid them into crevices, pushing them until stuck.

I used a mason's hammer and a sledge to break larger stones into pieces. Be sure to wear safety glasses to protect your eyes if you do so. That's very important! I used stone I found on my land, sedimentary stone that was layered and could easily be split into thinner layers. I used a sledge to tap the mason's hammer to split stones into thinner layers. Most of the stones I used were only one to three inches in thickness. I preferred oblong pieces, say twelve inches long by four or five wide. The sledge was useful for breaking big chunks into small ones.

Since my igloo is, in part, to be for the enjoyment of my grand-kids, the final step was to give it an inhabitant. Inside sits a statue of one of Snow White's famous dwarfs—Happy or Dopey, I'm not sure which.

My folly pleases me every time I walk by it and that's what garden follies are supposed to do. But if making a stone igloo doesn't appeal to you, perhaps you would like to make a different type of garden folly. How about a miniature Taj Mahal?

Daylilies

For some gardeners, daylilies are humdrum. Everyone has them, and the classic orange daylily appears everywhere—even along roadsides with the weeds. But daylilies really are wonderful, and much more diverse than is widely known.

Take bloom time, for example. Daylilies are generally considered midsummer flowers. But some start in early June, while others wait until September to start and continue into October. Recurrent daylilies like Stella d'Oro (a gold one) and Pardon Me (a nice red) will bloom off and on for much of the summer.

Early bloomers include one that has graced farmsteads for ages. It has small lemon yellow blossoms, and is a species all to itself—formerly known as *Hemerocallis flava*, now called *H. lilioasphodelus*. (Don't ask me why the folks in charge of Latin nomenclature do that. Just when you learn a name, they go and change it.) It is pleasantly fragrant, though most daylilies are not fragrant. Late bloomers that I like include Lime Lighter, a lemon yellow, and Hurricane Edouard, a violet pink.

Then there is size. I visited Olallie Daylily Gardens in South Newfane, Vermont, and was amazed by the range of sizes available. One known only by its Latin name, *H. citrina*, var. "vespertina," beckoned to me. Its delicate light yellow blossoms stand five to six feet tall, with foliage, which is only two feet tall. It's a dramatic flower that is perfect for the back of a flower bed.

According to Chris Darrow, the owner of Olallie Daylily Garden (and a third-generation daylily breeder), others are small enough to put in a garden of diminutive plants, with delicate leaves and flower scapes. Shortee, aka Stella Jr., a peach-colored recurrent type, has flower scapes just nine inches tall.

Daylilies come in a full range of colors, from nearly white to yellow and peach, while others come in pink, lilac, lavenders, and red. Some come in one color, but most are bicolored, with a throat or eye of a second color. Some, such as Fleur de Rocaille, have more than two colors. Olallie's catalog (www.daylilygarden.com or 802-348-6614) describes it as a "bright lavender-pink/strawberry yellow bicolor with a wine eye." Visiting Olallie in early August I saw one I liked called Mallard, which, despite its name, is nearly a pure red. (Excuse me, but are mallards coming out in red this fall? Designer ducks?) Flower shape varies as much as the colors. There is the standard trumpet. Then there are those with ruffled edges. And spiders, whose petals are narrow and spaced a little apart. Scorpio (developed at Olallie Farm) and Yellow Ribbons are nice ones. Doubles, such as Little Carnation and Shamrock Double Grape have their centers filled in with more petals.

Many people don't know that daylilies are great cut flowers. Because each blossom only lasts a day—hence the name—most people don't use them in flower arrangements. But I cut scapes that are just starting to bloom and have numerous fat, unopened buds. The buds will open in a sequence of blooms lasting up to a week, depending on the number of buds. This works most reliably if the arrangement gets some sunshine each day.

It is interesting to me that not all daylilies are programmed to open at the same time of day. According to Chris Darrow, some will open in the late afternoon and last until the next afternoon, while the more common ones open in the morning and close at night. The former are better cut flowers at the dinner table, obviously.

Large clumps can be dug up and divided, creating dozens of new plants. This can be done anytime, though I do it after blooming so as not to interfere with the show. Daylilies are extremely tenacious, so this is not a job for the faint hearted or feeble. It is best done with a sharp spade, and while still in the ground. Step (or jump) on your shovel, slicing the plants, roots and all, into four sections before trying to extract the clump from the ground. Much easier than trying to lever out a large clump.

For me, a good reason to grow daylilies is that they are indestructible. Even someone with a "brown thumb" cannot kill a daylily. Daylilies do best in full sun, but I have some common orange ones that bloom reliably in almost full shade. The more sun, the more blossoms, however.

Most insects don't eat them, though slugs will take bites if there's not much else offered for lunch. Thrips will sometimes suck their juices, but this just causes an interesting color change—splotches on the flowers. I've never seen one suffer from mildew or any other disease.

So if you are lazy, inexperienced, or lack confidence in the garden, buy daylilies. Daylilies, once established, will outcompete most weeds and grasses. Planted about two feet apart, they will turn into a solid planting of daylilies, stabilizing banks and keeping outsiders beyond their boundaries. And they will grow in any kind of soil. Hot, dry soil? Wet, heavy clay? Bring it on. Daylilies will do just fine. Peruse a daylily catalog such as Olallie's and you will surely see a daylily that speaks to you. But watch out: Before long you may become addicted to them—buying, trading, and hybridizing them. There are worse fates, of course.

The Garden as a Place of Comfort

In times of trouble and sadness I go to the garden. I find it comforting to spend time surrounded by flowers, many of which evoke memories of people I've loved. I find it therapeutic to pull weeds, to pick cherry tomatoes, or cut flowers for an arrangement. I have planted trees in memory of loved ones who have died. I say hello to my friend and mentor, Fritz Hier, once New Hampshire Tree Farmer of the Year, when I pass by the purple smoke bush *(Cotinus coggyria)* I planted for him on the day of his memorial service in August 1999.

July 2009 was a tough month for me. My vigorous sixty-five-year-old sister, Ruth Anne Mitchell, died unexpectedly on July 6 after eight days of strokes. We had hiked the Chemin de St.

Jacques de Compostelle in France just two years before. I had visited her in Namibia the year before that. We gardened and walked and talked and ate outrageous meals together. She was a soul mate. Then on July 23 my mother, nearly ninety-three, passed away. Mom was in a nursing home and had a long and wonderful life, but she was ready to go. She was in poor health and her death was a blessing.

So I spent some extra time in the garden. I have some of Ruth Anne's ashes and will place them in the soil here at the Creamery (my house was built in 1888 as a butter factory) where she spent countless hours pulling weeds and admiring the flowers. I want to plant special, unusual flowers in her memory. Below are some of the things I shall plant.

I went to E.C. Brown's Nursery (www.ecbrownsnursery.com) in Thetford, Vermont and got a yellow ladyslipper *(Cypripedium pubescens)*. I have wanted one for a long time—they are not inexpensive plants—and took this excuse to get one. It is a Zone 4 plant that will do well in a moist, neutral soil in light shade. I have such a place – it's under a wild apple tree.

I also called Cady's Falls Nursery (www.cadysfallsnursery .com) outside of Morrisville, Vermont and talked to Lela Avery, who is co-owner (with her husband, Don) of one of New England's most elite and wonderful nurseries—but one hundred miles from my home. I called to ask about the umbrella plant *(Darmera peltata)*, which I had seen there a couple of years ago. It has huge leaves—each two feet across or more—and does well in moist to wet acidic soil. Yes, they had some, and agreed to save me one. I asked Lela about the flowers. She explained that the flowers pop up out of the ground in the spring before the leaves. They form clusters of small pink flowers on long stems. My books tell me it is only hardy to Zone 5—tolerating no colder than minus 20 degrees. Lela said they are in Zone 3, with temperatures much colder than that, and that theirs had survived and thrived for twenty years.

I asked Lela for some suggestions for other special plants. She suggested the Himalayan blue poppy *(Meconopsis betonicifolia)*. I had tried and failed with this plant previously—it's very fussy. Lela said it likes shade with lots of humus in the soil and moderate moisture. It blooms at the time of the showy ladyslipper *(C. reginae)* and in the same conditions. I do well with the showy ladyslipper, so I decided to try again. Lela admitted that there is no specific formula as to where it will grow or not, but that it does not want to get too hot—it is a native of the Himalayas, after all. They have had some die and others do well.

My sister visited me at my cabin in Prince Edward Island years ago, and we probably saw bunchberry *(Cornus canadensis)* in the pine woods there—I know I did. It is a true dogwood, but not a woody one. It is a low-growing ground cover that only gets six inches tall or so, but has gorgeous white two- to three-inch flowers. Actually the flowers are tiny, but surrounded by four white "petals" that are actually bracts, or modified leaves. They look like the flowers of the dogwoods that grow in warmer places like Connecticut where my sister and I grew up. Cady's Falls sells them, and I will get a few. Lela says they are a bit tricky, but in the right spot they grow and spread nicely. They are hardy to minus 40 degrees. She suggested modifying the soil with peat to acidify it, and growing them in part shade, not too dry. I have a clump of pines near my brook, and will try them there.

Lela also suggested trying trailing arbutus *(Epigaea repens)*. A native wildflower, it is hardy to Zone 3 and may grow where bunchberry will, she said, as it also needs acidic soil. It has early pink to white fragrant flowers that are formed the summer before, waiting out the winter as buds ready to bloom early in the spring. Sounds delicious, I shall give it a try. I'm sure my Mom would have liked it, so I shall plant it for her.

Having great flower gardens means spending money and taking some risks. Some "iffy" plants will do well, others will not. I can modify soil and try to create microclimates that work. Nothing will heal my heart right now, but planting a few flowers in memory of my sister and mother will help.

Postscript, 2010: Some plants did well, others died. The Himalayan poppy was spectacular, blooming for two to three weeks. The umbrella plant is fine. The rest? They did not survive. The yellow ladyslipper got dug up by an animal sometime during the winter and the roots dried out. The others just didn't come back after the winter.

Standing Stones in the Garden

In 1972 while traveling in England I had the chance to visit Stonehenge before it was fenced off and turned into a site for throngs of tourists arriving in buses. As I wandered around the big grassy field I was filled with a sense of awe and wonder: How did people move these huge monoliths hundreds of miles in the days before John Deere tractors, before trucks and trains and cranes? How did they know how to arrange them so that the stones related to celestial events?

Standing stones have intrigued people for thousands of years, and Stonehenge is just one of many sites that have utilized stones for mystical or religious purposes. In the garden, standing stones can be used effectively to catch people's attention, or to lead people from one part of the garden to another. One summer I decided that I'd like one in my garden.

I cleared out some weedy alders that were growing around our stream, and created a small round grassy area (about ten feet across) with the idea of creating a quiet garden room for rest and reflection. I planted a small river birch at one side of the clearing, and cleared out the brush and weeds from the edge of the stream.

Elsewhere on the property I had a stone bench, but I rarely used it. I decided to move the bench closer to the stream, and to add a standing stone at the edge of this garden space to draw people to the stream and the bench.

Before I began work I pulled out my copy of Gordon Hayward's wonderful book entitled *Stone in the Garden: Inspiring Designs and Practical Projects* (W.W. Norton, 2001). Hayward is a highly regarded garden designer who lives in Putney, Vermont. I have seen his use of stone in the garden, and thought I should read his chapters on benches and standing stones before I got started.

Hayward explains that stone benches are not comfortable to sit on for very long, but are great for imparting a sense of permanence to a garden, for providing a sense of scale from a distance, or for drawing people into a garden room. He explained that it is human nature to want to sit with our backs protected—by a wall, or by a substantial planting. Perhaps that harkens back to the time when we were prey for big game. I snuggled my bench up to a green wall of leaves near the stream.

I found a nice stone in my woods, about four feet long and a foot wide and thick. Despite its weight—about 180 pounds per cubic foot—I was able to roll it onto a plastic sled and drag it downhill out of the woods. Once on the lawn, I pulled the sled with my riding lawnmower to its destination.

It's important that a standing stone be set firmly in place. Hayward's book recommends burying one third of a stone, but David Brandau, co-owner of Standing Stone Perennial Farm in South Royalton, Vermont told me that burying just one quarter is adequate, particularly if concrete is added in the hole. Brandau has set dozens of standing stones, including some eight to twelve feet tall. Their display gardens feature a variety of standing stones. They sell lovely stones for gardens as well as unusual, organically grown perennials.

I dug a hole twelve inches deep and twenty-four inches around with vertical sides. I undercut the sides with a hand tool (my CobraHead weeder) so that the concrete I planned to use would spread wider than the walls of the hole—forming a wide, stable base shaped like a mushroom anchor.

I slid the butt of the stone over the hole and tipped it in, then stood it up straight. I rotated it to find its best face, stopping to ponder its placement. Once it was in place, I knew that this stone was not going anyplace.

I removed the stone and put two inches of dry concrete mix in the bottom of the hole. Then I rolled the stone back over the hole, righted it, and rotated it a little until it was "just so." Then I shoveled in the rest of the eighty-pound bag of concrete mix. I packed down the dry mix around the stone and into the undercut area I'd created. I added a little water, but did not bother mixing it in. I filled up the rest of the hole with soil, and packed it down.

I finished the project by planting grass seed around the stone and, off to one side, a royal fern *(Osmunda regalis)*. Royal ferns like moist soil, and can grow to be the biggest of all ferns in New England—up to six feet tall or more.

I'm not sure what it is about my standing stone that pleases me so much. The shape, color, and texture are nice. But it might also be that I see it and remember what a challenge it was getting it there, and standing it in place. I doubt it, but maybe that's what the builders of Stonehenge wanted to do—give guys something to be proud of, and something to do on their days off.

The Killer Instinct

To be a good vegetable gardener, it really helps if you have a bit of the killer instinct in you. You have a big advantage if you don't mind squishing bugs or picking up snails and slugs to drop them in soapy water. It's all part of getting your veggies to harvest in good condition.

I know, there is another way to control bugs—but I don't choose to use chemicals. Yes, I could visit what I call "death row" at my local garden center, the row where they sell all those toxic powders and liquids. I could buy chemicals that would kill every bug that chews on the cukes, every snail that perforates my broccoli leaves, and every slug that sucks the juice out of my potential coleslaw. But I don't choose to.

Here's why: Broad-based pesticides don't kill just the bad critters, most of them annihilate everything that wiggles—including the good ones. For example, I recently learned that there's a tiny parasitic wasp that attacks Japanese beetles. If you see a single white spot on the back of a Japanese beetle that you're about to toss in soapy water, you may want to reconsider. Soapy water will kill the culprit today. The parasite may take another week or more to finish off the beetle, but I like to encourage the good bugs. I know I can't find and pick every Japanese beetle that's lurking in the raspberries, so I encourage the predators to multiply.

And then there's corn. I don't grow my own sweet corn because there's too much raccoon in my temperament: I'd want to stuff myself. But it's tough to find organic corn for sale. I asked my neighborhood grower why he sprays pesticides on his corn. He explained that customers want perfect corn. That finding a corn worm will shock and dismay some customers, and he fears they'll go elsewhere. So he sprays.

Me? I'm always delighted when I do find a corn worm. I mean, it only takes a quick flick of a sharp knife to get rid of the worm, and it means the farmer didn't spray that batch. I know the government has rules about spraying, and that properly sprayed corn is said to be 100 percent safe for me to eat. But it's not just about me. I wonder what the chemicals do to the farm workers, the birds and fish, and of course, the good bugs.

When I buy corn somewhere new, I ask if pesticides have been sprayed on it. I say that I'd be willing to pay more for unsprayed corn. If enough of us do that, we may influence the choices our local farmers make. I may be a cold-blooded killer in my own garden, but I do it just one bug at a time. That generally works just fine, and I won't starve if I lose part of my crop.

Spiffy Up the Garden and Have a Party

August is a great month for a garden party, and I try to have one every year. And although I try not to worry too much about what others might say about my gardens, I do want everything to look nice. Here are a few tips if you decide to entertain in the garden. I did all this before this year's party, and it really helped.

Cut the lawn a day before the event. Cutting the lawn is like making your bed: It gives the surrounding spaces a tidy look, even if there are less tidy spots nearby. You might even want to cut the lawn half an inch shorter than usual.

Use an edging tool or shovel to make nice sharp edges around flower beds. A little dry moat will keep lawn grasses from climbing into the flower bed, and add to the overall sense of orderliness. Pull weeds at the front of the flower bed, even if you don't get them everywhere. Pull all the tall weeds. Anything taller than your flowers will be noticeable. I have one kind of tall weed (I don't know its name) that attracts Japanese beetles. Each morning and evening I check these weeds and harvest a few beetles. So I leave them in place and point them out to my visitors. They're my "good weeds."

Add mulch as needed. Mulch is a great weed deterrent, though I often don't get everything mulched perfectly. Mulch in the front part of flower beds and on pathways through the vegetable garden makes everything look better.

Fill in holes created by weeding. This can be done several ways. Before my party I moved some spare bee balm and phlox into spaces where perennials I'd planted last year had not wintered over. Weeds had filled in, of course, so when I weeded there were gaps. I went to a bed of bee balm, and lifted a few plants and carefully moved them in. I did this in the evening, and watered well afterwards. If you have pots of flowers on the deck, or nice looking indoor plants, you can move them temporarily into the garden to fill in spaces. You might even want to keep them there for the rest of the summer.

Stake up tall flowers that have flopped, preferably a few days in advance of the party. Floppers often turn their noses up while lying on the ground, so doing this in advance gives them time to straighten up and fly right. I use bamboo stakes, which I use individually or in a circle around a group of plants. I like green string or the green twist ties that come on a roll. First I tie a Boy Scout clove hitch to the stake, then go around a tall stem in a loose loop that is not attached to the stem itself. This allows the plant to move naturally in the wind.

For clumps of floppers, like pink mallow or monk's hood, I encircle the clump, creating a support system all the way around, about two thirds the way up the stems. Four or five stakes may be needed, and they should be stiff and strong. Using my pruners, I cut off the tops of any stakes that are taller than flowers.

Do a quick pruning of trees and shrubs to correct any obvious flaws. I have a lovely purple smoke bush, for example, that gets damaged by the cold winds each winter. It grows vigorously, sending new stems up each summer, but it had some dead branches. Before the party I took my pruners and removed the unsightly dead stems. What a difference that made—I should have done it earlier. Fruit trees often grow water sprouts in summer—thin stems that stick straight up from branches. Remove them to open up the view through the trees. Save major pruning until next March.

Add some humor. I dug out Sister Mary Lou, my prize-winning scarecrow, and set her up in the garden just a couple of days before the event. She is a busty, full-bodied scarecrow that always turns heads—even mine. She distracts visitors who might notice the weeds. She is best displayed when partially hidden.

I like garden whimsy, and put little things in the garden in less noticeable places. I have a ceramic bird on a bamboo stake tucked in between a big clump of "Gateway" Joe-Pye weed and some cardinal flowers. And I have a brass toad, a good-size one, that is actually a watering device, that I snuck in under some overhanging leaves.

Arrange lawn furniture in conversation groups facing a good view of the garden. If you don't have an outdoor coffee table, find a wooden box and put a colorful cloth over it. I have even used a twenty-gallon pickling crock turned upside down as a small table. I visited writer Jamaica Kincaid's garden a few years ago, and I was struck by the bright colors she used on her lawn furniture. After the visit I copied her, repainting our Adirondack chairs bright magenta. Often the first words people utter on entering the garden is, "I love your chairs!"

Take a really good look at what is blooming in your garden. A day before our picnic I went around with a clipboard and wrote a list of everything in bloom. It served to make me notice unusual flowers, smaller things—and places that needed a little tune-up. Then I sat down and enjoyed a cold beverage and smiled. I was ready for company.

Wheelbarrows

I love wheelbarrows. I currently own eight—these include the basic one-wheeled barrow, an old fashioned wooden wheelbarrow, a metal folding wheelbarrow, a Smart Cart, and a standard plywood garden cart, among others. I use different barrows for carrying different loads—from fence posts to compost.

Everyone needs a basic barrow. It has a single wide tire in front, a body made of either plastic or metal, and two wooden handles. They come in various sizes and colors, and turn on a dime, literally, which is nice for delivering bark mulch or manure down a narrow footpath.

The basic barrow distributes weight equally between the wheel and gardener, so it can get very heavy if you are loading it with rocks or soil. It unloads easily: Just lift the two long handles, and it dumps out the contents. Plastic ones are less heavy, but metal ones are sturdier. I don't like those huge ones that have twin tires in the front—they are awkward when turning. And although a friend has one with hand brakes, I don't need that feature.

The one I use most often is called the Smart Cart. Made in Maine, it has a plastic body the pops in and out of a tubular aluminum frame. They come with either four-inch-wide wheels, which I have, or bicycle-tire wheels. I love the wide wheels because they don't sink into soft wet soil. And in the ten years I've had my Smart Cart, the tires have never gone flat—unlike all my other barrows. It is rated for six hundred pounds of load, and the balance is such that even heavily loaded it moves easily.

I like the fact that the bin part of the Smart Cart can be taken out of the frame. I used it recently to collect chicken manure from a friend, sliding the bin into the back of my little Toyota hatchback. Other barrows would not easily do the job. Or I can de-skunk a dog in it instead of the family bathtub. (See below for a good recipe for skunk odor remover). Available from the manufacturer for around $300, the Smart Cart is worth every penny of the cost. Contact them at 800-366-6026 or go to www.smart carts.com for more information.

Peter Shack's Recipe for "Skunk-Be-Gone":
1 quart hydrogen peroxide (3%)
¼ cup baking soda
1 teaspoon liquid soap

Pour all ingredients into a bowl and combine. Dip a sponge into the liquid and rub onto the pet's dry fur. After dousing the pet with the solution, give him a bath with a good skin-conditioning shampoo, because the peroxide will cause the skin to dry out.

Garden carts are good, too. I have the biggest size plywood garden cart made by Carts Vermont (www.cartsofvermont.com or 800-732-7417). They come in four sizes, from two hundred- to four hundred-pound load-carrying capacity, and from 4.0 to 13.6 cubic feet. Mine is great for carrying bulky stuff: Leaves, hay, or four snow tires at once, for example. It has bicycle tires, and is well balanced and rolls easily. I have never tipped one over by accident on a hillside, a common problem with the one-wheeled basic barrow. But emptying mine is awkward: The front piece does not slide out easily (it's a fifteen-year-old cart), so I rarely bother when tipping out a load of weeds. I end up unloading them by scooping them up in my arms. Not the best barrow for carrying manure.

I have a lightweight aluminum wheelbarrow that folds up so you can hang it on the wall of your garage or put it in the back of your car. Although I know people who love them, I rarely use mine except when I convert it to use as a pull-behind the lawn tractor cart, using a kit. Made by Tipke Manufacturing, they are not available from the maker but they can be found online from places like Amazon.

Polyethylene bin wheelbarrows come in a variety of sizes, shapes, and qualities. Big-box stores will sell you a little cheapie for under $50, or you can get a good one such as the long, sturdy one I have from Kadco, a Carry-It with bicycle tires. The plastic tub is forty-four inches long, twenty-four wide, and a foot deep. It holds water, so I use it to soak my logs that I use for growing shiitake mushrooms. I like the barrow: It has good balance and carrying capacity. Available by calling 800-448-5503 or online at www.kadcousa.com; they cost about $235.

My sentimental favorite is an Amish-made wooden wheelbarrow just like the one my grandfather had. It has removable sides, making it great for carrying long objects such as fence posts. Available from the maker, Ike Lapp, by calling 717-355-9366. An old order Amish, Ike generally doesn't answer the phone (which is in a little shed out in a field where it can't disturb family life), but you can leave a message. I got the metal liner with mine, which allows me to grow flowers in it without damaging the wood. That is an extra $45. Available in a variety of sizes and colors, the large deluxe wooden wheelbarrow costs about $259 plus shipping. Ike has no Web site, but to see them, go to www. horsetackinternational.com and search for Amish wooden wheelbarrows.

You probably don't need half a dozen wheelbarrows. I'm not sure I do. But one of my first memories in life is a ride in a wooden wheelbarrow, on top of a load of weeds. My grandfather scooped me up, popped me into the barrow, and raced us home ahead of a thunderstorm. I regularly give my grandson George a ride in one of mine, and I even let him float down our stream in the tub of my Smart Cart. After all, wheelbarrows are for fun, too.

Saving the Harvest and Putting Up Tomatoes

When I was a kid—back in the 1950s—there was only one option for saving your tomatoes: Canning them. It was hot work and time consuming, but our mothers and grannies did it. Now I save my harvest in easier, better ways.

Canning tomatoes or sauce is still good, but freezing whole red tomatoes is easier—and, from what I've read—preserves more of the vitamins than canning. That's right: Instead of slaving over a hot stove in August and September, I make my sauce as needed in the off season from fruit I freeze now. Canning sauce entails cooking the tomatoes and herbs, putting them in clean canning jars, and then keeping them in a hot water bath for forty-five minutes (for quart jars). All that cooking breaks down some of the vitamins and uses lots of energy.

Freezing whole red tomatoes is easy: Wash and dry your tomatoes and put them in the freezer. You can put them on a cookie sheet first and then bag them, but I put mine directly in gallon zipper bags. I use a standard milk straw for sucking air out of the bag when it's 99 percent closed. That helps to minimize frost inside the bag.

When I need tomatoes for a recipe I take a few out of the freezer and run them under hot tap water. I rub the skins and they come right off. I let the skinned tomatoes rest for five minutes to thaw a smidge, and then cut them in half. I cut out the stem point and chop up the tomatoes. Put them right in the pan and they act just liked canned tomatoes.

Another technique: Drying them. I grow a lot of cherry tomatoes that I dehydrate to make something like those sun-dried tomatoes from California that are sold in fancy stores for a small fortune. I cut clean cherry tomatoes in half, and place them cut side up on the trays of my food dehydrator. I set the thermostat at 125 or 130 degrees F and dry them for about twenty-four hours. Although my machine would do it faster if I pushed up the temperature, vitamin C breaks down more quickly at higher temperatures. Dried tomatoes are safe on a shelf for quite a while, but I usually keep them in zipper bags in the fridge or freezer.

A few words about dehydrators: I've tried four different ones, and have settled on the Nesco/American Harvest Gardenmaster Pro. It's the Cadillac of dehydrators, but not pricey—you can get one directly from the manufacturer for $140 or so (www.nesco .com or 800-288-4545). It has a heating element, thermostat, timer, and fan. It is round, and has stacking trays for the veggies. Buy the Clean-a-Screen inserts—they make washing much easier. Its only downside? It uses 1,000 watts of electricity per hour, so I only use it for large batches.

I also dry fruit, hot peppers, and garlic. Apples and pears I slice into quarter-inch slices and dry for snacks all winter. Don't overdry your fruit, however, or it gets so hard that chewing it is a struggle. Leave it a little chewy.

Hot peppers I dry until brittle, so that I can make hot pepper powder with them. When they're fully dry I put them in my coffee grinder and chop, seeds and all. By making a powder I can use as much—or as little—as needed, depending on who is coming to dinner. I process garlic the same way as peppers, making a garlic powder that stores well on the shelf.

I also make a lot of tomato paste and sometimes even some ketchup. To make paste, I first core tomatoes and squeeze out some of the juice and seeds. Then I cut the tomatoes in halves or quarters and put them in my food processor and puree them. I let the puree simmer all evening until I can stand up a spoon in it. I turn off the heat, and let it cool all night without a lid to evaporate a little more.

In the morning I spoon the paste into ice cube trays. When the paste is frozen, I pop out the cubes and store them in zipper bags in the freezer. I like making the cubes because I can use a small quantity whenever I want, and not have paste left over in the fridge picking up flavors or getting moldy. Paste is good for tomatoes that have bad spots—I cut out the defect and throw the good parts in the blender.

One word of caution when freezing: Be sure to use freezer-grade zipper bags. The storage bags are flimsy and don't store your food as well over the long haul. It's worth the few pennies extra to get the good ones.

Even if you didn't plant a forest of tomatoes this year, you can store tomatoes for the winter. Just go to your local farm stand and ask if they have a special price for canning tomatoes by the bushel. Most do, and it's worth the effort to put some away.

SEPTEMBER

Apples

This is apple season: The time for picking, for making pies and applesauce, for making cider, and the time for planting apple trees. Let's start with the chicken, not the egg: Planting them. Fall is a good time to plant because the weather is generally cool, the soil moist, and because tree roots are most active in the fall, even after leaf drop.

Apples require two different varieties in order to get good pollination—and hence, plenty of apples. If you have wild apples growing nearby—as I do—they will pollinate any tree you might plant. Still, I like to have cultivated apples of both early and late varieties so I can start eating apples in midsummer and continue harvesting right up until late fall.

Pick a good site in full sun for your tree. The old adage "Apples don't like wet feet" is true, I suppose, though I have apples growing in an area with a very high water table that do just fine. Orchards are often sited on south-facing slopes for good water drainage and for good air drainage. In spring when the apples are in bloom you can lose fruit to frost if you plant them in a cold hollow. Cold air slides downhill, so trees in a low spot may suffer from frost even when those a hundred feet away on a hillside may escape it.

Apples do best in soil rich in organic matter, but please avoid the mistake I made when I was young and ignorant: Don't dig a big planting hole and fill it with compost, rotted manure, topsoil, and fertilizer. This encourages the roots to stay in the rich-soil zone instead of wandering far and wide, which is what you want. Filling a hole with rich material can create what is known as the bathtub effect. Roots stay put, so if the bathtub dries out in a drought, the tree will suffer, and may blow over in a high wind.

The other mistake I made when I planted my first apple tree was to ignore the trunk flare, burying the base of the tree deeply. Often trees come from the nursery with soil covering the part of the tree trunk that flares out or widens above ground. Look at a mature tree in the forest—you will see roots taking off from a widened area, or flare, at the base of the tree. The bark will rot, the tree will sicken and may die in six to ten years if you cover the bark with soil, or even a mulch "volcano."

My fated first apple tree showed signs of stress by turning leaf color earlier in the fall than others. And then there were the tell-tale signs of tip dieback—the top branches of the tree had few leaves, even in summer. But I was ignorant, and ignored the problem. So eventually I pulled it out (easy to do since the roots never went anywhere) and it went onto the woodpile. If you've planted a tree that shows signs of stress, carefully scrape away the soil until you find the trunk flare, and regrade the area around it to keep it dry. It may survive.

If you wish to plant an apple tree and have truly crummy soil, dig a very wide hole—say ten feet wide—but not a deep one. The loosening effect of the digging will make it easier for the roots to extend. And yes, you can mix in some compost. Just don't make a very rich mixture—and no fertilizer, please.

If you have more apples than you can eat fresh, here are some ideas: First, buy an apple slicer. This is a wagon-wheel-shaped kitchen tool that you press down on the apple, slicing it into eight or ten pieces and separating the core from the slices in one quick motion. You might find them locally at a kitchen store, or if not, online from the Vermont Country Store (www.vermont-countrystore.com).

I make applesauce with extra apples, package it in zipper bags and freeze. I just cook the apple slices (skins and all, since the skins have lots of vitamins), add cinnamon, and mash with a potato masher. I add a little cider while cooking if the sauce is too dry. If you want a less lumpy mix, run it through a food mill.

Want wintertime apple pies? My friend, Cindy Heath, makes apple pie mix in the fall, fills pie pans with the mix, and puts them in the freezer—without the crust. She puts wax paper in the pan for ease of removal. Once the apples are frozen, she empties the pie pans and puts the preformed pies in zipper bags for storage. Later she makes the crust, and pops the frozen pie filling into it. She cooks it as she normally would, just adding some extra time.

Most cider makers will use your apples to make your own cider, for a fee. It's a lot less mess than pressing your own at home. Be sure to wash apples first if using drops from under the tree. I freeze lots of cider made that way. I'm careful to leave an inch or more of space for expansion when freezing cider. I have to break the seal on the plastic jug coming from the cider maker and pour some out to leave enough space on top.

So go plant an apple tree. Apples are among the least expensive, least labor-intensive foods you can grow. In five years you can be harvesting free apples—for the rest of your life.

Planting Fall Bulbs

Autumn is here. Fat pumpkins are sitting on the front steps. The potatoes and garlic have been harvested and are stored in the cellar. A few tomatoes are on the vines, but many more are in glass jars of sauce lining the pantry shelves, or stored whole in the freezer, like red rocks. Asters and mums are blooming, and my seven-sons flower tree *(Heptacodium miconioides)* is displaying clusters of white flowers, in one last gasp from the world of blooming trees.

Each year at this time I plant spring bulbs, knowing that by March or April I will be desperate for flowers. I like the early bloomers—my snowdrops, crocus, scilla, and glory-of-the-snow—but have enough now, so I don't bother adding any more. Tulips are glorious, but short-lived, and often prey to squirrels or other beasts. But one can never have too many daffodils.

Having planted dozens of daffies every year for twenty years or more, my biggest problem these days is finding a spot to plant more. Daffodils aren't too fussy. They prefer full sun, but will bloom in deciduous forests where they'll get some get some sunshine before the maples and oaks have large leaves. They look good at the edges of woods near the lawn, too. Thick pine forests would probably be too shady, but I've never tried planting them there.

Once I planted daffodils in the lawn, and every year I kick myself for doing it. They look glorious, but I can't cut that patch of lawn until July 1, or risk causing diminished vigor. On the other hand, I figured out that one of the best places to plant daffodils is between large clumps of hostas. The hostas leaf out and get big after the daffodils have finished blooming and hide the foliage nicely.

Planting bulbs is slow and tedious if you plant each bulb in its own hole. I prefer to dig a hole big enough to plant twenty-five or more at once, which is much quicker. To plant twenty-five large bulbs such as daffodils or tulips, I dig a hole roughly three feet long, two feet wide and six inches deep. If the soil is poor, I dig eight inches deep and place two to three inches of good soil mixed with compost in the bottom of the hole. I always remove stones and mix in a good quantity of compost with the soil that will go over the bulbs. When you dig the hole, place the soil directly into a wheelbarrow or onto a tarp to keep cleanup to a minimum.

I don't buy "bulb booster" because it's expensive, comes in small bags, and I haven't found any rated for use by organic gardeners. Instead I use my favorite bagged organic fertilizer, Pro-Gro, and some green sand. Green sand comes in fifty-pound bags and contains lots of micronutrients from the sea—it was deposited by the sea in New Jersey, eons ago. A cup of organic fertilizer and half a cup of green sand scratched into the bottom of the hole will give your bulbs a good start in life.

A commonly asked bulb question is this: When the directions say plant bulbs six inches deep, is that to the bottom of the hole or to the top of the bulb? Answer: To the top of the bulb. And why do some bulbs never produce flowers? Poor drainage is the primary reason why bulbs fail—heavy clay soils hold water in winter, and the bulbs rot. Amending the soil with compost to provide drainage is the solution to that problem. Of course, some rodents feed on bulbs, too, particularly tulips.

I believe it's okay to plant bulbs close together, not the six inches apart that most bulb companies suggest. I like a big splash of color, and have never seen any adverse effects of tight planting. Planting close together also means you'll have space for more bulbs for the same amount of work. And even after I cut flowers for the table, the clump is still bodacious.

After setting the bulbs in place, carefully cover them with soil. When the tops of the bulbs are covered with soil you should pat the soil down to firm it up. Then just shovel the rest of your soil/compost mix into the hole and press down lightly with a foot. Don't tread on it, just pat it down. Water well if the soil is dry.

Sometimes the very thought of short days and interminable snow puts this gardener in a funk. But planting bulbs is a sure cure for the blues. And come spring? Every bulb will be worth its weight in gold.

Using and Storing the Harvest

I was chatting with a friend outside the village post office the other day, talking about our gardens. My friend mentioned that she was going to make a stodge with her leftover vegetables. A stodge, I asked? Yes, she said. It's a soup of all the garden vegetables she has on hand—including those that are damaged and need to be used up right away.

I looked it up when I got home, and sure enough, a stodge is a thick, filling soup or stew. I guess I've been making stodges for years, and never knew it. Got some cabbage, potatoes, carrots, kale, beets, and onions? Add water, simmer, and you've got a stodge.

My vegetable garden is running out of steam, and cold weather is just around the corner. It's time to finish putting up food for winter. Potatoes store well, and we usually can eat them all winter long, and still have enough for planting a new crop in the spring. They keep best in a cool location with high humidity. I keep mine in the basement where the temperature stays between 40 and 50 all winter.

If you have a dry basement, you can assure a higher humidity for your spuds by storing them in plastic pails and putting an inch of moist sand in the bottom of each. They'll need air circulation, so don't put a tight lid on the bucket if you do this. And if you have a warm basement, try keeping the buckets near the bulkhead doors—but keep an eye on a strategically placed thermometer during cold snaps; frozen potatoes are no good. I try to keep mine at 40 degrees. This means the potatoes will taste sweeter than when first picked. I've been told by a professional grower that below 50 degrees, some of the starches turn to sugar.

I've never had much luck storing pumpkins or winter squashes much past Christmas. This week I'll try to find time to steam my Blue Hubbard squash, then scoop out the flesh and freeze it in bags. I love squash in winter soups, especially one I make with fresh ginger, peanut butter, and hot peppers.

My garden provides me with much more than fresh vegetables in summer. It gives me exercise from April to October, a taste of the garden in winter, and something to dream about once the snow flies. I'm not ready for winter yet, but a nice bowl of stodge might put me in the mood.

Fall in the Flower Garden

It seems to me that many gardeners ignore the fall as a season of flowers. As much as I love fall chrysanthemums and Sedum "Autumn Joy," there are many other flowers to please us and grace our tables. Now is the time to visit your local nursery or garden center and take advantage of their fall sales to add some color to your flower garden.

You surely know black-eyed Susans, also called gloriosa daisies or yellow ox-eye daisies, and many of these are still looking wonderful. Their genus (their closest relatives, in the terminology of scientists), *Rudbeckia*, contains many species and varieties. The black-eyed Susan is of the species *R. hirta*. These can average in size from the diminutive Becky, that is just eight inches tall, to others thirty-six inches tall. Gloriosa daisies come in both single and double varieties. My favorite is Prairie Sun with green eyes (centers) because they bloom profusely for months on stiff stems. They make fabulous cut flowers, but I find the plants tend to die out after a winter or two. No matter, I'll always buy more.

Then there is *R. fulgida* "Goldsturm" (botanists often save space by using just the first initial of the genus) which is one of the best and best known. A plant or two planted in full sun and rich soil will form a clump five feet across and two to three feet tall in just a few years. Want a tall one? For me *R. nitida* "Herbst-sonne" grows up to six feet tall, and has all-yellow flowers, including the center eye. Because of its height, it needs a little staking to support the stems.

I bet that Darwin would explain that fall flowers tend to be taller than spring flowers because they need to be taller than the grasses of their native prairies. One of my favorite tall flowers is called snakeroot or bugbane (*Cimicifuga* spp.). These flowers are very fragrant, attracting bees—and even making passersby turn their heads. I love the smell, though not everyone does, just as not everyone loves the taste of anchovies. The flowers, on stems up to eight feet tall, are like fuzzy white bottlebrushes, with lots of smaller bottlebrushes on side-stems that bloom a little later. Snakeroot also comes as purple or black-leafed varieties: Hillside Black Beauty is one of the best, a real beauty. Grow it in full sun in dry or moist soil.

Another plant with bottlebrush flowers is Canadian burnet (*Sanguisorba canadensis*). This is a native plant that likes full sun and moist, rich soil. I grow it near my stream, and it is quite dramatic now—six feet tall, and a clump eight feet around after ten years of growing. The flowers are best appreciated outdoors as they don't do well in a vase—they shed white fluff almost immediately. Greater burnet (*S. officinalis*) is smaller and has dark red blossoms that are tidy and look great in a vase with snakeroot.

Pink turtlehead (*Chelone lyonii*) is looking fabulous in my shady, moist primrose garden right now (in the shade of apple trees), and will bloom through the month and into October. It stands three to four feet tall and has half a dozen or more pink blossoms on each stem. As I was photographing it, bumblebees were crawling inside the "mouths" of the blossoms, and buzzing like crazy, and going in and out of each flower more than once. I am not used to bumble-bees being vocal. Were they singing, perhaps? Or complaining? I'd like to think they were having a good time, maybe even tipsy. I also grow it in full sun where it started blooming in mid-August and is now starting to look bedraggled. They key to success? It must have wet to moist soil. It also comes in a white variety *(C. glabra)*, which I have seen in the wild. I don't grow the white ones as they're not a pure white and tend to just look dirty. They're much shorter, too. Turtlehead is a great cut flower.

Joe-Pye weed *(Eupatorium purpureum)* is blooming along-side my stream in full sun, and has been for a month or more. It's tall—up to seven or eight feet. I grow a cultivar known as "Gateway" and it outperforms the native varieties that also grow there: Bigger flower heads, better color, longer lasting in a vase. I took mine out of my flowerbed after five years—but only with difficulty, and the help of a pick ax. Its root system is immense, so I recommend planting it where it can spread and never be moved. I have seen it in dry locations where it is less vigorous but still pretty.

Another great fall plant is sneezeweed *(Helenium autumnale)*. It does not make you sneeze. According to my favorite reference book on flowers, *Manual of Herbaceous Ornamental Plants* by Steven M. Still (Stipes Publishing, 1993), it is named after Helen of Troy whose face allegedly launched a thousand ships—and a war. It is three to six feet tall, depending on the cultivar and growing conditions; it is in the aster family. It varies in color from pure yellow to orange and brown, with slightly reflexed petals (they are bent backwards) that are an inch or two in diam-eter, with a central button.

My new fall favorite is a blue gentian, *Gentiana makinoi* "Marsha." I bought one last year and it wintered over nicely even though it has been reported on the Web as only hardy to zero—or hardy to minus 40! It has intense true blue flowers—rare in the plant world—and lots of them. I grow it in afternoon sun where it is fairly dry. It produced about twenty blooming stems, each about eighteen inches long. It's a great cut flower lasting over a week in a vase.

So go get some new varieties of fall flowers. There are plenty, and this is a good time to plant them.

Saving Seeds

There are several levels of gardening: Beginner, steady intermediate, serious, and mad dog. I'm a mad dog. Sometimes it's good to jump up from one category to another. And some activities usually done by serious or mad dog gardeners can easily be done, and with great satisfaction, by beginners. Saving seeds for next year is one of those activities that anyone can do, but is most often done by the obsessed.

Let's start with one of the easiest seeds to save and use: Annual poppies. If you had some annual poppies this year, their seed pods should be dry by now. Go collect a few pods and put them in a small plastic bag or an envelope. Once you turn the pod upside down the seeds will fall out, so don't collect any pods that have fallen over, only erect ones. Test a pod to see if tiny black seeds will shake out of it. Store the seeds in a cool, dry spot for planting next year. I love to plant them in midwinter: I sprinkle the fine seeds over the snow where I want a few to grow next year, and they do the rest. You may sprinkle a hundred seeds to get one plant, but it couldn't be easier.

I save seeds from a few strains of tomatoes each year, and start them indoors under lights, starting in April. Most beginning gardeners don't want to be bothered growing seedlings indoors. But I have a few strains of tomatoes that are worth growing, and that are not commercially available, so I save the seeds. And I like starting seedlings in the spring.

If you read a book on saving seeds you will be told that you need to make a slurry of tomato seeds in water, let it ferment, and then clean and dry the seeds. Nonsense. I once had a father-in-law who told me to pick the best tomato from a plant, scoop out some seeds, and let them dry on a paper towel. I've been doing that for decades. Thanks, Charlie. I write the variety name on the paper towel before I spread out the seeds.

Modern hybrids are not suitable for seed saving. They will not breed true to form the way the heirloom varieties do, and you probably will get something that does not resemble the parent plant at all. So you need to know the name of the variety, and then look it up on the World Wide Web. You will probably find lots of people trying to sell you seeds, but they will also have the information about where it comes from, how long it has been around, and pictures for comparison.

Bill Poland, a farmer who sells at the farmers market in Cornish Flat, New Hampshire, gave me a nice dark-skinned tomato to try, and I liked it a lot. He called it a "Black Russian." I should have asked him where he bought the seed, but didn't. Later I Googled "Black Russian tomatoes" and learned all about them—they've been grown for at least a hundred years, so I know it's not a hybrid. I saved a few seeds and started them the next spring. They produced early large fruit that tasted great.

One year I grew some paddy rice and I saved seed so I could do it again the next year. The Japanese farmer who taught me how to grow rice in a five-gallon pail told me to be sure to pick grains that are fully ripe, and to save those that produced early in the fall. That's good advice for any seed saving. Even with global warming our seasons can be pretty short—some years we've have had frost in both June and in September. Selecting seeds from plants or fruit that mature early in the season is better than selecting those that wait until the end of the season to ripen. Doing so for many generations may help to create varieties that develop faster.

Not all vegetables produce seeds in their first year. Beets, cardoon, carrots, celery, leeks, and parsley, for example, go to seed their second year. I worked as a farm hand for three weeks in the summer of 2005 on a big organic farm in Idaho that sells organic seeds, including carrots. Fred Brossy, the farmer, told me that each fall he pulls his seed carrots and stores them in a walk-in cooler. Then he replants them outside once winter is done, and they produce seeds their second year. If you try this, cut off and discard the tops of the carrots and store the roots in a cool, humid place where it stays in the 35- to 50-degree range. Same for beets.

I've had both cardoon and parsley overwinter in the garden, but neither is edible their second year. Last fall I cut the top off a cardoon plant but did not pull the roots. Then I dumped a wheelbarrow full of leaves from the lawn on the spot—not to protect the roots, but just to get rid of the leaves. This spring, much to my surprise, the cardoon (which is a big leafy plant related to artichokes) sprouted when I raked off the pile of leaves. I let it grow, and it began to show unusual proclivities early on. Instead of staying low and bushing out, it grew tall, reaching nearly five feet tall. Then it bloomed, producing numerous gorgeous blossoms. It is in the thistle family, with beautiful blossoms like big thistle heads. I saved those seeds and supplied many gardeners—but, oddly enough, most seeds did not germinate. Go figure.

So just do it. Save a few seeds, and plant them next spring. You'll feel like a serious gardener if you do—or maybe even get promoted to "mad dog" gardener.

Share the Vegetables Day

Even though I'm past sixty, I try hard not to be a curmudgeon. This means I'm not supposed to lecture young people about how things used to be, or even to make comparisons to life in the

1950s. However, when I was growing up we knew all our neighbors, and that isn't the case anymore. In today's world, neighbors come and go almost as often as the Canada geese. I'm embarrassed to admit that I don't know all my neighbors within easy walking distance of my house.

I'm a gardening guy, so we generally have more vegetables than we need. And although I share tomatoes, potatoes, lettuce, and zucchini with friends and family, I've decided to share some with those neighbors I don't know. This seems like a good way to meet them. So I'm declaring the second Saturday in September "Share the Vegetables Day." I'll put together a nice selection of fresh veggies and go door to door, giving them away. Maybe I'll load up a wheelbarrow with zucchinis, pumpkins, and winter squashes, and push it through the village of Cornish Flat, making new friends and visiting old ones.

Even after I share the harvest, I'll still have more vegetables than I need. So I'll bring some to organizations that serve the needy, such as The Upper Valley Haven and The Good Neighbor Health Clinic, both in White River Junction, Vermont. They're always glad to get some fresh veggies to share, as are the soup kitchens around the state.

Nonetheless, I like to store vegetables for the winter, and will put away plenty. I'll freeze some, can some, and store some in the cool basement. There is something wonderful about eating my own garden produce in midwinter. I know it has never encountered pesticides or chemical fertilizers, so I know it is wholesome—and tasty.

I grew up hearing about starving children in other parts of the world, and met some hungry people during my time with the Peace Corps in Africa, so it pains me to throw away food. I like the idea of a day each year to share the vegetables, but I also realize than any day is a good day to meet some new neighbors and to share the harvest. I hope you'll share some, too.

Fire Cider

Last winter I never suffered from the flu (bird, swine, regular, or high-test) and I avoided the seasonal plagues (colds, coughs, fevers, and congestion). I attribute this to several things: I have no school-aged children; I do not work in an office full of coughing coworkers; I eat well, exercise daily, get plenty of rest . . . and I regularly imbibe a variety of herbal concoctions. I make my own elderberry elixir, and have a spoon or two most days. I eat plenty of garlic (which also helps to keep Typhoid Mary at bay in the checkout line of the grocery store). And I sample something called "fire cider" daily.

Fire cider is not for the faint of heart—or palate. It is made from ingredients that, individually, are powerful tastes: Cider vinegar, horseradish, garlic, ginger, onions, and cayenne. Together, they are wonderful. Horseradish is said to have antibacterial properties and stimulate digestion; garlic is believed to kill microbes and support the immune system; cayenne is thought to increase circulation; ginger is said to fight off colds and coughs. Here is the recipe I used:

Fire Cider
    Combine in a glass jar the following ingredients:
    1 quart cider vinegar (preferably local and organic)
    $\frac{1}{2}$ cup horseradish, grated
    $\frac{1}{8}$ cup minced garlic
    $\frac{1}{2}$ cup finely chopped onion
    $\frac{1}{2}$ cup fresh chopped ginger
    1 teaspoon cayenne pepper

Before putting a lid on the jar, cover the top with wax paper to prevent the fumes from corroding the metal lid. This is seriously strong stuff. I allow it to cure in a cool dark place for six to eight weeks, then strain.

I grew or made all the ingredients myself except the ginger (and some of the cider), and maybe next year I will have my own ginger, too. Sylvia Newberry of the Healing Arts Clinic in Windsor, Vermont gave me a potted ginger plant last fall and explained that it is easy to grow from grocery store ginger. Just get a good fresh piece and pot it up a couple of inches deep in rich soil. In a year it is ready to harvest, she said. Use a pot that is eight inches deep.

The horseradish needs to be thoroughly washed and then peeled with a potato peeler before using. I cut it into chunks and ran them through the slicing/shredding blade of my food processor. I processed the ginger (after peeling) and onions with the slicer blade, too. After slicing the ginger and horseradish, I then chopped them finer with the regular blade of the food processor.

Growing horseradish is easy. Getting rid of it is not. So, come spring, if you decide to grow your own, give some careful thought about where to plant it. A friend in Unity, New Hampshire planted some in a corner of her vegetable garden. It spread. It got mangled by a rototiller and parts of the roots were spread around the garden. She has been fighting it ever since. It has a deep taproot—it can go down three feet or more and will break off before you can pull the entire root. I found that planting it between a stone wall or foundation and a lawn works well. For directions on how to grow horseradish, see my article in the November chapter.

I called Vermont's preeminent herbalist, Rosemary Gladstar of East Barre, who confirmed that she had developed the fire cider recipe some thirty-five years ago, but noted she had "adapted it from hundreds of years of herb use." She also suggested adding honey to mellow the flavor. After straining the fire cider, she said you could heat up honey (making it liquid) and add up to a quarter cup of honey for each cup of the vinegar solution. She suggested using it as part of a salad dressing to make it even easier to tolerate. Her lovely book, *Rosemary Gladstar's Herbal*

Recipes for Vibrant Health (Storey Publishing, LLC, 2008) is full of wonderful herbal concoctions you may wish to prepare.

I like making my own remedies from plants I have grown. Fire cider may not be as good as getting a flu shot . . . but then again it might be better.

Putting the Garden to Bed

It's not enough to put away the wheelbarrow and rake up the fall leaves. Weeding in the fall is important, especially for perennial weeds that will come back next spring. Use a shovel or garden fork to loosen the soil before you try to pull weeds with taproots—even the smallest tip of a root will survive and return next spring. Weeding is best done after a rain or when the soil is moist.

Some grasses can be a real nuisance, so pull any that have gotten into your vegetable or flower beds. I like using a Cobra-Head weeder (www.cobrahead.com or 866-962-6272) as it lets me get under clumps of grass and helps me tease out long roots. Keep weeds with seeds (or flowers) out of the compost pile. Most compost piles never heat up enough to kill weed seeds, and weed seeds are often viable for years.

Any plant that had a fungal disease this year needs special care—tomatoes, apples, and phlox are common examples. Haul diseased plant debris and fallen fruit far from the garden or put it in the trash or in a pile for a bonfire this winter after snow flies. Bonfires are great because a) they're fun and b) they get rid of fungal spores, insect eggs, and overwintering bugs. If you've got brush from pruning or wind storms, you can load up the pile with potato plants, squash vines, rotten fruit, and anything else that might harbor pests. Raking up leaves and fruit from under your apple trees will make a big difference next year.

I like to prepare my vegetable garden beds now, so I won't have so much to do in the spring when the soil is waterlogged.

After I get rid of all the plants and weeds I add an inch or two of compost, and rake it into the top two inches of soil. Then I cover the beds with leaves that I have run over with the lawnmower. That helps to prevent soil erosion and weed seeds from germinating in the spring.

I've already dug up my dahlia tubers and gladiola corms, but it's still not too late to do until the soil freezes. I store mine in a cool upstairs bedroom in a black plastic bag that has many holes punched in it. I add some lightly moistened cedar gerbil bedding to keep the roots from drying out too much.

Some folks are compulsive about cutting down all perennial flowers and pulling the annual flowers. I'm not. I like some to stand up all winter above the snow, offering birds some seedy treats and reminding me that our New Hampshire winters don't last forever. But it does make sense to cut some back if you have the time now. That also allows you to see what needs to be divided come spring, and to pull the weeds that have snuck into the beds.

I like to use a sharp, serrated knife for cutting flower stalks, not my pruners. It's faster, and less likely to cause hand pain. Years ago I bought something called a root knife from Lee Valley Tools (www.leevalley.com or 800-871-8158) that does the job nicely, but even a serrated kitchen knife will work.

I sometimes use hedge shears to cut down tall flowers—either the old fashioned kind, or the electric kind. If you use electric shears, be sure to plug into a ground fault interrupter (GFI) plug—the kind with a reset button. I once cut off my extension cord with my electric hedge clippers, and the GFI saved me from death or injury (though I still uttered a few words about my own stupidity that I will not repeat here).

Fall is also a good time to feed the soil. You can top-dress your flower beds with organic fertilizer or compost. By that I mean sprinkling it right on the surface of the bed—you don't even have to stir it in. If you have mulch on your flower beds, however, you do have to push it aside before you top-dress them. And it makes sense to loosen the soil and stir in the amendments before putting back the mulch.

Sheep, goat, llama, and rabbit manure are all good soil amendments. Unlike cow and horse manure, they're not full of weed seeds, and can be added to the soil fresh. So if you can get some, spread it out on your flower beds. Shredded fall leaves are great soil amendments, too, both in the vegetable and flower gardens. Earthworms love them, and will carry their goodness into the soil.

If you have raspberries or blackberries, fall is the time to cut back the canes that produced fruit this year. Once they have bloomed, they won't produce again. I like using a pole pruner to reach in to the very base of the canes to cut them back. I've learned how to use the pole pruner to grab on to the cut cane and pull it out. How do you know which canes to cut? Those that produced fruit look brown and dead, and probably have a few dry berries on them. Next year's canes will show green if you scratch the bark.

Crisp fall days with blue skies are a gift. Accept the gift, even if it means playing hooky from your work, and get out in your garden. And if your boss complains? Blame me. I'll stick up for you.

OCTOBER

Giant Pumpkins

When I was growing up in the 1950s and 1960s, a giant pumpkin was one that was bigger than a bushel basket. Or one that was a struggle to pick up and carry to the front steps. I visited Karen and Steve Cutter of Cornish to see their 225-pound pumpkin, which, they explained to me, is really a very small giant pumpkin. Like restaurant meals, pumpkins have been supersized.

The Cutters explained that there is no magic involved in growing giant pumpkins. Or, actually, there is: It's all about the seeds. Genetics, as in having a child grow to NBA size, matters a lot. You can't get a giant pumpkin from pie pumpkin seeds, no matter how good your soil. The Cutters told me that the seeds that produce the biggest pumpkins were developed by Howard Dill, a grower in Nova Scotia. I called Mr. Dill, a fifth-generation farmer, a couple of years before he passed away in 2008 at age seventy-four. He gave me some tips on how to grow the big ones.

First, get top-quality seeds. Seeds can be ordered online at www.howarddill.com, or by calling 902-798-2728. The Cutters, like most growers of giant pumpkins, use Dills Atlantic Giant seeds.

Next, select a site that gets full sun all day long. The more sun you have, the more your pumpkins will grow. You could select a site now, while you're thinking about Jack-o-lanterns.

In our climate it's smart to start seeds indoors three to four weeks before the last frost date. Mr. Dill uses four-inch peat pots, and tears off the sides when he plants, trying not to disturb the roots.

Mr. Dill recommended building a mound about the size of the pitcher's mound, say, ten feet in diameter and a foot tall at its peak. A space twenty-five by twenty-five feet is all you need to grow a giant pumpkin, though one year Mr. Dill let a vine grow to be seventy feet long.

Unlike many giant pumpkin growers, Mr. Dill is not a believer in chemical fertilizers. Good rich soil with lots of organic matter is all you need, he said. Work in plenty of two or three-year-old dairy cow manure, six inches or so. He thinks beef cattle manure is not as good as dairy cow manure, and that horse manure is awful. He stockpiles manure, and applies it in the spring. You could get some now. He tests his soil pH once a year in late winter to be sure it's about neutral.

Mr. Dill explained that pumpkins have both male and female flowers, with males outnumbering the females by ten to one. Although you can let bees do the pollinating, Mr. Dill goes out at 6 AM to pollinate any females that have opened that day. He uses a small paint brush, and keeps the flowers covered for a day.

Although many growers, including the Cutters of Cornish, use black plastic to keep down weeds and increase the heat, Mr. Dill does not. If you are going to use plastic, you probably need to add a drip irrigation system under the plastic. Systems are available from your local garden center, or from Gardeners Supply Company (800-427-3363 or www.gardeners.com).

Once your plant has set fruit, you need to select one pumpkin and cut off the others. Choosing the best is intuitive since you need to do this when they are between the size of a baseball and the size of a volleyball. Sometimes Mr. Dill will look at them in the afternoon and not know which to pick. "I'll think, nope, I want to sleep on that," he explained. Bigger is not necessarily better, as not all the pumpkins will be pollinated on the same day. A potentially huge pumpkin might be smaller—but only because it's younger—which means choosing the best one is tricky.

After the main vine is eight to ten feet long, he covers parts of it with soil to encourage more root development. Side vines get the same mounding, but sucker vines off those get pruned off.

Watering every three to four days in hot weather is about right. Mr. Dill does this with watering cans, giving each plant six to eight cans of water. Watering too often can inhibit growth, according to Dill. "Know when to hold 'em and when to fold 'em," he said. He believes you have to get to know your plants, and when they need water.

Shading pumpkins and providing windbreaks can be important for growing a prize winner. Reemay is an agricultural fabric (row cover) used by the Cutters and many others to provide light shade, in an effort to keep the pumpkins from cracking. Mr. Dill even uses thin sheets of plywood to shade his pumpkins.

So why grow a giant pumpkin? Well, "It's fun," said Karen Cutter. And she is competing against her dad, who also grows them. There is big money to be won or lost, too. Some seeds have sold for as much as $500, and prize money can be significant. The Ontario contest each year awards a new pickup truck to the winner.

In 1980 Mr. Dill won the triple crown of pumpkin growing: Philadelphia, Ohio, and Ontario, but back then prizes were mainly ribbons—and bragging rights. In his later years he just tended his pumpkins and worked on developing better color and shape for big pumpkins. He loved to see people get involved. "It's good clean fun," he said.

In Praise of Leaf Mold

Most people think of mold as the yucky stuff growing on the forgotten broccoli in the back of the refrigerator. But leaf mold is a term used by soil scientists for decayed leaves that have broken down and turned into a wonderful soil supplement. Now is the time to make some.

Making leaf mold takes time—generally two years or more. When you are done you have a rich dark material that no longer looks like leaves. You can use it as a mulch, dig it into the soil or use it with your houseplants. As mulch it will hold in moisture, attract earthworms, and slowly become part of the soil. Add a layer of chopped leaves each year to your flower gardens and your soil will become rich in organic matter, drain well but hold moisture, too. It will become the soil plants dream of.

I don't bag my leaves in the fall, but put them directly in their final resting place—the vegetable garden or in a flower bed. But if you wish to be tidy, you can collect them and hold them in "corral" for a couple of years until the leaves turn into leaf mold. A chicken wire fence will hold the leaves in one place and keep them from blowing around. Use wooden grade stakes or pipe and three-foot wire mesh fencing to make a four-foot-diameter circle. Pack down the leaves as you add them.

The great thing about mowing the lawn and chopping up the leaves is that it adds fresh green grass, which is high in nitrogen. Leaf mold is not created by magic, but by microorganisms. Fungi and bacteria need both carbon and nitrogen to make the proteins needed to grow and multiply. Leaves are very high in carbon, but low in nitrogen. If you rake your leaves without first mowing the lawn, your leaf pile will decompose slowly unless you add a source of nitrogen, just as your compost pile will never get hot without a source of both carbon and nitrogen.

One easy way to get a leaf pile "cooking" is to sprinkle some bagged fertilizer on it as you build it up—a couple of pounds for every six inches of leaves would probably do. Organic fertilizer is good for that, but it's an expense you can avoid. Got sheep? Got friends with sheep, llamas, or goats? Get some manure and add it to the leaf pile. Horse manure would do, though I avoid it because it is so full of weed seeds. In principle, a working compost pile gets hot enough to kill grass seeds, but I try not to take chances and avoid fresh horse and cow manure. If you have a source of spent hops from a brewery or coffee grounds from your local coffee shop (most will give the grounds away), they will add nitrogen, too.

The other factor needed for a working compost or leaf pile is moisture. Too dry and nothing happens, but in our climate that should not be a problem. Too wet and microbial action stops.

You can use your leaf mold in flower pots to great success. Most potting soils are largely peat moss, which provides very little nutrition to plants, hence the need to add liquid fertilizers. But if you use a mix of leaf mold, compost, and 10 percent perlite or vermiculite, you can make your own potting mix that will make your house plants smile—and grow.

Vermiculite and perlite are soil additives that are made like popcorn, but at temperatures high enough to make the minerals pop. Perlite is the white stuff in potting mixes; it is inert and has a neutral pH. It holds water on its surface. Vermiculite is also inert, but brown and shiny. It absorbs water, up to sixteen times its own weight, so it can create a soggy soil if you use too much. It varies in pH, and may be quite alkaline. Both help to keep soil in pots from getting compacted, but are not recommended for use in the garden.

So get to work before the snow flies. Create a good leaf pile—even stealing some bagged leaves from your neighbors.

Fall Asters

On a lovely October afternoon under a sky clear and blue, I had tea in a brightly colored Adirondack chair in the garden. Nearby was a row of tall perennials that included a fair number of tall fall asters in full bloom. In addition to great numbers of serious, industrious bees, there were two monarch butterflies bopping around from one blossom to another like teenagers at a dessert buffet.

Asters are generally big plants with lots of small flowers that bloom in the fall. Purples dominate the aster color palette, but colors range from white to pink and blue. Farm stands and grocery stores sell asters now, generally short deep purple ones, along with the ever-present fall chrysanthemums.

Those short farm stand asters do best in rich, well-drained soil, though they aren't fussy. Like most asters, they will do fine in a variety of sun and soil conditions. What you may see next year, however, is a much taller plant with fewer blooms than the one you purchased. The growers of these asters cut them back during the growing season to make them bush out, stay short, and produce more blooms.

I planted a short farm stand aster last fall—two, really, but one expired during the winter—and gave it a haircut twice this year: once in early June, again in early July. Each time I trimmed off the top third of the plant. It is now twenty inches tall, two feet wide, and loaded with deep purple blossoms.

The two species of asters most commonly sold by nurseries as landscape plants are the New England aster *(Aster nova-angliae)* and New York aster *(A. novi-belgii)*. Both species include many tall varieties, though the New England aster tends to be taller (four to six feet) than the New York aster (generally three to five feet, with some shorter ones). As a group they have one notable fault: They have bad legs. That is to say, the leaves on the lower branches turn brown and ugly over the course of the summer.

But if they are placed behind other plants of medium height, their flaw remains hidden.

Most of the asters in my garden are New England asters, and I don't know their cultivar names, having gotten them as gifts from gardening friends. Most are purple, blue, or light pink, though this year I bought a deep rose-pink variety known as "Alma Potschke." I like plants named after people, and tend to think of them by their first names, like friends. Alma is one I've ogled for years, but despite promises of a division from various gardeners, I'd never gotten one until very recently. Its color is radiant. Like any first year perennial, Alma is shorter this year than it will be next.

A clump of New England asters will soon spread to three to five feet in diameter, and can eventually take over a garden space. Their roots are constantly moving out and sending up new stems, so they do need to be controlled—with a shovel.

Another aster I love is the bushy or rice-button aster (*A. dumosus*). Its lower leaves don't seem to be affected by the fungal disease that turns New England asters brown, and so it can be displayed anywhere. Its leaves and stems are shiny and a very dark green. It is usually the last aster to bloom for me, only starting in late September or early October. The variety I purchased is known as "Wesley Williams." It is four to six feet tall, with intensely purple flowers about an inch across. Like many tall things, it needs to be staked to prevent flopping, particularly in rich soils where it grows tallest. I admit that I didn't do a good job of staking it this year.

Several varieties of wild asters are in bloom now—they are common along roads and at the edges of the forest. My reference text on native flowers (*The Illustrated Book of Wildflowers and Shrubs* by William Carey Grimm; Stackpole Books, 1993) lists twenty-nine species. I have hundreds of these wild ones growing at the edge of the lawn right now, short ones (eighteen to twenty-four inches) with bluish-white blossoms. I believe they are the common blue wood aster *(A. cordifolius)*, which is usually a light blue or lavender. The differences between wild asters can be minute, and there is much variety within a species, so they could be the white wood aster *(A. divaricatus)*, which is also common in New England. It doesn't matter, they're lovely.

I suspect many gardeners mow down these lovely wildflowers at the edges of woods as "weeds" before they bloom. Tidiness is overrated, I think. Biodiversity—including those weeds and wildflowers we all get at the edges of our cultivated areas—is important for feeding wild things, from the regal monarchs to unnoticed greats like the parasitic wasps that keep "evil" pests like the tomato hornworms in check.

So let them grow, and add a few New England asters somewhere on your property to provide the monarchs a taste of nectar before they leave for Mexico—and a great visual treat for you.

Growing Garlic: Now Is the Time to Plant

Garlic: I've read it's good for keeping away vampires. I've heard it's good for preventing colds. I know it's good to make almost any tomato-based dish taste better. I've been growing my own for more than fifteen years, and have not bought any since I started. It's a real money-saver as well, particularly if you eat as much garlic as I do. Now is the time to plant it.

Garlic is one of the easiest crops you can grow. Since it is planted in the fall it uses space that is not being used for other crops while it gets started. It is harvested in mid- to late summer, freeing up space for late-planted crops like fall radishes or late spinach or broccoli.

There are two types of garlic: Hard-neck and soft-neck. Soft-neck garlic is the kind you generally find at the grocery store, and some of it now comes from China. Most soft-neck garlic is pretty much the same in terms of flavor. It stores well and can be braided, but soft-neck garlic is adapted for growing in warmer climates, so it may not do as well for you as the hard-neck varieties.

Hard-neck garlic is so named because each bulb has a stiff stem that is surrounded by the cloves. There are several distinct types (Purple Striped, Porcelain, and Rocambole, among others) and each has its own distinct flavor.

Plant garlic by separating the cloves of a head (or bulb) of garlic, and planting it in rich soil well amended with compost and a little organic fertilizer. Cloves should be planted about two inches deep, pointy end up. Space them three to four inches apart in rows that are six to eight inches apart. Grocery store garlic has probably been treated to prevent sprouting, so do not plant it. Buy from a local grower because even organic seed garlic grown in California will not do as well as varieties that are adapted to your climate.

Here is the key to success: Mulch your garlic bed well with straw or mulch hay when you plant. A six- to twelve-inch layer of well-fluffed mulch hay accomplishes two things. First, it insulates the ground as the cloves of garlic get their roots started. The soil is warm now and the roots will grow until the soil freezes. You want as much root growth now as possible, and the mulch will hold in the heat, allowing a longer growing period before the soil freezes. Second, the mulch will keep weeds down next summer. Garlic doesn't compete well with weeds, so keeping it mulched keeps it happy. I plant, I mulch, I harvest. That's it. I do virtually no weeding.

Your fall-planted garlic will establish its roots and may even send up shoots before snow flies—but don't worry about that. Come spring it will send up new leaves. Garlic will push up through your layer of mulch, but most weeds won't.

Garlic scapes—the flower stalks—will shoot up in mid-summer, twisting and turning in sculptural forms, with an understated flower on top. Some gardeners believe that cutting the scapes will increase bulb size, though I have never noticed that it really makes a difference. The scapes make wonderful components in flower arrangements, and are tasty in a stir fry, until they get woody (so pick some early on).

Michael and Nancy Phillips of Groveton, New Hampshire are herbalists and organic apple and garlic growers. They explained to me that garlic produces chemicals that help to prevent cancer, but that you should smash or crush your garlic and then let the garlic rest for ten minutes before putting it in the frying pan to get the benefits. So for years now I have prepared it, set it aside, and let it rest before using. It can't hurt to do so.

Michael also taught me that garlic needs to cure before you cut off the tops. Harvest it, and then let it hang in a cool dry location for a couple of weeks before you cut off the tops. Apparently the bulbs will reabsorb some of the nutrients in the stalk while it cures. I used to keep my garlic hanging in groups of ten all winter in a cold basement, but now I have decided that it keeps better in an unheated room upstairs where it is a bit warmer and much less humid.

If you have excess garlic, here is a simple recipe that I love:

Roast Garlic with Goat Cheese

Peel several cloves of garlic—four or five for each dinner guest—and place in a small ovenproof ceramic baking dish. Drizzle with olive oil and sprinkle with herbes de Provence. Bake at 400 degrees for half an hour or until the garlic turns golden brown and slightly translucent. Toast slices of a baguette and spread with feta or any soft cheese. Spread the now-soft garlic on top. You'll see that the sharpness of the garlic has disappeared. Yum!

Looking to buy some seed garlic? Try your local farm stand first. If none is available locally, you can get some from Michael Phillips at his Web site (www.herbsandapples.com) or from Johnny's Seeds (www.johnnyseeds.com or 877-564-6697).

Garlic may not really keep away vampires, but it's so tasty

and so easy to grow you should try it. Once you do, you'll grow it forever.

Fall Is the Time to Prune Deciduous Shrubs

You may think you're all done with gardening for the year if you've pulled the weeds in the vegetable garden, cut down the tall perennials, and cleaned up the leaves on the lawn. I haven't done so, but congratulations if you have. There is still work to do outside while the nice weather holds: This is the time to do some pruning of your deciduous shrubs and hardwood trees (those that drop their leaves).

Many good gardeners like pruning only slightly more than preparing Federal Tax Form 1040. I guess their aversion is due to an anthropomorphic view of pruning: They feel that taking off limbs of trees is like amputating an arm or leg. Or maybe it's due to the fact that pruning is absolute: Once removed, a branch cannot be reattached.

Trees and shrubs thrive when pruned. They do better when the clutter of too many small branches is reduced. Taking out branches opens up trees, allowing sunshine to reach the surface of every leaf; it also allows breezes to dry wet leaves, minimizing the chance of fungal diseases. Don't be afraid to take big branches: Removing one bigger branch is generally better than taking six small ones.

Let's look at shrubs. You need to decide how your shrub should look and how big it should be. So, for example, rhododendrons are often planted in front of the house, but then get so big they cut off the light coming in the windows. Lilacs and forsythia can send up many branches from the ground, forming an impenetrable mass with no recognizable shape. This is not acceptable to me.

Start by taking a good look at a shrub before cutting any branches. Walk all the way around it. Sit down on the ground near the base, and look up through it. Look for branches that are dead, and remove them first. If you are unsure if it is alive or dead (because there are no leaves on a branch at this season), scratch the bark with your thumbnail. If you see a green tinge, it is alive.

Next, remove any branches that have no future. Is a branch growing into the center of the bush, or rubbing against other branches? If so, off it must come. But don't cut it off in a way that leaves an ugly stub. Follow the branch back and remove the entire thing. If it is shooting up from the ground, cut it off at ground level.

Unless you have a hedge that you want to be flat-topped and regular, you should not reduce the height of a shrub by just giving it a buzz cut with electric hedge shears. Generally doing so will result in lots of new growth next spring—often three to five new stems starting up from each cut tip. Not only that, you will leave bare ugly stubs showing.

To reduce the height of a shrub, remove some of the oldest, thickest stems first. They are the least vigorous and generally the least healthy. You can cut some of them all the way to the ground. Others you should prune back to where they join another branch—even a small branch that can replace it eventually. Stagger your cuts to give a layered look, the way your hairdresser may do for you. By this I mean, follow tall stems back to a "Y" or "V," and remove one side of the fork. These cuts will all be at different heights, creating that layered look.

Prune not only for plant health, but beauty. Make your shrubs pleasing to the eye. An unpruned forsythia is as messy as a teenager's bedroom, but it is a thing of beauty if pruned to a lovely vase shape, with cascading branches. Remember that pruning for looks also opens up the tree or shrub, allowing it to reach its full potential.

Don't be bashful when pruning. Bill Lord, the pruning guru at University of New Hampshire Extension for many years, likes to point out that if you take off a branch in an "oops" maneuver, another will grow back to replace it. Just don't remove more than 20 to 25 percent of the wood of a tree or shrub in any given year.

This is also a good time to remove root suckers. These are straight young stems that pop up from the ground around trees, often from the root stock of grafted trees. Crabapples and apples, for example, are not grown on their own roots—they are grafted onto roots that determine the ultimate size of the tree. Dwarf trees have one type of roots, semi-dwarf or full-size trees have others. The roots are not the same variety as the top of the tree, and would not produce nice fruit even if you let the root suckers get huge. Cut these suckers off close to the ground to keep the tree looking tidy and to prevent non-fruit-bearing stems from getting large.

If you prune spring-blooming trees now, you'll lose some blossoms. Apples, lilacs, forsythia—trees and shrubs that bloom before the Fourth of July—form their spring flower buds the summer before. But you aren't overly busy right now, so go get the work done, even if it means you will lose a few flowers in the spring. I love to look out my window in winter and see perfectly pruned apple trees. I think of pruning as sculpting my landscape.

Noble Trees

About fifteen years ago I took a course at Vermont Technical College to increase my knowledge of trees and shrubs used in the landscape business. The book we used was *Manual of Woody Landscape Plants: Their Identification, Ornamental Characteristics, Culture, Propagation, and Uses* by Michael A. Dirr (Stipes Publishing LLC, 1998). The book has been my bible of "woodies" ever since, so it was a pleasure recently to meet Professor Dirr and to attend one of his workshops sponsored, in part, by Green Works, the Vermont Nursery & Landscape Association. He is as impressive in real life as he is in writing—and humorous, too.

Professor Dirr came to Middlebury, Vermont, to talk about what he calls "Noble Trees." He made a very convincing case for planting trees that will achieve a magnificent size and that will survive long past the people who planted them. He gave several criteria for noble trees. First, they should get big. They should span generations (he showed us a photo of a tree planted by George Washington). They should have great architectural form, like the elms that once lined Main Street America. Each should be, in his terms, a "Skyway to Heaven"—tall and broad.

Two of Dirr's criteria are not quantifiable, but you'll know what he meant: Noble trees should be spiritual and inspiring. Many is the time I have paused in the woods to look up at an old sugar maple and wonder what went on during its 250-year life span. I find big trees awe inspiring, literally. But so few of us plant the noble trees—many Americans want trees that grow fast and look good immediately. Maybe we should all rethink that, and start planting trees for the future generations. Here are some of Dirr's candidates for noble trees to plant.

Sugar maples *(Acer saccharum)*. It's true that many of these are struggling (acid rain washes out much of the calcium in the soil that is needed by maples), and that these are not trees that you can plant close to the street. They don't do well in compacted soil, but they are magnificent trees, and everyone who has the space—and deep rich soil in full sun—should have one—or many.

White oak *(Quercus alba)*. Full-size white oaks are fifty to eighty feet high and wide, according to Dirr's book. They are very cold hardy but, like the sugar maple, don't do well with soil compaction. They like a deep, fertile soil in full sun.

River birch *(Betula nigra)*. This is a trendy landscape plant because it is relatively fast growing (thirty to forty feet in twenty years) and has interesting bark. It is not prone to leaf miners, the way white birch is. The national champion is 111 by 96 feet, growing in Lamar County, Alabama. It does best in rich moist soils and will not do well in dry, sandy soils but is the most tolerant of all birches to adversity.

Kentucky coffeetree *(Gymnocladus dioicus)*. Hardy to Zone 4 (minus 30), this little-used tree gets to be sixty to seventy-five feet in height with a spread of forty to fifty feet, which qualifies in my book as a noble tree. It is slow to moderate in growth rate: ten to fourteen feet in ten years. It is quite adaptable to harsh conditions, even surviving in cities and under drought conditions. Most cultivars sold now are male, and lack the nuts that settlers used as a coffee substitute.

Tuliptree *(Liriodendron tulipifera)*. I love this tree, having observed it many times in New York City's Central Park. According to Dirr it is hardy to Zone 4, but never achieves the size and grandeur here that it does in warmer climates. Trees over 150 feet tall have been documented. It is fast growing: fifteen to twenty feet in a six- to eight-year period, according to Dirr's book. I use a few of the ornate seed pods as decorations on my Christmas tree.

Black tupelo *(Nyssa sylvatica)*. Like the tuliptree, this one is hardy to Zone 4 but never gets really big here. There is one in Louisiana over 140 feet tall, but we might be lucky to grow one thirty to fifty feet tall. It likes acidic soils (pH 5.5 to 6.5), which we have, and will grow in places as tough as cold mountain swamps. It is tap-rooted, so you need to buy a small plant. It will grow twelve to fifteen feet in a ten- to fifteen-year period. Its fall color rivals that of the sugar maple, and I intend to plant one this year.

Linden *(Tilia cordata)*. One of my favorite trees, this tree offers nice shape and form, and fragrant (but not showy) yellowish flowers in July, with lovely shiny leaves. It can be sheared and shaped if you so desire, and some are made into nice lollipops—if you like that sort of thing. Hardy to minus 35, it gets to be sixty to seventy feet tall and thirty to forty feet wide. Another excellent street tree.

There is something to be said for planting big trees, trees that my grandchildren's kids will look at and say, "Awesome! Did your Grampy really plant that?" It's a good feeling to plant a tree that will be big enough, eventually, to provide carbon offsets for all those jet trips I take. And most of all, there is satisfaction in nurturing one of America's magnificent trees.

Planting Trees Right

Fall is well upon us and most gardening tasks should be done. But this is a good time of year to plant new trees, for a number of reasons. The weather is generally cooler and wetter than summer, so dehydration—a major reason for tree failure—is less likely. And tree roots do much of their growth after leaf drop.

Although a few nurseries here still grow some of their own trees, most trees are grown south of the Mason-Dixon Line— they grow much faster there, and time is money. They are grown close together in rows, like corn. When they reach a certain size they are pulled up and put in pots or wrapped in burlap and shipped north to our nurseries.

It is important that the base of the trunk that was above ground when it was growing in the field be above ground in your yard. Unfortunately, that part of the trunk, which is called the trunk flare, is often covered with two to four inches of soil in the pot or burlap ball when you buy it. You need to expose the trunk flare at planting time because otherwise bark rot can occur after six to ten years, and your tree will suffer and eventually die an untimely death. Go outside and have a look at trees you have planted in recent years. If they are turning color earlier than other trees, or if the tips of the top branches are barren of leaves, your trees are stressed—which may be due to covering the trunk flare.

Whether correcting a bad planting or starting anew, you need to recognize the trunk flare. Start by looking at trees planted by

Mother Nature. You will see that trunks near the ground fatten, and then flare out, often with roots traveling a little way above ground. That is the right way. If you do not see any flaring, you need to remove soil until you do see it. There may be some small adventitious roots coming out of what should be above ground, depending how long the tree has been in the ground or in the pot. Cut them off. The flare on a small tree is sometimes hard to recognize.

A client showed me a tree he planted seven years earlier. He said that the tree was that same size when he planted it, and he wondered why it had not grown. I got out my CobraHead weeder and started to loosen soil around the trunk. The trunk flare was covered by soil, so I worked at finding the flare and exposing it. In the process of doing so I found that the tree had been planted in the burlap that it had been purchased in—so the roots were confined to a very small space.

I know nurserymen who will argue with me, saying that it is best to leave a larger tree in the burlap so that roots are not disturbed at planting time. They say burlap is made from natural fibers and will break down in a year or two. Well, this burlap was seven years old, and was still in great shape. The roots of that poor tree had been confined for seven years, unable to reach out for nutrients and water. It is like putting a teenager in the same pair of sneakers for years—day and night.

If you buy a good-size tree in a plastic pot you will probably notice that some roots have grown so long, and been confined for so long, that they are circling the pot. You need to loosen them up and let them straighten out in your planting hole. In Woodstock, Vermont, I did some excavating around a twelve-inch-diameter maple tree that had a girdling root—a circling root that was growing over another large root, strangling it. The offending root was an inch in diameter, and I had to carefully cut it off with a hammer and chisel. If I had not discovered the offending root (which I found while exposing the trunk flare) a significant portion of the tree would have died.

Do not fertilize trees when you plant them. I add a couple of cups of rock phosphate, a mineral I buy in bags, because it is good for root development. It will not push top growth the way a nitrogen fertilizer would. I also add two cups of green sand that will help my tree grow thick cell walls and resist drought and extreme cold. I want my new tree to develop good roots before it starts growing new branches and leaves.

If in doubt, plant a tree a little high in the hole rather than too deeply. Dig a nice wide hole. When you refill the hole, the soil won't be compacted—allowing roots to extend more easily. Be sure to place the root ball on unexcavated soil so it won't settle later. A hole should be three to five times the width of the root ball. And again, remember to have the trunk flare above ground level!

Please do not make a mulch volcano around your tree. Mulch against the bark can rot it as easily as soil, maybe more so. Leave a donut hole in your ring of mulch, keeping the mulch about six inches away from the trunk.

Fall is generally cooler and wetter than summer, but water your tree if we have a dry spell. Roots will continue to grow after leaf drop, and will need moisture until the ground freezes. And water it next summer, too.

Planting trees is not rocket science, but doing it right makes a big difference. Your grandchildren will enjoy a tree that you plant well, and you might even hang a hammock from it.

NOVEMBER

Building a Pagoda-Style Garden Entry

The gardening season is about over. Hard frost has put even the most cold-resistant flowers and vegetables into their inevitable decline. But we gardeners don't have to stop yet. If you've finished your chores for the year, perhaps this would be a good time to build a welcoming entryway to your garden.

I built a cedar pagodalike garden entrance in 2004, and it is still in good shape. It is about four feet wide and the peak of the roof is about eight feet. The roof has a low rise and overhangs the sides by two feet on each side. I built it in about eight hours, and the material costs were well under $100.

In past years I've always had a bentwood arbor made of maple saplings as an entrance to the garden, and used it to support annual vines. But maple rots out in three to five years, so I decided to build something more permanent. I used cedar posts, which last much longer, and was able to get some small-diameter cedar poles and branches. Locust resists rot, and would also work well.

My local feed and grain store sells cedar rails for fences. These rails are ten feet long, and appear to have been run through a machine to make them round and pretty much the same diameter from top to bottom. I cut off the ends, which were made to fit holes in fence posts, so I ended up with nine-foot posts.

To increase the life span of the cedar posts I painted the bottom three feet with linseed oil. If you use regular cedar posts, you should peel the bark (as rot will begin first under the bark) and then paint with linseed oil.

I wanted the structure four feet wide (for easy passage of my garden cart), so I cut a piece of plywood forty-eight inches by thirty-eight inches, which I placed on the ground. This guided me when digging the holes for the posts. I used a two-handed post hole digger, and was able to get my holes twenty-four inches deep. If your soil is rocky, you'll have to make do with whatever depth you can reach, though twelve inches should be a minimum.

I set the first pole, and used a level to see that it was vertical in two directions, and backfilled around it. I did the second pole, towards the back of the entry, then joined them together with a crosspiece thirty-six inches above the ground. This was a two-inch diameter cedar pole that I attached to the uprights (on the outside of the entry) with long galvanized Phillips screws.

Next I attached two more crossbars, one near the top, one near the bottom: I placed a "top plate" four inches below the top of the upright poles to catch the rafter poles; the other I attached twelve inches off the ground. This made a sturdy start to the entry.

My screw gun has lots of "guts," but you may need to predrill the holes if yours doesn't. You can lubricate the screws by dragging them across a bar of soap, which also helps.

After setting verticals and crossbars on the other side of the entry, I temporarily attached a piece of strapping across the top of the opening to keep everything stable while I worked on the roof. Then I was ready to set rafters. I cut ten rafters, sixty-inch poles that were about 2½ inches in diameter at the base, and one four-footer for the ridge pole.

It is important to get the roof looking right. I had a friend help me while I set the first two pairs of rafters. Standing on a step ladder, I crossed the first two rafters (setting them side by side) so that they made a "V." I let them overlap each other by about ten inches, and fastened them temporarily in place with copper wire.

To make sure the roof was level from front to back, I set the second pair of rafters at the back of the entry, and then placed a piece of plastic pipe in the "V" formed by the two sets of rafters. I used pipe instead of a pole because it's straighter and smoother than poles, making it easier to check the level.

I screwed through the rafters into the top plate, then through the crossed rafters, and then through the rafters into the ridge pole (which replaced the piece of pipe). Next I added the three remaining pairs of rafters: One in the middle of the space, and the others at equidistant spacing.

Since I wanted to grow vines up this structure, I added vertical branches for them to climb. I used one-inch-diameter branches, and realize they may rot out before the bigger poles. However, the branches do not touch the ground, which helps prevent rot. They are attached to the lower crosspieces, and start six inches above ground level.

The beauty of building a structure that will last twenty years is that I can grow perennial vines on it, not just annual ones. I planted a white-blossomed fall blooming clematis vine, *Clematis paniculata,* that is very vigorous and has a wonderful scent.

On the other side of the entry I planted a wisteria. Most wisteria will not bloom this far north because they bloom early in spring on buds that were set the summer before. Our cold weather kills the buds, but not the vines. But there are two varieties that will work here: One called Blue Moon, the other Amethyst Falls. I put an Amethyst Falls on this entry and the Blue Moon on another vine structure. Both have done well, blooming every year.

So if you are looking for a nice fall project, think about building a garden entryway. Mine pleases me all year long, but especially in winter when there is little to look at in the vegetable garden—except for this welcoming entry.

A Frog Lends a Hand to Rhododendrons

For the past four years, Dr. Mark Brand has been inserting genes derived from an African frog into rhododendrons, trying to create a plant with extra resistance to the root rot caused by *Phytophthora cinnamomi*. A common soil fungus, *Phytophthora* does hundreds of thousands of dollars of damage to rhododendrons every year.

Dr. Brand is a horticulturist and a director of the plant biotechnology facility at the University of Connecticut in Storrs. And he is able to do what seems impossible to an old-fashioned gardener like myself: Implant something he cannot see—a modified frog gene—into something else he cannot see—the DNA of a flowering bush.

Creating a transgenic plant is so far beyond what traditional gardeners and hybridizers have done it seems, at first, incomprehensible. But Dr. Brand was able to make it seem, to use his words, more like baking a cake. Or almost.

Genetic modification has stirred protests in Europe, and some environmentalists believe it presents risks that outweigh benefits. But scientists are unlikely to stop experimenting, and from talking to Dr. Brand, I began to see why. The technology offers scientists the chance to create their dream plants.

Dr. Brand chose to introduce a frog protein because other scientists had already noticed that it worked against other fungi. The challenge was to take the gene that creates the protein and fit it into the genetic sequences of a rhododendron.

Though university labs are able to create DNA sequences,

these days a researcher can pick up the phone and have a biotech company send one over for about $50. Once Dr. Brand had the frog protein DNA sequence in hand, he inserted it into *E. coli* bacteria, which enabled him to easily create all the DNA he needed.

After determining which bacteria had been successfully married to the new gene, Dr. Brand placed them in a rich broth, allowing them to reproduce many times over. He was fattening them for slaughter. The unsuspecting bacteria were centrifuged and lysed with an enzyme, splitting them open so that he could harvest the DNA.

The next step was shooting the DNA into rhododendron cells with the potential to develop into complete plants. Dr. Brand's gene gun is nothing like the six-shooters that boys have been known to lug around in second grade. A small plastic and metal box that fits easily on the counter, his gene gun is powered by high-pressure helium.

His ammo is gold dust covered with frog DNA. It goes onto a thin piece of red Mylar that sits on a screen above the tissue sample. A burst of helium knocks the gold off the Mylar, sending it flying at the speed of sound.

The target is a petri dish with callus cells from a rhododendron leaf. Callus cells are the equivalent of stem cells in animal research. Each can multiply quickly, developing into an entire plant if given the right signals by plant hormones.

If all goes well in the petri dish, a few cells are penetrated by motes of gold carrying the specially prepared DNA. Some cells will incorporate the DNA into their own gene sequence at this point, copying it into every cell of the plants-to-be.

Eventually, after considerable testing to see if the gene is indeed in the plants, these test tube babies grow into ordinary-looking rhododendron plants. The ultimate test is to inoculate them with the *Phytophthora* fungus to see if they will develop root rot—or not. Dr. Brand does this by contaminating their soil with kernels of ordinary Uncle Ben's rice that have been inoculated with *Phytophthora*, thirty-six grains per pot. Controls are grown, too.

Dr. Brand said other scientists were genetically modifying roses in hopes of developing varieties resistant to powdery mildew and black spot. Still others imagine a rose with a new perfume, or maybe an unusual hue. (But if you are picturing a perfect black rose, don't count on that happening soon; roses are difficult to work with, and black is the toughest color to create.)

Easy-to-manipulate petunias and geraniums have been changing colors in labs for years. How soon will they, or the new improved rhododendrons, appear at the local garden center? Not soon at all. Testing will take about eight years, and more time will be needed for government approval of commercial products.

But success seems likely in the end. Dr. Brand is determined to build a better rhodie, and the technology is there to do so. He pointed to a row of quart-size pots in a temperature- and climate-controlled chamber at his lab with the proud look of a new father. The shiny-leaved young rhodies looked pest-free to this gardener.

Postscript: In September of 2010 I called Dr. Brand to see what had happened since this article appeared in *The New York Times* in 2003. He explained that the research was never completed as it became clear that the government was not going to easily approve the release of transgenic plants. Even if UConn spent the money to generate the information required by the USDA, it was still likely that their plants would not get approval. Public opinion about genetically modified plants is such that approval would be very difficult, he said.

Horseradish

Shrimp cocktail? Rare roast beef sandwiches? If you like them spicy, you've got to have horseradish. For most people, horseradish comes in a small bottle that languishes forever on the door of the refrigerator. But, just like tomatoes, the fresh homegrown kind is better than store-bought, so you may wish to grow your own. This is the time of year most people harvest horseradish, though you can do so almost anytime.

Horseradish is one of the few perennial vegetables we can grow in New England. But you should know that once you have it, you will always have it—even if you decide you don't want it anymore—so think where you want it before planting. Fortunately, a small patch doesn't increase in size very quickly. About the only way to get rid of horseradish (or at least for an organic gardener who eschews herbicides) is to turn the patch into lawn. Even then, new shoots may come up through the lawn a decade later.

Once established, the roots go down two feet or more into the soil. Because the roots branch and they are brittle, one can never get all the roots out. Even a scrap of the root will re-sprout, so the plants are there for life. Horseradish is as persistent as it is piquant.

Horseradish is in the cabbage family, but unlike its kissing cousins, it is the root, not the leaves, that you eat. And unlike other crucifers, horseradish is not started by seed, but by planting a cutting. The Johnny's Selected Seeds catalog (www.johnny-seeds.com or 877-564-6697), one of very few that offer cuttings, explains that the seeds are not viable. They ship cuttings in April, "after danger of freezing in transit has passed." But you can also get cuttings from a friend who is harvesting now and plant some this fall.

Prepare a horseradish bed by working in some well-rotted manure or compost. That will improve soil texture and keep the soil looser—for ease in future harvesting. Horseradish, which is essentially a weed, doesn't need high levels of nitrogen, phosphorus, or potassium.

To prepare a cutting for planting, slice off the leaves and the top two inches of the root. Plant the cuttings (those two-inch chunks of root) a foot or so apart, and cover with about two inches of soil. Water well, and surround with mulch to keep down the weeds. In a year or two you will be ready to begin harvesting. Horseradish does best in well-drained soil, but really will grow anywhere. It will be most vigorous in full sun, but four hours is plenty.

To harvest, loosen the soil around a plant, either with a garden fork or a drain spade. Drain spades have blades that are about sixteen inches long and five inches wide, and are great for digging out deep-rooted things like horseradish. A mature root will challenge even the strongest backs, so you may need to sever the root with your spade to remove it.

Prepare the horseradish for making sauce by hosing off the dirt, then peeling the dark brown skin to reveal its white interior. A potato peeler works just fine for that. The fumes of horseradish are very pungent, so think about working outdoors on a breezy day.

Slice the horseradish lengthways into sections the diameter of your index finger, then chop into pieces about three quarters of an inch in length. Use a food processor (or even an old yard-sale blender) to prepare the sauce, blending the chopped roots with vinegar. One medium-size root yields about two cups of chopped root. Begin by adding a half cup of vinegar and pulsing until the horseradish is coarsely chopped. Add more vinegar—about another half cup—and blend for two minutes or until the consistency is moist and creamy. Add salt if you are so inclined. Put in a glass jar and store in the fridge.

The strong flavors of horseradish tend to create strong feelings: You either love it or you hate it. The nice aspect of horseradish, for gardeners who want it for their kitchen, is that it is essentially labor free. Plant it, and walk away. The outer leaves, which are a bit coarse-looking, will sometimes get brown and scraggly looking, and slugs will occasionally nibble them, but the plants are trouble-free. They'll be there, just waiting for you to harvest the roots.

Henry's Shrimp Cocktail Sauce
    4 ounces tomato ketchup
    1 to 2 tablespoons fresh, homemade horseradish sauce
    Juice of half lemon
    Dash or two of Worcestershire sauce
    Black pepper and salt to taste

Blend ingredients in a small bowl, sampling and adjusting until perfect. The sampling/adjusting process is perfect for getting a bit more than your fair share of the shrimp.

Growing horseradish might be the perfect first step for folks who think that gardening is beyond them. So if you're harvesting now, think about sharing some horseradish tops with a nongardening neighbor who likes shrimp cocktail. Now, if someone would just develop corn and tomatoes that were so undemanding, everybody would garden.

Forcing Bulbs

Winter, I regret to inform you, is here. No, not by the calendar. But it's cold and raw outside and it gets dark early, and I've taken out my long johns and flannel-lined jeans. So I say it's winter. We'll all get used to it, but I doubt we'll see a shorts and T-shirt day until April. That's nearly half a year. But there is much we can do to avoid the winter blues. Planting bulbs for forcing is one of them, and now is the time to do it.

Tulips are an impossible dream for many gardeners. Planted in the fall, the bulbs are eaten by rodents during the winter. Or if they come up in the spring and are ready to bloom, the deer arrive and have them for pre-dinner appetizers. But if you grow them indoors, you can enjoy their splendor—and enjoy them while there is still snow on the ground.

Here is what you need to do: Buy some tulip bulbs, plant them in a large pot, and keep the pot in a cool dark location for sixteen weeks. But you need to read the packages carefully. Always buy bulbs that are labeled "Early Spring." Midseason or late-season tulip colors may make you swoon, but if you want tulips for forcing indoors, pick early blooming ones. The same goes for daffodils and other bulbs, although those only require a twelve-week cool period.

Plant bulbs for forcing near the soil surface in their pots. Instead of planting tulips or daffies six to eight inches deep—the way you should outdoors—plant their little pointy noses just beneath the soil surface of your pot. I make up a mix for forcing bulbs using 50 percent compost and 50 percent potting soil (the kind that that comes in a bag). Or I'll make a 50-50 mix of sandy garden soil and compost, and add some perlite to lighten it up. The planting soil should be lightly moist at planting time, but not soggy or the bulbs may rot.

There is no need to leave space between bulbs for future offsets (bulblets) to grow, nor do you need to fertilize them. These bulbs are going to be used once in the pot, then either tossed out (tulips) or planted outside (daffodils). Squeeze as many as possible in the pot for a good display—plant them shoulder to shoulder.

I plant our window box with daffodils each fall, then bring the box inside to store it in our chilly basement. Ideally you will find a place that is between 32 and 50 degrees. If you have a garage or entryway that is protected but not heated, or if you have a cellar bulkhead, you probably have the right conditions. I've read that you can keep bulbs in the fridge for twelve weeks, then plant them in pots and bring into the warmth immediately—but who wants tulip bulbs in the fridge for three months?

Forced bulbs can survive if the temperature goes a little below freezing, but they won't survive in a pot outdoors—at least not in my Zone 4 garden where temperatures routinely go to minus 25 degrees. One year, as an experiment, I planted the window box with daffodil bulbs and left it on the deck, but the box got too cold and all the bulbs were ruined.

Most homes are prone to occasional rodent incursions in winter, so it makes sense to protect your bulbs. I once had all my tulips, crocus, and scilla dug up and eaten—in the basement. So cover the pots with wire screen, but be careful: After you cut wire mesh, it can have razor-sharp edges. Daffodils are poisonous to rodents, so they are not interested in eating them—though they may dig them up looking for tastier things.

Check on your sleeping beauties from time to time throughout the winter. The soil shouldn't get totally dried out, so some years I give my pots a light watering in midwinter. And wait at least twelve weeks before bringing forced bulbs up into the house—even if they send up shoots. When the time is up, put them in a sunny window and watch them develop. Tulips need to sleep until March.

If you long for spring blossoms and can't wait for your forced bulbs, get some paperwhites. These fragrant beauties are in the daffodil family, and are ready for action on day one. Instead of planting them in soil, most people just arrange them so they sit on small stones in a bowl of water. Let the bottom of the bulb just kiss the water, and in a few days the roots will extend down into the water. For best results, let the roots and shoots develop in the dark for a week, and then place them on a sunny windowsill.

Paperwhites, for me, vary considerably in how long they take to blossom. I've had them bloom in a month, but six weeks is probably average; I've had to wait eight weeks on occasion. Once in bloom they are very fragrant and look good for a number of weeks—I like them even after they have passed their peak. These bulbs are not for outdoor planting here—they are only hardy to Zone 8 or 9—so when they are finished, just toss them in the compost.

So don't despair. Spring is only six months away. And we can have blossoms even sooner.

Potatoes

Potatoes—I love 'em. I'm over sixty years old, and have eaten them every Thanksgiving Day of my life but one. That one exception occurred when I was a young man hitchhiking through Tunisia, and none were on the menu. I had a spicy chicken couscous instead, and, truth be known, I felt somewhat deprived and a little bit homesick that day. I've substituted chicken or duck for the turkey several times while working in the Peace Corps. But potatoes? Only that once. To me, potatoes are an essential part of Thanksgiving.

Potatoes are amazing producers of food. A single potato, if kept until late spring, can be divided into two or three sections and planted. Each new plant will produce anywhere from one to five pounds of food—an amazing return for just a little work and a spot in the garden.

When potatoes were introduced in Ireland, they were a contributing factor in the population surge that ended when the potato blight hit in the 1840s. The Irish potato famine was caused by a fungus that wiped out all their potatoes virtually overnight. Back then, there were no relief organizations to help feed the hungry, so many either starved or fled the country.

There are, in Peru, over three thousand kinds of potatoes. But the Irish grew just one kind, and it was highly susceptible to *Phytophthora*, a fungus that, in its various species, causes potato blight, late blight on tomatoes and root rot in rhododendrons. Who knows what would have happened back then if they had been growing a hundred different kinds? In all likelihood, a few varieties would have survived, along with some of those poor people who starved to death. It might have changed history.

I grow a lot of potatoes, and have figured out how to store them well. It's not tough to properly store potatoes you can eat all winter and start next year's crop from this year's. I have some

Red Pontiacs, a wonderful and productive potato that I grew from my own seed potatoes for at least fifteen years.

Potatoes store well at temperatures between 33 and about 50 degrees, with high humidity. I store my potatoes at about 40 degrees. We have an above-ground portion of our basement (our house is built into a hill), which I keep cold, but above freezing. I built a cement-block bin with a plywood lid to store root crops. This maintains the humidity, minimizes temperature fluctuations, and keeps out any rodents that might want to share the harvest. The easiest way to store potatoes, I suppose, would be to buy a secondhand fridge, and keep it in the basement. Carrots, beets, and potatoes would all be happy there.

Each year I grow four or five varieties of potatoes. I always grow Red Pontiacs and a purple potato that, when cooked, is blue and white, with patterns like a tie-dyed T-shirt. Most years I grow Yukon Gold. I like white potatoes, too, and have tried several including Kennebecs, which are classic New England potatoes. This year I grew one called All Red, which cooks up to be pink inside, and was very productive. Some years I grow fingerlings—they are less productive than other potatoes, but yummy.

We don't have much trouble with the Colorado potato beetle, that striped critter that loves to munch potato leaves. Instead of spraying toxins, I patrol the potato patch regularly, removing and drowning the bugs and their orange larvae in soapy water. About ten years ago, I sprayed *Bacillus thuringiensis* (Bt), a bacterium that infects larvae of the potato beetle, and it greatly reduced their numbers. It doesn't kill them as a chemical would, but it makes the larvae sick—they stop feeding and die. I like to joke that it affects the adults, too ("Not tonight, honey, I'm not feeling so good."). There are several strains of Bt for a variety of beetles, and they remain among the best tools for organic farmers. I plant my potatoes later than my neighbors, and that may help too—the local beetles have already found something tasty. I plant them two weeks after last frost, even though they could go in the ground a month earlier.

As an organic gardener, I believe in diversity in the garden. The more kinds of things I grow, the less likely that a pest or disease will wipe out my entire crop. I enjoy having different colors and flavors of potatoes, too—even if that doesn't provide insurance against a blight. And each year I like to give thanks to the Incas of Peru, who domesticated the potato and whose descendants still grow many kinds.

Protecting Your Soil

By nature, I'm a bit impatient. I try hard to remember that growing plants, like raising good kids or dogs, takes time and patience, but sometimes I forget. One sunny day in early November I was ready to give the lawn out back a final haircut. We'd had a month of wet weather, and the ground was still soggy despite three days of sunshine, but I said to myself, "Aw heck, it won't matter."

I should have waited. Good soil structure is an important factor in growing anything well, even a lawn. When I was done mowing, I could see the tracks of the lawn tractor, indentations which meant I had compacted the soil in neat rows. This was not a death knell for the affected lawn, but it was careless, and I knew better.

Organic gardeners often have healthier plants than gardeners who depend on chemicals, in part because we nurture our soils. We regularly add compost, which feeds the soil organisms that help to create good soil structure, keeping the soil soft and spongy. This allows the soil to breathe—plants obtain oxygen from their roots, not their leaves—and it allows excess moisture to pass through.

A compacted soil, in contrast, has little space for air. There are fewer passages for water to drain out, so it tends to stay wet and soggy longer. For sensitive plants, things like delphinium or tulips, this can be fatal. Their roots rot or they just plain drown.

If you are, like me, still finishing up gardening tasks, pulling weeds and cutting back perennials, you need to be careful where you walk. Some of my flower beds are wide enough that I can't reach everything while standing on the lawn or a pathway. If the soil is soggy, I place a plank between plants to distribute my weight. I use a board six inches wide to walk on.

As you go about your tasks this fall and winter, don't always walk the same paths. Wet or frozen soil is very sensitive to compaction. Game trails in the forest exist because animals— even things as small as a fox—compact the soil so that most plants won't grow there.

Cleaning up my vegetable garden is easier than the flower beds. I have defined walkways with wide raised beds in between them, so there's no danger of compacting the soil. I don't rototill because I don't want to disturb the microorganisms living there, nor disturb the soil structure.

It's true, of course, that I disturb the soil even though I don't rototill. Pull a broccoli? Plenty of soil comes up with its roots. Planting disturbs the soil, too. Recently I added a couple of wheelbarrows of compost when I planted 160 garlic cloves for next year's crop. I stirred in the compost with my potato hoe. But that is nothing compared to the whirling and tossing done by a rototiller.

Most of my raised beds are not contained by planks or timbers. I just mound up the soil. Initially, I raked loosened soil from the walkways onto the beds, and added lots of compost. Now the beds are pretty much static. Some soil washes down into the walkways with hard rains, but not much, because I mulch heavily. And some soil gets used up or carried away with weeds or at harvest time. So I do build up the beds with soil from the walkways in the spring or fall when I add compost.

Roots from vegetables and flowers extend far beyond what you might think. What you see when you pull up a carrot or a daylily are only the gross roots. They also have fine roots that extend long distances. Root hairs, the parts of the roots that actually absorb air, water, and nutrients, are too small to be seen with the naked eye. By growing my vegetables in wide raised beds, I know that I am not stepping on the fine roots of my plants.

Each fall I like to topdress our garden beds with aged manure, and with leaves I've run over with the lawn mower. Both of these provide organic matter and help to protect soil from erosion. I just layer them over the bare earth. Leaves are great for keeping early weeds from germinating in the spring, too.

This is also a good time of year to get your soil tested by your state university extension system. The test will give you the soil pH and more. You will probably need to make adjustments to the soil pH by adding limestone or wood ashes. Your goal should be a pH of 6.5 to 6.8, just slightly acidic.

I always argue with people who say they don't have a green thumb. "There's no such thing," I say. Folks who don't do well in the garden usually haven't taken care of their soil (or improved it enough), but that's easy to fix. Tread lightly on the earth and nurture your soil with compost and fall leaves. You'll have a green thumb in no time.

Learning from Mistakes in the Garden

I believe that paying attention to the details of the garden can be as important as taking classes and reading books (even mine!). I like to pause at the end of the growing season to think about what I've learned, and store away the useful information somewhere up above my ears, or on the computer. I've been gardening for over sixty years, if you count "helping" Grampy in the garden starting at age two, and I'm still learning—and learning from my mistakes.

One lesson I never seem to learn is that most plants (except weeds, of course) need plenty of space in order to thrive. Even though I have a couple of acres to grow things in, I never seem to have enough space to grow everything I want. So I crowd things. This summer I was given some lovely David Austin roses to see how they would do in this climate. I tucked a couple of them into my front flower bed, but they were competing with a variety of perennials including phlox, daylilies, and a big, juicy euphorbia.

My roses bloomed, but were nothing spectacular. I planted one of the same roses at my friend Cindy's house in a flower bed that has more space, more sun, and fewer other plants nearby. The result? That one bloomed and bloomed and bloomed. On November 20, it still had two lovely blossoms. I guess I will have to remove some of the perennials around my roses if I want them to thrive.

I know that potted plants left out all summer can cause problems when brought inside to spend the winter. Inside they are soon covered from top to bottom with aphids. I know I need to wash them outside with the hose before bringing them in to remove aphids and their eggs. Usually I do. This year I did some, ignored others. And sure enough, I had to carry the unwashed ones back outdoors for a nice cold shower because I saw the signs of aphids—goop on the leaves (excrement) and tiny white critters underneath the leaves (aphids themselves).

I know that no matter how carefully I look for aphids before bringing them in, I need to wash every plant, every leaf. Here's my theory: While outdoors, aphids are not a problem because there are predatory insects that eat them and keep their numbers low. Indoors? Those lazy ladybugs looking for a warm place to sleep all winter do nothing to help, and the other predators are left outdoors. So next year I will do a better job of washing the plants before they come in the house.

If you have big plants that are infected with aphids, you can spray them with a dilute soap solution that will dehydrate them while not damaging the leaves or spreading poisons around the house. I use Murphy's Oil Soap, at the rate of one teaspoon to a quart spray bottle of ordinary water. Don't get carried away and make an "extra-strength" solution; too strong a dilution can ruin the leaves or even kill a plant. And don't use dish detergent—use a real soap. Commercial insecticidal soaps such as Safer (www. plantnatural.com) also work well.

This summer I let the weeds in my vegetable garden get ahead of me. I know that I need to mulch the walkways and around my plants by July Fourth weekend. I know I need to put down layers of newspaper and cover them up with leaves, straw, or mulch hay. But I didn't do it. So the weeds got big and my production went down. Many thanks to my friends who came to rescue me in August, pulling weeds before they totally took over. So I learned, "Practice what you preach." Don't let the weeds get ahead of you. Mulch.

I learned that even good organic gardeners can get late blight on their tomatoes and potatoes. The weather created a perfect storm of conditions and many of us got hit. I've read that the spores only survive the winter on living tissue—which includes potatoes. I've been growing potatoes from my own saved potatoes for over twenty years, but I guess I need to start over. If you had the blight, try to get all your little potato "escapees" pulled out in the spring when they first sprout up.

Celery: I decided I will never grow it again. Celery grown in dry years is tough and bitter. This year we had plenty of rain, but my celery still was not very good. The slugs and bugs liked it better than I did. I've read that if you only buy a few organic veggies, celery should be on that list, as it's sprayed with strong chemicals more often than most other plants.

A good alternative to celery (with similar flavor and great shelf life in the fridge or cold cellar) is celeriac. It's a root crop with a bulb the size of a baseball or larger. Same family, easy to grow and store. I planted twenty and will be eating it all winter.

I tried not to get discouraged this year with the cold, rainy weather that made gardening difficult. By spring I will have forgotten all about that, I hope, and will be starting seeds indoors. And I'll try to remember a few of the lessons I learned.

DECEMBER

Poinsettias

Poinsettias are, for most of us, a standard part of the holidays. They are those bright red "flowers" with green leaves that are present in every church and supermarket—and in most homes at this time of year.

Poinsettias actually have just tiny flowers, little yellowish things smaller than peas that grow in clusters surrounded by colorful bracts. The bracts are modified leaves that give poinsettias their allure. Bracts come in red—the standard color—but also in white, pink, lemon, cinnamon, plum, burgundy, and more. Some poinsettias such as Christmas Rose or Kris Krinkle have extra bracts that are crinkled and bunched, making them look, from a distance, a bit like giant roses. Some retailers even sell poinsettias that have bright blue or purple bracts, but those have been treated with dyes to make them even more outrageous (or perhaps to match Martha Stewart's idea of upscale holiday colors).

Poinsettias grow wild in Mexico, and were first brought to the United States in 1828 by Andrew Jackson's ambassador to Mexico, Joel Poinsett. It was grown outdoors in warm parts of the United States for nearly a hundred years before a clever nurseryman recognized its potential as a holiday plant.

In 1923 Paul Ecke, a grower in southern California, started growing poinsettias commercially and selling them to greenhouses around the country, shipping mother plants by rail to local growers, who took cuttings and produced more. By the 1960s poinsettia breeding had produced durable, colorful plants that were happy living in pots, and traveled well.

Paul Ecke was not only a trained horticulturist, he was also a marketer who made sure that television shows like *The Bob Hope Christmas Special* and *The Tonight Show* with Johnny Carson always had poinsettias on their sets. Today, 70 percent of all poinsettias in America start their lives on the Ecke Ranch.

It's good to know what to look for when selecting a poinsettia to bring home. Look for plants that have nice rigid stems and perky leaves. They're shipped in cellophane sleeves to keep cold drafts from shocking them, but plant quality deteriorates with time if left in those sleeves or crowded together at the store. Avoid plants with wilted leaves or bracts—wilting is a sure sign of stress. And don't pick a plant with waterlogged soil—too much water will rot roots. Bring your purchase right home in a closed bag or sleeve to keep it warm.

Poinsettias are popular because they don't require much special treatment. They don't need direct sunlight, so a table top with about six hours of indirect sunshine is fine. Like most of us, they hate being cold, and do best at 68 to 72 degrees. Temperatures below 50 are fatal—but few of us keep our houses that cold anyway.

The worst thing you can do to a poinsettia is overwater it. Once a week is good, and then only if the soil feels dry to the touch. Overwatering can cause root rot, or send plants into shock from lack of oxygen. Bottom watering is best—set the plant in a dish of water and let it absorb water for five to ten minutes. You don't need to fertilize them at this time of year.

Poinsettias are photoperiodic plants. That means that they decide when to bloom based on the length of the day. Theoretically you can get them to rebloom year after year, though it is a bit tricky. Start by cutting them back to eight-inch stems after they start looking ratty in April. Fertilize with a balanced all-purpose fertilizer every two to three weeks, and keep them indoors until the nights are above 55 degrees, and then put them outside. By October your plant will be thinking about blooming, but will only do so, the experts say, if it is totally dark for fourteen hours a day.

Supposedly even car headlights or interior lights can interfere with blooming, and I've read that one should put poinsettias in a totally dark room or even in a large box to keep away stray rays of light. But, as the song goes, it ain't necessarily so. I've summered them over outdoors and had them rebloom without any special treatment. Full disclosure: Some years they've rebloomed for me, but other years they have not.

Although the poinsettia growers have done a good job of convincing Americans that poinsettias are the ideal holiday plant, they are hindered by a persistent myth: That poinsettias are poisonous. Many cat lovers (including my mother, no matter what I told her) are afraid to bring them in the house—even though few self-respecting cats would eat them.

Ohio State University and the Society of American Florists did a study which showed that poinsettias are not poisonous. Elsewhere I've read that even if a fifty-pound child ate five hundred poinsettia bracts, it would not be dangerous. My friend Liz Krieg, a commercial grower from Bethel, Vermont, admitted tasting the white sap when she was a child, with no ill effects. "If you feed your kid and your cat well," she said, they're not going to eat many leaves." And I can't imagine they'd be very tasty.

Protecting Plants for the Winter

It won't be long now before snow flies and we'll be in the throes of winter overnight. I keep puttering in the garden, hoping for another week of warm weather. There are still a few chores that you should consider doing to protect plants over the winter.

First, protect your young trees, especially fruit trees, from vole damage. Voles are the bad boys (and girls) of the garden—they kill young trees by chewing on tender new bark during the winter, though they rarely bother mature trees. If they girdle a tree by chewing all the way around it and eating the tender, green, cambium layer, the tree will not survive. The cambium layer of bark is the layer that grows and provides new tissue in the trunk.

Voles resemble mice, but have smaller ears, short tails, and blocky bodies. If mice are ballerinas, voles are hockey play- ers. They live aboveground, hiding in leaf litter, long grass, or mulch—you've probably seen their trails in the lawn after the snow melts. They are active all winter and are the primary winter food source for many of our predatory birds.

There are two measures you can take to protect your trees: First, pull back any mulch that is close to the trunk, leaving only a six-inch ring around the tree. This will remove any nesting material near the tree, and leave it free of hiding places. It will also eliminate the bark rot that, after several years, can be fatal to trees that are subjected to the "mulch volcano" look that some landscapers like.

To be sure your tree is protected, you must encircle the lower trunk with a wire mesh called hardware cloth. It is like chicken wire but is stiffer and has much smaller openings—too small for voles. Ideally the base of the mesh collar will be buried in the ground a little, and extend above the snowline. I use eigh- teen- or twenty-four-inch-wide hardware cloth, which is some- times buried in snow, but have never had a problem. The biggest liability is forgetting it is there for five years and getting the wire embedded in the bark. You need to remove it before that happens.

If you have flower beds near your driveway or road, they may get sand, salt, and gravel plowed onto them each winter. There is little we can do to keep the salt out of the beds, but you can do something about the debris. Get a roll of burlap, and spread it over the bed to catch the sand and gravel after you have cut back your perennials. Then in the spring, just drag it onto the driveway and dump the detritus out. If you cut the burlap into six-foot sections, it will be easier to handle than one long piece in the spring.

I'm sure you have seen those plywood teepees some folks put out to protect shrubs that are planted under the eaves of the house. If you have plants where they can be damaged, they will be—unless you protect them from the ice and snow that falls off the roof. A better solution? Dig them up and move them next year, or get rid of them. The front of the house is a good place for flowers, but an awful place for shrubbery if the roof slants towards it.

Trees and shrubs you planted this fall can benefit by a four-inch layer of bark mulch spread in a wide circle around them. The idea is to keep the ground from freezing for as long as possible. Roots are actively growing on most woody plants until the ground freezes, and the more the new roots grow now, the better.

Then there are those tender perennial plants you are growing that are a zone north of their comfort zone. Some will make it through the winter if you give them protection. Here's my method: I wait until after the ground has frozen solid, then cover them with cut evergreen branches, and straw, hay, or leaves. Hemlock, spruce, pine—all are fine. Or I'll use my Christmas tree branches after I take it out of the house in January. The branches won't smother the plants, and will support the straw I place on top. The ground will stay a bit warmer—even if there is not much snow cover.

Tender, early blooming shrubs and vines have buds that were set this summer, and the cold winds of January can freeze and dehydrate the buds, killing them even when the shrub or tree shows no sign of damage. Small things like roses you can wrap in burlap, or protect with cut evergreen branches as described above. I've done it, and it works.

Gardening is a dance. We put one foot forward, but then sometimes we take two steps back. I lose a few plants every winter, or grow plants that just don't thrive in our climate. After a few years, if a plant is just limping along, I get rid of it. So do what you can to protect your plants—or let them go to the great compost pile in the sky.

Starting Tropical Trees from Seed Indoors

Given the state of the economy, no one I know is going to the tropics this winter—especially not me. But you could start your own tropical forest—indoors, for practically free. Judy Durant has a number of hot-climate trees growing in her house on a cold hilltop in Meriden, New Hampshire. And she started them from seeds she extracted from ordinary grocery store fruit. It is not, apparently, as tough to do as you might think.

In their living room Judy and her husband have a six-foot-tall date palm that she started about ten years ago. In the sunroom there is a six-foot-tall avocado tree, and two rubber trees— including one that she started herself from a cutting. In the dining room is good-size grapefruit tree and another, smaller, avocado tree. She has tried to germinate mango seeds, but without luck.

Judy's basic approach to starting most seeds is to germinate them wrapped in a moist paper towel. She places several seeds on the towel, and places them in a plastic container that she keeps near the kitchen sink so that she will remember to check them daily. She places a lid on the container, but doesn't snap it shut. Once the seed germinates, she plants it.

I asked Judy how she knows if the seed sends out a root first, or a shoot. Roots come first, she said. So she plants the seed with that little root pointing down. Shoots tend to turn green very quickly, which is another clue you can use to properly orient the seed if a seed sends both a root and a shoot at the same time. How deep does she plant a seed she has never tried before? She plants them about three times the length of the seed.

Avocados have huge pits (seeds) that Judy germinates by suspending them in a glass of water after poking them with three toothpicks for support. She allows the pointed upper end to remain in air while the base is in water. In recent years Judy reports that most grocery store avocados have not germinated for her, so I went on the Web and learned that avocado seeds are only viable for two to three weeks—but the fruit has a shelf life considerably longer than that. So you need a fresh one!

After her seeds have sent out roots, Judy plants them in ordinary potting soil (that comes in a bag) mixed with some composted cow manure. She told me that she doesn't offer fertilizers to her plants very often, so she likes a nice, rich planting mix.

Judy's trees all sit near south-facing windows, so they get good winter light. Depending on the height of your window, you probably will need to place them on a table to get them up to the height of the sill, so they can take advantage of the sunshine. Most of Judy's trees are large plants by now, and are growing in pots that are a one foot or more wide and deep.

Maintenance is pretty basic for trees: Water sparingly. Check regularly for aphids or other bugs. Root-prune as needed. Judy doesn't pamper her trees, or fuss over them much. It's important not to overwater trees—you don't want their roots to rot. She waters most things once a week.

She keeps a spray bottle of Safer soap (which is a commercial soap that dehydrates soft-bodied insects and is nontoxic to us and our pets; www.saferbrand.com) in her sunroom to fight off aphids if they show up. But last year somehow the aphids took over and she took a radical approach that worked: She amputated the entire top of her avocado and grapefruit trees, leaving two- to three-foot-tall stubs, bare and leafless. You would never know that she did that. Her avocado, which was already a large tree with an extensive root system, pushed out tons of new growth—almost three feet of it in one year. It started three new branches from dormant buds, and is a great looking tree.

Root-pruning is needed every year or two for large houseplants if you don't want to keep increasing their pot size. Last year Judy's date palm was pushing itself out of the pot, and had become so root-bound that there was no space for water.

Here's how Judy root-pruned her date palm: She pulled it out of the pot and saw that the roots had gone around the pot, looking for somewhere to go. She took a serrated knife and attacked mercilessly. She cut off about two inches of root mass everywhere around the rootball—which was in a pot fifteen inches wide and twelve inches deep. She repotted it in the same pot, adding new soil mix in the bottom and forcing it in around the sides.

You can't think of your tree in human terms—cutting off roots is not painful to it. Think of it like a haircut. When I root-prune, I put down an old sheet on the kitchen counter to contain the mess.

When I was an eight-year-old boy I started a grapefruit tree from a seed and tended it until I went to college. Now, more than fifty years after that first effort, I'm ready to start another indoor tree. I crossed the Sahara as a young man, and have fond memories of the date palms growing in lush green oasis towns, so I think I'll try growing a date palm. And eating the fruit to get some seeds won't be a hardship, either.

A Very Special Gardener

As I sit here, counting my blessings, I reflect on all gardening does for me. The exercise of it helps to keep me healthy; the vegetable harvest supplies me with healthy organic food; and the flowers, trees, and shrubs provide beauty throughout the year. Gardening also helps me to make friends, and sometimes lifelong friends. Donna Covais is one of those friends. She is a wonderful gardener and a very special person.

Donna has the gift. She grows mountains of flowers and vegetables in a tiny strip of land between her driveway and the house she rents in downtown Burlington, Vermont. She grows houseplants that make ordinary houseplants look anemic. She makes gorgeous flower arrangements, and has twice won city-wide prizes for her garden. And yet, for almost ten years, Donna has been completely blind.

Donna has had diabetes most of her life, and she always thought she managed it quite well. But then in 1996 her eyesight started to go, and quickly. Despite a number of operations, she lost her sight, and descended into a deep funk. She lost her business, a florist shop and nursery, and wasn't sure how she would make a living, or support her two children. Life seemed pretty grim. Two things saved her: She met her husband, Joe, and she started gardening again.

While running her flower business and raising her two children, Donna had also volunteered her services to help others. She worked with special needs students, bringing them to her flower shop and teaching them skills they could use to get a job. She taught them how to tend plants, and how to prepare cut flowers for the shop. She worked with the elderly, bringing plants to nursing homes and hospitals, doing demonstrations and encouraging patients to interact with plants. It was then that she first learned about horticultural therapy.

After Donna lost her sight, she met and married Joe Covais, who is also blind. They moved to Burlington, Vermont. A friend of Joe's mentioned to Frank Oliver, Merchandising Director of Gardener's Supply Company in Burlington, that Donna had once been a great gardener but no longer did any gardening. Frank called her, and then stopped by their house. "Donna was pretty despondent," Frank told me. "So I brought by some gardening stuff and asked her if she would try it." She agreed.

Mr. Oliver got Gardener's Supply to donate some raised cedar beds, self-watering planters, tools, and even a talking thermometer. He cut grooves in the cedar beds and put strings in them so she could plant seeds in straight rows. He delivered good compost and soil because the soil between her house and the driveway was pretty awful. Before long, Donna's spirits had lifted, and she was figuring out how to garden again. The local Master Gardener program sent people by to help her. Life was good.

Donna's garden is a strip of land no more than eight feet wide. In it, she raises tomatoes, lettuce, peas, beans, chard, cukes, garlic, and dozens of types of flowers. Among her favorite flowers are heliotrope, for its "incredible smell—like vanilla," hollyhocks, zinnias, morning glories and moonflower, Angel's Trumpet, cleome, and sunflowers.

As an organic gardener, Donna believes in companion planting. "I plant things together that belong together," she said. Donna also rotates her vegetables through the garden, planting tomatoes on one side of the steps this year, on the other side the next. She believes that gives her a little insurance against the pests. "I'm a strict organic gardener, but I don't have a pest problem."

She also understands that healthy plants start with a healthy soil, and that an organically nurtured soil is healthier than one pumped up with chemicals. Donna only buys plants that are raised locally. "It's very difficult to get people to recognize quality," she said. "Some people just buy by price. But you get what you pay for." So Donna avoids the big-box stores, buying from local growers or starting her plants from seed. She can tell how her seedlings are doing by running her fingers down the row, and it almost seems as if her plants can feel her love—and respond.

Texture, smell, and shapes are very important to Donna, though she also plants according to color combinations with the help of sighted friends. "I was lucky, I saw for forty years. Every night I say the name of the colors I can remember. I try to keep them in my visual memory." After watering a flower bed sometimes she runs her fingers through the foliage, fluffing it up like a hairdresser. "Even though I can't see, I want it to look good."

Once gardening had helped Donna to recover her spirit she decided to finish the college degree that she had started years before. "My plants and horticultural therapy gave me my life back, especially professionally," Donna said. She is now a registered Horticultural Therapist, and a motivational speaker. I feel very lucky to be able to count her among my friends.

Postscript: I spoke with Donna in the fall of 2010. She has received the first grant given by the State of Vermont for horticultural therapy. She is working with residents at Starr Farm Nursing Center in Burlington, Vermont, to research and document the benefits of horticultural therapy. Not only that, she got a grant for a florist's cooler to assist her in her work.

Creating an Arboretum in Your Backyard

It's winter, and time to dream. Looking out the window at his bird feeders, Bill Shepard of Thetford, Vermont, can see a dream come true. Not only are there birds galore, his yard is full of trees and shrubs that feed and shelter birds. Many years ago Bill Shepard had an idea, a pipe dream. He wanted to create an arboretum, a collection of trees that would not only please him, but would nourish and nurture wildlife.

In 1985 Bill bought an old rundown farmhouse, and even though it was barely habitable, he didn't just focus his attentions on the house—he started planting trees right away. He is an avid birder and he loves trees. So he decided that over the course of his life he would create his own arboretum and every year he would plant a few trees, particularly those that nourish wildlife.

The first tree Bill planted was a thornless honey locust *(Gleditsia triacanthos* var. *inermis)* sent to him by The Arbor Day Foundation. Since that time he has planted another forty or fifty trees, concentrating on native species. He has a few that, while native to the United States, are outside their normal habitat. He dug up a little pitch pine *(Pinus rigida)* from his sister's place in Cape Cod, and a lodgepole pine *(P. contorta)* he got while in Montana—and both are doing well.

Instead of planting trees and shrubs that are seen in every new subdivision, Bill has looked for more unusual things. He loves his beaked filbert *(Corylus cornuta)* not for the delicious fruit that the squirrels get before he can, but for the male catkins in winter, and for the delicate magenta blossoms that grace this multistemmed shrub in April—blooming even before his shadbush, one of the earliest bloomers. Others he likes are mountain maple *(Acer spicatum)* a small understory tree with interesting bark, and common hackberry *(Celtis occidentalis)*, a fast-growing, full-size tree that produces drupes (fruit) enjoyed by birds in the fall.

Although he has twenty-nine acres, Bill has thirty species of trees and shrubs growing on the half acre surrounding his house—but has not given up his lawn. He has added trees that will be large at maturity along the edge of an existing woodland at his property line, then added understory shrubs next to them. Witchhazel, elderberry, pagoda dogwood, red osier dogwood, blueberries, and hobblebush are great animal food, and take up very little space.

Bill has spent very little on his arboretum. His family and friends know that he collects trees, and have let him dig seedlings on their properties. But he doesn't try to transplant trees and shrubs the size most nurseries sell. Bill thinks small: He digs up seedlings that are generally just twelve to twenty-four inches tall. He explained that small trees do better than larger trees because they lose a much smaller percentage of their root systems when dug. Normally he digs two or three of the same species, and immediately heels them into his vegetable garden. Later he moves them again—once he has found good places for each.

Even sumac, a plant I consider a nuisance, has a place on Bill's property. He has it because it provides food in the spring for robins and other birds when there is little else to eat. It spreads by root suckers, but his has not spread aggressively—perhaps, he explained, because it is at the edge of the woods so it is not as vigorous as it might be in full sun.

Although many experts advise planting trees in the fall, Bill plants most of his in the spring. He likes to get them established before the harsh Vermont winter arrives. The key to success, he explained, is to water at least twice a week. He knows that if they dry out, they won't survive. Of course, that is another reason to have so many trees near the house—they're close to the hose.

Deer are a problem in Bill's neighborhood, so he protects all his young trees with chicken wire or bird netting. He noted that the growing tip (or leader) of a tree is the most important part to protect, so he keeps it screened up to a height that deer can't reach. Later, if a deer nibbles a branch or two? Well, that's just some volunteer pruning.

Not every tree that Bill plants is a success story. Near the bird-feeders is a dead sycamore *(Platanus occidentalis)* that lived for ten years, then mysteriously died. He lives in USDA Zone 4 (minus 20 to 30 in winter), and sycamores should be hardy there, though they are rarely seen in the wild in his part of Vermont. He keeps it for the birds, which rest in it, and perhaps to remind himself that it's worth trying to grow lovely trees even if they don't all make it.

So take time to dream this winter. You don't have to be an expert to start your own arboretum. As Bill told me, "I don't make it rocket science. I'm just an enthusiast, not a botanical wizard." Me? I'm dreaming about getting a beaked hazelnut with those early magenta blossoms.

Picking Stems to Grace the Table in Winter

Like many gardeners, I grow flowers because I like their colors, forms, and fragrances. I like them outside, and as cut flowers in the house. Starting with snowdrops in March and going to colchicums in October (and some years, saffron crocus in November), I cut my own flowers to grace the table.

Now the gardening season is over, so it's off to my local florist for flowers. But I also use ferns, evergreen branches, and dried flower stalks in table arrangements. I like mixing them with purchased flowers to save money, and to remind me of the outdoors. If you take a look around, there's actually a lot to use.

White pines are common in our New England woods, and work well in arrangements, holding their needles and looking good for a month or more. They have five long needles per cluster. Canadian hemlocks are also common, but have short flat needles that fall off almost as soon as they come indoors.

Balsam fir and blue spruce are commonly sold as Christmas trees, and hold their leaves well indoors. Save any branches you trim off, and keep them fresh in water—even if you don't need them immediately. Cedars and arborvitae work well in arrangements, too.

Color can come from not only flowers or leaves, but also berries. In swamps or wet places our native deciduous holly, winterberry *(Ilex verticillata)*, is currently displaying bright red berries. Some years they produce magnificently, though this year I seem to have few. A good domesticated variety is called Sparkleberry.

Viburnums also have good red berries, though the birds often make short work of them. They also tend, in my experience, to drop their berries on the tablecloth more quickly than winterberry.

A little used, but useful, fruit is from the staghorn sumac *(Rhus typhina)*. From now, through the return of the robins in the spring, sumacs have clusters of reddish-brown berries on the tips of their branches. In past years I've used them in dried flower arrangements, but found them messy. But, when kept in water, sumacs don't shed berries nearly so much. An arrangement of three spider mums (tall, big-blossomed chrysanthemums) from the florist looks pretty meager, but very nice with a few freshly cut stems of sumac added to the mix.

The Christmas fern (*Polystichum achrostichoides*) is a low-growing evergreen fern that generally grows in shady woodland areas, often under evergreen trees. It is still looking good outdoors, though by spring the leaves may be a bit ratty. Don't pick all the leaves off one plant, but harvest just one or two stems from each. Leaflets alternate on a central stem, each leaflet ever-so-slightly resembling a Christmas stocking, with a little toe bulging out and upward. I use the fronds at the base of an arrangement, as they tend to flop.

Depending on the temperatures you've experienced, you may still have some nice-looking ivy, myrtle, or pachysandra outdoors in the garden. Last year I remembered to pick pachysandra in mid-fall and rooted it in water. When rooted, it can be used at the base of arrangements all winter.

Mosses are often used by florists to cover up "Oasis," that green foam stuff used to keep flowers from moving around in arrangements. If you want to harvest moss from the woods around your house, it's easy to do. It will peel off a log, the ground, or a rock with just a little encouragement. But remember that, as with any wild plant, you should harvest only small amounts or it may disappear.

Stems of trees and shrubs can also be used in arrangements. Red-twig dogwoods and red osier dogwoods (*Cornus sericea* and *C. alba*) are grown as decorative shrubs, but also grow wild in wet places along roadsides. They need to be pruned back severely each year so that they will coppice (send up several stems where one was cut) and display a nice red color. Red twigs look great in window boxes with greens.

Beech trees produce beautiful gray-barked branches with cigar-shaped buds that look good indoors. Native cherry trees often have nicely branched dark stems, particularly if growing in the shade. The tree with the most interesting, finest branching is the hophornbeam *(Ostrya virginiana)*. It is a small to medium-size understory tree. I keep a branch of it on the ceiling above my computer, where I can see it when I tip back my chair to search for a word.

This fall I cut stems of flowers with interesting seeds, saving them to use now. But you may still have some in your garden if you didn't cut everything down. Wild cattails are great in arrangements—but they're beginning to open and shed fluff by now. Goldenrod is pretty, but sheds seeds, as do wild asters.

So go outside on a nice day, see what is interesting in shape or texture, and bring some inside. They're not a substitute for peonies or daffodils, but they're better than nothing. And the price is right.

Removing Big Tree Branches

Sometimes I wonder if my boy, Josh (the illustrator of this book), was a bear in an earlier life. He can hunker down for the winter, close the blinds, and not be bothered by short, gray days. He doesn't exactly hibernate, but close to it. Not me. I need all the sunshine I can get, so I recently spent some time pruning the branches of a white pine and a Canadian hemlock that were blocking out the few rays of sunshine that try to brighten the north side of our house.

Back in 1972, before I knew anything about planting trees, I dug up half a dozen small evergreens—pines and hemlocks—and planted a row of them for privacy near the house. They flourished. Even though the closest trees are twenty to thirty feet from the house, their branches were beginning to touch it and block out the light. It was time to bring back the sunshine.

Removing a big branch takes some planning. First, it's important to have a good sharp saw, gloves, and safety glasses. If using a ladder, as I was, it's important to have it well placed so that the branch will not fall on you, and so that the ladder will not tip or slide. It's best to have someone at the base of the ladder while you work.

Both pine and hemlock are fairly brittle, and will snap long before you saw through big branches. Bark will tear, scarring the trunk and opening it up for disease and insects, so it's best to make three cuts instead of one to remove a long, heavy branch.

First, a word about saws. I have a twenty-one-inch curved pruning saw with good, stiff teeth. It is ideal for taking on bigger branches or small trees. I got mine for about $40 from OESCO (formerly Orchard Equipment and Supply Company; www .oescoinc.com or 800-634-5557). I could have used a bow saw for my recent job, but they are much less adaptable, and can't get in tight spots.

Here's how I removed the offending branches: First, I made a cut on the underside of the branch, an inch or two deep and about sixteen inches from the trunk. Then I severed the branch about twenty inches from the trunk with a cut from the top. The undercut stopped the ripping that occurred in the bark when, with a loud crack, the branch snapped off when I was barely halfway through the top cut.

I then had a tree with a long ugly stub. But this was relatively lightweight and easily pruned off near the trunk. Not at the trunk, as flush cuts are not recommended. I cut just beyond the branch collar, which is a swollen area with wrinkled bark. It extrudes outward from the trunk, and is the site for healing.

My project was an easy one, in terms of deciding what to do. I was removing branches on the back side of the tree, and opening up the sky over my deck. The road side of the tree still has adequate branches to serve as a screen. But what to do if someone planted a blue spruce in the front of your house twenty years ago? You can't just prune off all the lower branches in order to keep them from blocking your windows.

The answer is one most homeowners won't like: You can cut down the tree, or you can live with a tree that keeps you from seeing out, and that rubs paint off your house when the wind blows. Many people have the problem, and just don't do anything. My vote? Cut down the tree.

If there is a moral to this story, it is this: Don't plant evergreen trees near your house. If you love their look, plant them well away from the house. If you need light in winter, plant deciduous trees and shrubs near the house—after all, they lose their leaves in fall. I particularly like a short-lived, native, understory tree that never gets much taller than twenty feet, the pagoda dogwood *(Cornus alternifolia)*. The branching is exquisite, particularly as seen against snow. Their blossoms, though not dramatic, are nice in early summer, and the birds love their clusters of dark blue berries on red stems in the fall.

Another great one is the Japanese red maple *(Acer palmatum)*. It is borderline hardy in Zone 4 where I live, so it stays small. It has gorgeous red leaves all summer. In warmer climes it gets to be a full-size small tree, but my winters keep it to about six to eight feet tall and wide. I've had mine since 1970, and it survived the winter of 1984 when we saw minus 38 degrees. It lost some branches that year (and other years) due to the cold, but the trunk is about six inches in diameter.

Now that winter is closing in, get outside and prune away branches that block the light from your windows. Unless, like Josh, you plan to hibernate. If so, maybe I'll see you in the spring.

Holiday Gardening with Kids

This holiday season, I've been busy with shopping, parties, and scurrying around like that mythical battery-powered bunny that never stops. On a recent snowy afternoon I paused to think about the gifts I've received during my lifetime, and about ways I can give back to others. The gifts I mean are not material things, but gifts of time, of knowledge, and of love.

I was lucky enough to have a grandfather, John Lenat, who was a wise man—and a good gardener. He was a tailor who came over from Germany about a hundred years ago and may never have gone to high school. But he spoke several languages and could make people smile in any one of them. He was a gentle and loving man. Grampy taught me the value of a good compost pile and a sun-ripened tomato, and he made me a lifelong gardener. He never asked me to weed, but gave me jobs in the garden I enjoyed, like stirring the manure tea and ladling it onto the tomatoes.

I hope to impart that same love of gardening to my grandchildren, George and Casey Jeanne-Marie. George started gardening when he was three. He loves to eat carrots and cherry tomatoes, so that's what we've grown. One year I built a little raised-bed garden for George, and he planted purple carrots in it. George not only loved the carrots, he won a blue ribbon with them at the Cornish Fair. That was a good start for a young gardener.

So what can I do now? Well, we'll plant amaryllis bulbs together. Amaryllis are big, dramatic indoor flowers that send up tall stalks and bright colored flowers in the course of just a few weeks. And they're essentially foolproof. Grocery stores and garden centers sell them in kits, and I've gotten one for George and one for his sister, Casey.

The kits come with a little compressed disk of coir, an alternative to peat moss that's made from coconut fiber. Put it in a bowl with a couple of cups of warm water and it quadruples in size in just a few minutes. This is fun for a kid.

The bulbs are about three inches in diameter—which is much easier for a child to handle than carrot seeds. It needs to sit with at least half of the bulb above the soil line. I'll guide the kids and they'll plant them just right. And when they bloom, I think they'll be their pride and joy. I bet they remember those first big blossoms when they're my age.

Call me a Luddite if you wish, but I don't like video games, robots, and battery-powered toys that make loud noises. I understand that my grandchildren like them, but I'm doing my best to introduce them to the joys of gardening. And I know that my Grampy, if he's watching, will approve.

JANUARY

Stone Walls

In recent years gardeners have come to appreciate the beauty of a well-made stone wall. But having someone build you one is an investment that may preclude sending your child to college. However, if you are fit and ambitious you could build a stone wall yourself, and this is a good time to do some dreaming, planning, and research.

On a cold day that hinted of snow, Travis Callahan of Cornish, New Hampshire took me around to see some of the dry stone walls he has built in my area. He is a master dry stone wall builder certified by the Scottish Dry Stone Walling Association. Dry stone walls are built using no mortar, the type recommended for gardens; the earth moves each winter and spring, so mortar cracks. Travis figures his dry stone walls will last a hundred years or more with little or no repair.

He explained that there are several types of good walls, but all rely on the same basic principles:

1. Create a good base, free of organic matter or soil that might compress. Dig out the topsoil—a foot or so—and replace it with crushed stone (but never round pebbles), or just start building on subsoil.

2. Select large stones for the foundation. In a retaining wall, a stone that is three feet long and two feet wide should run from front to back, so that the two-foot face is facing out of the wall.

3. Make sure the top of any flat stone is level. A stone that tilts will tend to make the next course slide down.

4. Use stakes and strings to keep the wall straight. A retaining wall should slant slightly back; each side of a two-sided wall should slant toward the middle. That way gravity helps keep the wall together. Walls can have a camber (tilt) ranging from one-in-six to one-in-twelve. Gritty things like granite grab well, and don't need as much camber as walls using smooth or round stones.

5. For the second course of stones, be sure that each space between the foundation stones is bridged with a stone. A running joint—one that is repeated in two courses—is a prescription for trouble.

6. Each stone, once in place, must not wiggle when you put pressure on it. Flat shim stones should be slipped under stones as needed.

7. A two-sided wall is built from both sides at once. The center is filled with hearting. This means using small stones and rubble to fill up the center space with junk you would have to get rid of otherwise.

8. The third course of stones should include a throughstone every three feet. Throughstones

are long enough to pass all the way through the wall, or at least to reach the middle of the wall.

9. The fourth course repeats the second. And so on.

10. The top of the wall can be finished in several ways. Capstones, which are large and flat, are ideal. They shed water and look nice—and are a nice place to eat lunch in the sun. They are the most common tops for both two-sided walls and retaining walls.

Travis Callahan took me to a freestanding wall he and David Fielder built in Meriden, New Hampshire. The wall is unusual, in that it is turf-coped. This means that instead of capping the wall with stone, it is covered with turf. They cut turf from the field nearby, and placed two layers on top of the wall. The first layer, destined to provide soil and retain water, they placed upside down. The second layer went right side up.

The wall was built in full sun in a dry year, and the grasses all died. But Mother Nature stepped in, and two years later there are native grasses and flowers, such as wild black-eyed Susans, growing on top of the wall. Of course, a serious gardener could also create a fine rock garden there.

Many of the walls lining roads and fields were built in the nineteenth century to define property lines, keep in animals, or to make plowing easier. Generally farmers didn't bother making fancy two-sided walls, but just stacked stones atop each other, creating "single stone" walls. Travis brought me to one he had recently rebuilt in Cornish, New Hampshire.

A single stone wall is just that. Each stone shows through on both sides of the wall. This also means there are places where you can see though the wall. But it is just as important to bridge all joints, and to shim stones to keep them from wiggling.

To see more stone walls, go to Travis Callahan's Web site (www.drystonewalls.com). A good reference book is Vermonter

Gordon Hayward's *Stone in the Garden: Inspiring Designs and Practical Projects.*

Years ago when I was young(er) and (more) foolish, I built an eighty-foot retaining wall to create a terrace for fruit trees. I asked a neighbor what to do, but didn't get all the information I needed. Now the wall I built is in bad shape, and this winter I'm thinking I should rebuild it in the spring. Of course, it's easier to dream than build. At least now I know what to do.

Postscript: I *do* dream better than I work. Years later that eighty-foot stone retaining wall of mine is still waiting to be rebuilt. I have built some others, however, using what I learned from Travis, and they are doing just fine.

New Year's Reflections

I like the idea of making resolutions near the beginning of each year. I've been making them for decades, but don't usually talk about them. That way, you see, no one will know if I don't succeed. But this year I'm pretty sure about meeting my goal.

My resolution is simple: This year I'm going to help six nongardeners to grow tomato plants. We have a daily electronic newsletter in Cornish, New Hampshire, called *Cornish Connect.* Sometime in May I'm going to place an ad in it saying, "Wanted: Gardeners."

I'll explain that I'm willing to help seniors, children—or anyone, really—to grow tomatoes, one plant per person. That there will be no cost, and not much work. I'll provide seedlings—I always start way too many, anyway—and we'll plant one together. The soon-to-be-gardener need not even have a proper garden. We can plant a tomato in a five-gallon pail with a few holes drilled in the bottom. All a gardener needs to provide is a sunny location and a little water in dry spells.

Why grow a tomato? Many reasons. First, in my opinion, is the taste of homegrown tomatoes. Few flavors can beat the taste of a sun-warmed tomato, ripe and red, eaten right off the vine. And gardening—whether planting a tomato or a maple tree—is also a statement. It says "I care about the natural world." Nurturing plants is the polar opposite of mayhem and destruction. I'm always shocked and saddened when I hear of soldiers bulldozing olive trees in the Middle East as punishment to their enemies.

By growing something we are expressing optimism, a belief in our future. I know a woman who planted three small crabapple trees at the age of ninety. She believed she'd live to see them blossom, and I bet she will. Gardening is a great way to stay young.

I was lucky as a child. I had two wonderful grandfathers, and one was also a great gardener. He got me gardening at an early age, and I've never stopped. Gardening has been my passion. It has bolstered my spirits in hard times. It has given me great joy. I smile when I see a bumblebee deep inside a tulip, and I've been known to shout with glee when my magnolia tree first blooms in spring. If I could help some people to garden, it would give me great joy.

Columnist Anna Quindlen once wrote, "Look around at the azaleas making fuchsia starbursts in spring; look at a full moon hanging silver in a black sky on a cold night. And realize that life is glorious, and that you have no business taking it for granted. Care so deeply about its goodness that you want to spread it around." Helping a few others to garden, even on a small scale, will be my way to spread that goodness around.

Growing Unusual Vegetables

This is the season for studying those seed catalogs and planning what to do in the garden this summer. It is easy to get into a rut. Plant Big Boy tomatoes, Kennebec potatoes, Bolero carrots, and black-seeded Simpson lettuce. All sure winners. But you can also think about new varieties and new species of veggies. Do you grow rutabagas, celeriac, artichokes, and broccoli raab? What about tomatillos for your salsa, and fennel for salads or the seeds in stews? Here is my theory: Some gardeners stick with the old favorites because they do not know what to do with bok choy, burdock root, or even Brussels sprouts.

This winter I've been enjoying two wonderful books that may help to get you to be more adventurous. They offer tips for cooking and storing less common produce and provide lovely recipes. The first is *From Asparagus to Zucchini: A Guide to Cooking Farm-Fresh, Seasonal Produce* by the Madison Area Community Supported Agriculture Coalition. The second is now out of print, but available from used booksellers and some independent bookstores. It is *Uncommon Fruits & Vegetables: A Commonsense Guide* by Elizabeth Schneider (William Morrow, 1998). I have learned from these two books, even about veggies I grow.

Let us start with one of my new favorite veggies. For years I made rutabaga jokes because the word rutabaga is, to me, essentially funny. And they are these big, clunky veggies that look like food served in Siberian forced-labor camps (actually, they probably were). But they are tasty, easy to grow, and provide lots of food for little garden space. Both books offer all kinds of rutabaga ideas, but this one from the A to Z book is terrific:

Mashed Rutabaga with Orange

Start with 2 pounds of rutabagas, peeled and diced. Cover rutabagas halfway with water and cook until soft. Drain. Mash or puree in a blender. Then add 1 tablespoon butter, salt and pepper, and 3 tablespoons of concentrated orange juice, thawed but not diluted. Garnish with a little orange skin zest and/or slices of orange. The book notes that this recipe goes will with pork dishes. I tried it, and it's lovely.

Kohlrabi is one of those awkward-looking veggies that most cooks pass by at the grocery store, and that few gardeners actually plant. I grow the purple-skinned ones and like them raw in salads or cooked in stews. What I didn't know until reading these books—but should have since I knew it was in the cabbage family—is that the leaves are edible, too. As fast growing as radishes, the edible part of kohlrabi grows above ground and is actually a thickened stem. Plenty of recipes for them can be found in these books.

Broccoli raab is often misunderstood. American gardeners think that it is just another form of broccoli and are disappointed by the meager florets—I know I was. But Chinese and Italian cooks understand that you use the entire plant, not just the flowers. According to *Uncommon Fruits and Vegetables*, "it packs an assertive wallop," noting that if you anticipate a "ferocious pungent-bitter taste, quite unlike that of any other vegetable, you might be happily surprised." The author notes that the flavor can be made more subtle by blanching in salt water before cooking, and that it should never be eaten raw—which is how I first tried it—and decided it was not for me! Ms. Schneider provides recipes for broccoli raab with spicy Italian sausages, cooked in salads, and with nuts, eggs, and brown rice as a main dish. I am going to grow it again this summer.

I've grown radicchio (pronounced rahd-EEK-ee-oo) and enjoyed it in salads. It is a very sturdy-leafed green, and *Uncommon Fruits and Vegetables* explains that it is also good as a cooked green, which I have never tried.

Ms. Schneider gives a recipe for a pasta sauce using radicchio that sounds great: Brown 2 to 3 tablespoons of minced garlic in olive oil and briefly cook a pound of slivered radicchio until wilted. Mix with cooked spaghetti, a 2-ounce can of anchovies, 2 tablespoons of minced chives, and a quarter cup of minced flat-leafed parsley. Lastly, mix in a half cup or more of grated provolone. Not for the faint of heart, but I love the idea of it and will try to find the ingredients this winter—and grow radicchio next summer if I like it.

Next summer I shall plant tomatillos. I only grew them once before, and used them raw, like tomatoes. Silly me. Tomatillos, both books assure me, can be eaten raw, but are best roasted or sautéed and used in salsas. Salsa verde, one of the classic salsas, needs tomatillos and hot peppers—poblanos or serranos if you can get them.

We don't live in the right climate for growing hot peppers, generally, but I love hot stuff and always grow some. I do well growing Hungarian Wax peppers, and a pepper I learned to love in southwest France, the Espellette. I have grown it for two summers and gotten good production—even on a summer that was cold and wet.

So get a copy of one or both of these books and plan your garden according to the recipes you like. I'm dreaming of broccoli raab with sausage, and radicchio with anchovies and provolone. I can barely wait!

Decorating the Landscape for Winter

Winter is here, and there's not much for gardeners to do outside. All we can do is sip tea, tend houseplants, read gardening books, and dream of spring. I try to avoid the blahs by making my outdoor environment as cheerful as possible.

I love the holiday lights, and keep mine lit longer than most people consider reasonable, I suspect. No inflated Santas or snowmen for me, just tiny lights in trees. I consider them winter lights, something to brighten those sixteen-hour nights. And I don't string them all where the world can see them. I decorate my Dr. Merrill magnolia—hidden behind the house—with tiny blue lights.

I love greenery, both indoors and out. I used to bring boughs of Canadian hemlock indoors because we have plenty to spare. But I've learned the hard way that hemlock branches are terrible as cut greens—they lose their needles faster than almost anything, even if used outdoors in a wreath. Balsam fir and blue spruce are used as Christmas trees for good reason—they hold their needles better than most. White pines, while generally not used as indoor trees, hold their needles quite well, and are plentiful.

Some years I make wreaths, but this year I was too busy. Instead I cut pine boughs and the berry-covered branches of our native holly, winterberry *(Ilex verticillata)*. I made a simple door decoration—a spray—by arranging short branches of pine as background, and adding stems of winterberry. I bound the stems with copper wire, and trimmed the cut ends square. The red berries stand out brightly in contrast to the greens. I also put berries and greens into the soil of a whisky barrel planter near the front door, where they are beautiful emerging from the snow.

Winterberry grows best along streams and in wet places. It's a dioecious plant, meaning that some plants are male, others female—and you need both to get berries (duh), even though the males don't produce fruit. I bought "improved" varieties, but I notice that wild winterberries in roadside swamps are often better producers of berries than mine.

Crabapples are self-decorating trees, which is part of the reason they are so popular. Their leaves fall off, but the fruits stay on like tiny reddish decorations. Some varieties are loved as food by birds, notably Snowdrift, Indian Summer, and Indian Magic. They are eaten early in the season. Others such as Donald Wyman are largely avoided, so the fruit stays on until late winter or early spring when food is scarce. If you don't have a crabapple, you can decorate any tree with those apples that went squingey in the back of the refrigerator. You know, the ones that are soft and wrinkled. Tie them onto a tree as bird food, and in the meantime, they are decorations. Better than just throwing them out. If they lack stems, just cut up metal coat hangers into six-inch pieces. Poke the wire through, and bend a hook on either end with a pair of needle nosed pliers. They're good for a laugh when hung in a pine tree.

A few years ago I bought a crabapple that was trained to grow in an ascending spiral, and planted it outside the kitchen window. It is more interesting now than midsummer when its leaves obscure the form. Other trees of unusual shape or bark texture are becoming increasingly popular with gardeners for their winter interest including twisted willows and contorted hazelnuts. This is a good time to read up on trees and decide on one to plant after the winter is over.

In my experience, contorted hazelnuts, also known as Harry Lauder's walking stick, is barely hardy here in Zone 4 where temperatures of 20 to 30 below freezing occur. It is a cloned tree made by grafting a scion, or twig, on the rootstock of the common hazelnut. Mine failed—the top died, and all growth has come from the rootstock—completely straight.

My friend, Anna, who runs a game preserve in the Ural Mountains of Russia, taught me another way to decorate trees for the winter. She taught me to take muffin tins or Jell-O molds, fill them with water, add a few drops of food coloring, and put them outside to freeze. I put a piece of string into each to serve as a hanger once frozen. This works wonderfully, catching sunlight and making an otherwise ordinary shrub into a colorful, cheerful bush—at least until you get a rain or a thaw. I usually do it for the solstice, but the January thaw often does them in, leaving red and blue splotches on the snow beneath the tree.

Although I finally took pity on Mary Lou, our scarecrow, and lugged her into the barn, I have left other durable garden ornaments outdoors. I have a lovely blue ceramic birdbath in the garden, which stands out nicely against the snow. I left the pole bean structure up for the same reason—it breaks up the monotony of winter. It's still a long time until spring, and I like to see some reminders of warmer times.

Growing Bananas and Other Unusual Plants from Seed

I'm thinking about ordering banana seeds from a catalog. Despite having spent nine years in Africa and being a self-proclaimed banana connoisseur, it never occurred to me that one could start them from those tiny, pale, barely visible seeds in fresh bananas. In Africa, bananas were started from offsets—shoots growing up alongside a mother plant.

The catalog in question, from Chiltern Seeds, is entitled *Grow Something New from Seed*. And boy, do they have unusual stuff. Bananas would be a challenge, especially since I don't have a heated greenhouse, and the banana plants I knew were much taller than my ceilings. But I've rarely been one to let ridiculous ideas go untried. There are lots of practical plants to grow, too.

Let's start with the bananas. They have eleven different varieties, starting with *Musa balbisiana*: Given rich soil, plenty of water and summer warmth, this species has been described as "almost dangerously fast growing. Tolerant of cool conditions. When young it is well suited for indoor culture. At Versailles they move this plant outside for summer in enormous containers, presumably with the aid of a forklift truck." Hmm. No forklift, better not order that one.

Then there's the Snow Banana, grown at 8,800 feet in China and Nepal. "With a thick, waxy blue trunk, it bears large and noble waxy gray-green leaves, six feet and an awful lot more long." Nah, too big. Maybe the Flowering Banana, which they describe as being of "manageable proportions" with red-veined, rich blue-green leaves that are "only" six feet long. And it produces fruit that starts red, and ripens to yellowish-red. A bargain at only three pounds thirty for seven seeds, or about a dollar each.

Chiltern Seeds, by the way, is a British company that I learned about from illustrator Tasha Tudor, who regularly ordered from them. You can contact the company by phone at 011-44-1220-581137, e-mail them at info@chilternseeds.co.uk or visit their Web site (www.chilternseeds.co.uk).

I have a love-hate relationship with delphinium. I mean, it's a gorgeous plant, but staking it to avoid breakage by heavy summer showers is a pain. So I was delighted to see that Chiltern Seeds has some short ones that range from eight inches in height (*Delphinium chinensis* "Blue Butterfly") to twenty inches (*D. grandiflora* "Blue Mirror"). Another, the plant mother of the "Pacific hybrids" commonly sold here, grows to six feet tall but has smaller flowers and "needs no staking." It is a form of *D. elatum* that they call "True Wild Form" from the Tatra Mountains of Slovakia. I've got to give it a try.

The Chiltern catalog has two flaws: First, the print is small and light, so in bad light I have to use a magnifying glass. Secondly, it doesn't give the zone hardiness for American gardeners. Those lucky Brits have a pretty mild climate, and the catalog is aimed at them.

Common milkweed *(Asclepias speciosa)* grows well in unmowed fields near my house, but I've never gotten around to trying any of the cultivated varieties—even though I've meant to. I looked up *Asclepias* in *The Flower Gardener's Bible* by Lewis and Nancy Hill and found that two other species, *A. tuberosa* and *A. incarnata* are hardy to Zone 3 (minus 30 or 40), so I looked them up in the Chilvers catalog. It had four varieties, two of each, and they sounded interesting. Swamp milkweed, *A. incarnata* "Soulmate," is a perennial that will produce flowers from seed in as little as three months, and produces rose-pink flowers on plants that are two to three feet tall. The catalog's writer keeps descriptions lively, noting that "You will doubtless be pleased to know that you don't have to have your very own swamp" to grow swamp milkweed.

Chiltern Seeds also sell a cousin of swamp milkweed known as butterfly weed, *A. tuberosa* "Gay Butterflies." It sounds interesting and is sold in packets of seeds that should produce a mix of colors: Gold, orange, red, and pink. It is said to be excellent as a cut flower.

Pincushion flowers (*Scabiosa* spp.) are wonderful flowers that come as both perennials and annuals. One summer I grew some *Scabiosa atropurpurea*, an annual, that produced nearly black flowers. Chiltern sells it, along with three other colors and packets of mixed colors. They have several perennial varieties including two that are hardy for us: *S. caucasica* and *S. columbaria*.

When I lived in Africa I learned that all bananas are not created equal: Some are naturally tiny and extra sweet, while others are big and bland; some travel well, but most are best consumed where they were grown. I'd love to grow my own and eat them right off the plant. It remains to be seen, however, if common sense will prevail, or if I'll order some banana seeds. But either way, lounging in a deep chair with a good seed catalog such as that of Chiltern Seeds is a good way to spend a long winter evening.

Postscript: Since that winter musing, I purchased a small banana plant in 2007 from a nursery. It was about a foot tall with three large leaves and a single stem. Now, three years later, it's four feet tall and wide, growing in a twelve-inch pot. The tag called it *Musa* "Cavendish." It has sent up side shoots and could be divided into four plants. I put it outside in full sun in summer, and in a west-facing window in winter. It's a delight, but no fruit—or not yet, anyway.

Goodbye and Good Riddance to Invasive Shrubs

It's official. As of January 1, 2007, the Norway maple officially became a thug. The Japanese barberry has been declared a bad boy. Say bye-bye to buying burning bush, that brilliant, red-in-fall shrub that performs even in years when the maples sulk in pallid tones of brown and yellow. According to New Hampshire law, it is now illegal to sell, propagate, or transport those three plants. And I say good riddance. You are not required to ax your plants, but you may want to.

"But, but . . . " one friend sputtered when I told her of the law, "they're pretty, and even I can grow them." True enough, perhaps, but they are (in some places) taking over the woods of northern New England.

Bill Guenther, the Vermont state forester for Windham County, described barberry's invasive potential. In 1996 he visited a site in southern Vermont with a few Japanese barberry alongside a stream, but not in the nearby woods. When he visited the same site seven years later, the barberry had invaded the pine woods, creating a thicket so dense with the thorny barberry plants that even with heavy jeans and chainsaw chaps he could not walk through it. The area affected covered several acres, and was expanding.

An isolated case, not worth worrying about? I don't think so. I cross country ski and see barberry bushes in the forest far from any bushes planted by gardeners. They will grow in full sun or full shade, and in nearly any kind of soil. They produce berries that birds eat, but the seeds are not digested, so they turn up where birds alight—almost anywhere. Little by little, they are sneaking into the woods.

And what about burning bush *(Euonymus alatus)*? I've seen fewer instances of invasion, but in parts of Massachusetts the forests have been taken over by them. Kathy Decker, Forest Protection Specialist for the Vermont Department of Forests, Parks and Recreation, reported to me that she has found wild infestations in northern Vermont, near St. Johnsbury. She reported seeing burning bush growing at the edge of a field, and creeping up into the woods.

Norway maple comes in various leaf colors; its most popular version, 'Crimson King,' is a deep maroon-purple, but the seeds usually produce green seedlings—so it's easy to mistake them for sugar or red maples. If you break off a leaf and look at the stem, you will see it oozing white liquid if it's a Norway maple. Like most thugs, Norway maples will grow in sun or shade, are fast growing, and tolerate a variety of soil conditions. Their roots spread very far, sucking up moisture and soil nutrients—and depriving other plants of water and needed elements.

So what do you need to do? First, recognize that these plants are capable of taking over the landscape—given enough time and an adequate number of plants producing seeds. Kathy Decker, speaking about the Norway maple, said to me, "Do you like maple syrup and fall foliage? If so, get rid of the Norway maple because it has the potential to take over the habitat of the sugar maple."

Vermont, despite its good environmental record in other areas, has not outlawed these three thugs, even though New Hampshire, Maine, and Massachusetts have done so. They are on the "Watch List" for problem plants as described by the Vermont Exotic Plant Committee. Banning a popular plant is never a popular move, but I hope that the Vermont legislature will ban them soon.

No matter where you live, you need to rid your land of invasive plants. To see photos and descriptions of these invasives and others you can visit a Web site such as www.ct.nrcs.usda.gov/invas.factsheets.html. Some invasives such as glossy buckthorn are rampant in some areas, but nonexistent in others. By familiarizing yourself with all the invasives, you will be ready to deal with invaders before they multiply.

Pulling small trees is one good way to eliminate them. There is a tool for pulling saplings called a weed wrench. I've used them, and they really work. A weed wrench of the proper size allows a 150-pound office worker to pull out trees that otherwise would be impossible to yank. It has a gripping mouthlike part, and a long handle to provide leverage.

You can look at weed wrenches on the web at www.weed

wrench.com. They range in size from the mini (for trunks up to 1 inch) to the heavy, which will pull trees up to 2½ inches in diameter; they range in weight from five to 24 pounds, and in price from about $90 to $200. This is a tool that might be purchased by a garden club or environmental group and shared among members.

Girdling trees is another way to kill them. Take a saw and cut two rings around the trunk of an invasive tree about a foot apart, cutting into the green cambium layer, but not down to the hard core. If done this winter, the tree may survive one more year, then die the following year. Some invasives (buckthorn, for example) will re-sprout from their stumps or roots if they are cut down. But girdling doesn't prompt the same response if done properly.

According to Doug Cygan, Invasive Species Coordinator for the New Hampshire Department of Agriculture, neither barberry nor burning bush should re-sprout from their roots or around their trunks if cut down—though Norway maple probably will.

No one will arrest you for keeping your invasives, but winter is a good time for bonfires—so think about cutting down your barberry and burning bush—and burning them. And Norway maple makes good fuel for the woodstove.

Midwinter Thoughts About Pesticides

People who sell pesticides like to say that they are perfectly safe if used as directed. Proving otherwise is often difficult for many reasons. Part of the problem is due to the nature of scientific studies. No one can ethically design and execute a study that administers pesticides to humans. Often rats are used as subjects of studies, but pesticide proponents tend to discount these.

Another part of the problem (of proving cause and effect) is the difficulty of measuring pesticide exposure. It wouldn't be possible to analyze the pesticide content in every bite of food that a thousand subjects ate over a period of three years, for example. Nor would it be possible to measure how much herbicide and insecticide is absorbed through the skin of a three-year-old playing on a lawn treated with lawn chemicals.

Not only that, the safety tests done by pesticide manufacturers are done using just their product. In the world of commercial agriculture, often pesticide cocktails are mixed and sprayed. If one insecticide will only knock out 98 percent of a bug population, for example, farmers will add a second and maybe even a third chemical to kill them all. These chemicals together can have a more potent effect on you, too.

So it was encouraging (for this proponent of organic gardening) to read a report done by the Ontario College of Family Physicians. The report is a review of all peer reviewed studies done on the effects of pesticides worldwide between 1992 and 2003 in English, French, Spanish, and Portuguese.

The report (available in full at www.ocfp.on.ca) advises physicians to counsel patients to "avoid exposure to all pesticides whenever and wherever possible." It cites evidence of serious and harmful effects on the human body including cancer, and negative effects on the reproductive and nervous systems.

The report also notes that even if cause and effect relationships are not fully understood, precautionary measures should be taken. The burden of proof should be on the manufacturers of chemicals that their products are safe, not on doctors or consumers to prove that they are harmful. These are sane ideas, even if our government doesn't buy into them completely.

Lawmakers in Hudson, Ontario, passed a law in 1990 restricting the use of pesticides for "cosmetic" purposes. The town was promptly sued by two chemical manufacturers. After more than a decade of litigation, courts upheld the laws. Toronto and Halifax now have laws restricting pesticide for cosmetic use. Even so, the report stated that 45 percent of Toronto homeowners admitted to using pesticides in the last two years.

As gardeners we face countless episodes each year where pests damage our flowers, lawns, trees, or vegetables. It is a natural reaction to want to "nuke the so-and-so's." But try to remember, that when you spray poisons on the bugs you may be inhaling it, absorbing it through your hands or feet. Your pets and children may also be affected.

Instead of reaching for pesticides when bugs attack our plants, it's good to wait and see what happens. Tent caterpillars were a problem one year recently, and some gardeners felt they had to spray pesticides to save their trees. I checked with a friend who had resisted the urge to spray pesticides. Her apple tree was totally defoliated, and she was sure that would be the end of the tree. But it wasn't. Dormant buds erupted with new leaves, and the tree is doing fine.

Hand-picking of beetles and bugs that are damaging your plants is still the best choice for home gardeners. Regular inspections of the garden will help you diagnose the problem before it gets out of hand.

You can encourage toads—voracious insectivores—to live in the garden by creating a toad-friendly environment. They like a cool dark place to hide during the heat of the day, and a saucer of fresh water slightly buried in the soil. A six-inch clay pot with a door knocked into the side with a hammer will make a nice toad house, though cute ones are also for sale commercially.

Each summer in August we can expect some mildew to attack phlox, lilacs, and some vine crops. Instead of reaching for a chemical fungicide this year, you might wish to mix one part milk with nine parts water and spray it on susceptible plants before you see an outbreak. I've read that it helps, particularly on cucumbers and zucchini. A one-quart hand sprayer will serve to apply it. I've never worried too much about mildew and have never tried the milk spray. It's my understanding that sprays for mildew—both chemical and organic—are not effective once an outbreak has occurred.

One last warning: Botanical pesticides like rotenone, sabadilla, neem oil, and pyrethrin are approved for organic gardeners, but that doesn't make them 100 percent safe. I won't use them as at least some of them can be toxic to us, or to fish or beneficial insects—and it's hard to know their long-term effects. Wear a mask if you spray them, and cover up bare arms and legs.

Even if your own doctor hasn't warned you about using pesticides, try to remember what the good doctors of Ontario are telling their patients. Even "relatively safe" pesticides are only that: Relatively safe. I don't need them—do you?

Study Your Landscape and Make Plans

In *The Inward Garden: Creating a Place of Beauty and Meaning* (Bunker Hill Publishing, 2007) landscape architect Julie Moir Messervy of Saxtons River, Vermont, explains that each person craves a specific kind of landscape. I need views and open spaces. Someone else may need a shady garden enclosed by dense vegetation that creates the feeling of a cave. Either way, winter is a good time to look at the bones of your property—the hardscape—when you are not distracted by flowers and leaves. This is a good time to see if your landscape provides you with what you like best and make plans to work on it if it doesn't.

Although I don't live on a hilltop, I try to clear out and clean up wooded parts of my landscape so that I don't feel closed in, and so that I can get as much view as possible. In nature trees grow willy-nilly. Where a seed lands is largely determined by chance. It is unable to know if it is six inches or sixty feet from another tree. If it germinates and grows, it might be in a good place, or it might be smack-dab next to another tree, or your house.

Your property, if you have a wooded portion, probably needs some help from you if you want it to look nice and have healthy trees. Here is what you can do as your garden project for the week: Go outside and really look at the trees growing on your property with a critical eye.

Ask yourself this question as you walk around your property (or look out the window) at your trees: What is the future of this particular tree? What will it look like in ten years? In fifty? Is it too close to its neighboring trees? Are there trees closing in on it that you need to remove? I'm a tree-hugger, but I have no problem cutting down trees. This is the time to plan on some careful thinning of trees to improve the health of others.

Before you start marking trees for culling you need to learn to identify the trees on your property, another good winter project. *A Guide to Nature in Winter* by Donald Stokes (Little, Brown & Co., 1998) is a wonderful book that will help you with that. The Stokes book identifies trees by their bark, shape, and buds—which is helpful since at this time of year there are no leaves on the hardwoods. (It also teaches much about all the other living things out there in the woods from snow fleas to goldenrod ball galls to deer and everything in between).

Trees that I cull from my woods include poplars (*Populus* spp.), boxelder *(Acer negundo)*, and alders (*Alnus* spp.). These are fast-growing trees that are short-lived and produce lots of seedlings. Even though they are deciduous trees, their wood is not much good for the woodstove—they produce less heat and burn faster than standards like maple and ash.

Trees that I revere are sugar maples, oaks, beech, birches, and hornbeam *(Carpinus caroliniana)*. I would think long and hard before cutting down one of them. But if a fast-growing poplar were growing within eight or ten feet of one of my favorites, I would not hesitate to cut the poplar down. Trees need plenty of space to do well.

Hemlocks and pines often grow so densely that their lower limbs die out because the sun never reaches their leaves (needles). Removing those lower branches opens up the landscape—another task for winter, if you wish. When cutting off branches, don't cut flush to the trunk, but don't leave stubs, either. Cut just past the swollen area of the branch that is known as the branch collar, and it will heal up nicely.

Working with a ladder in the snow really isn't as bad as it sounds. Just be sure to get the footing of the ladder firm before you go up, and don't go up too high. To be on the safe side, have someone steady your ladder. The good part of working on your trees now is that if you fall, you'll have a nice soft landing in two feet of snow!

So shake off the winter doldrums and get outside. Study your landscape, and make plans to make it a little nicer.

FEBRUARY

Groundhog Day

I think Groundhog Day should get more recognition than it does. I don't mean the Groundhog Day of Punxsutawney Phil and weather forecasters with fake smiles and plasticized hair. I think we should take time out to recognize that February 2 is halfway through the winter. The worst is over. That's worthy of celebration.

We really only have two months of winter. December is too busy and full of fun for me to consider it winter. There are the Winter Revels, the Garden Club Christmas Tea, the hordes of family and friends visiting, and First Night celebrations.

And March? By then the sun has strength and the days are longer. Skiing home at dusk, I'm able to enjoy the perfect Maxfield Parrish blues and purples in the sky behind Mt. Ascutney without risking frostbite.

January is the worst of winter, the longest nights, the coldest temperatures. It's the month the pipes freeze if they're going to, and the month I worry about my tender plants suffering from frostbite. We've made it through January.

February is also winter, and can be dreary, so we need a little fun to start off the month. So here's what I propose for Groundhog Day, at least for gardeners: First, let's get out last year's seed packets to see what we have, and what we need to buy.

Most seed packets have many more seeds than one can plant in any given year, so I store mine in the fridge or a cool spot in zipper bags. I found that most seeds are good for three years, though I've used some that are up to five years old. Germination rates are lower, but for most things that doesn't matter.

Then, let's make lists. Lists of what we plan to grow in the vegetable garden, and what seeds we need to buy. Let's get out all those glossy seed catalogs, and drool. Let's dream. Let's select some flowers and veggies we've never tried before, and order them. Let's be a bit frivolous. After all, if we have too many seeds, we can always save them for next year, or start extra plants to give away or trade with our gardening buddies.

And, for Groundhog Day: Let's go in the pantry or dig around in the freezer and bring out vegetables and sauces we made with last year's garden produce. Let's cook up a storm, invite over friends, and have a party. Maybe I'll even open a bottle of that hard cider I made from all those extra apples I picked in 2005.

It's still real winter, and too early for starting seeds indoors, but in a couple of weeks we can start our onions and leeks. Then, by the first of March I'll plant peppers and artichokes. And before you know it, spring will be upon us, with snowdrops and crocuses. I can barely wait.

Seed Catalogs: What to Think About Before You Order

On a snowy Saturday in February I went outdoors and planted my first seeds of the season. I had been sorting out my seeds saved from previous years, working up a list of what I needed, and wishing for spring. I decided to plant a few seeds outdoors that day. I sprinkled poppy seeds on the snow, knowing that at least a few of them would germinate in my flower bed, come spring.

Each spring after planting flowers and veggies I tend to throw all the partially used seed packets in big Ziploc bags, willy-nilly, and put them in the fridge, where they keep better than they would if I just left them out.

Playing with seed packets and seed catalogs is a good way to fight the winter doldrums. This year I threw out any seeds that were more than three years old, even though many seeds might still be viable. But given limited space for starting seedlings, I like to be sure of relatively good germination rates, so I throw out older seeds.

I try to buy all my seeds locally, but can't find everything I need, so I do buy some from the catalogs. If you are inundated with catalogs, here are some things to look for when selecting a catalog company.

1. Look at package size. You probably don't need three hundred Early Girl or Big Boy tomato seeds. Even though seeds will hold over for a few seasons, mini packets are nice. You could share a bigger packet, of course.

2. Look at price. Not just the price of the seeds, but also the price of shipping and handling. It's only fair that companies bill for mailing, but there is quite a range of prices for a small order. A quick look at half a dozen catalogs shows me that if I were buying just a single package of seed, this might cost me anywhere from $2 to $4.50 to ship.

3. Look at the information that is provided with each description. A good catalog will tell the quirks of each variety. It's not good enough to say "Superb flavor" or "Big fruit." After all, what are they going to say, "Pretty good flavor, but mealy?"

When I visited Mariquita Farm in Watsonville, California, I tasted an absolutely fabulous radish. No bite, great flavor, and the size of a baseball. I had a hard time minding my manners. Andy Griffin, the farmer, peeled it and served some up with a little olive oil and vinegar. It was all I could do to keep myself from hogging the whole plate. He calls it a "watermelon radish" because the interior is pink, with a white layer outside the pink, then a green layer.

I found the radish in the Johnny's catalog (www.johnnyseeds.com or 207-861-3901), as Andy said I would. It is called Red Meat radish, and contains this advice: "For summer to fall sowing only; will bolt to seed from spring sowing." That is the kind of information a catalog should be dispensing. Not only what to do, but why—so I won't be tempted to plant it in the spring.

Looking at a Johnny's Selected Seeds catalog, I notice that it had a graph indicating optimal temperatures for germinating tomatoes. (Eighty-six degrees is best, so start them on a heating mat if you want a quick start). It also has symbols to indicate "easy to grow," varieties, cold tolerance, heirloom varieties, disease resistance, organically grown seed, and those suited for container growing or in greenhouses. You're not expected to know all this, but many catalogs don't tell you.

4. Look for truth in advertising. Even Johnny's has two best small, early tomatoes: Early Cascade ("Best flavored saladette") and New Girl ("Taste tops the charts"). Look at varieties you have grown before. See how their descriptions compare with your results.

5. Variety. I love to try new types of vegetables, especially tomatoes. Some catalogs are full of hybrids, others specialize in heirlooms. Some have both. I try to order from one company that has everything I want.

No one company supplies all my "must have" veggies, so I take turns. I have to have Kwintus pole beans because they are good even when the pods get to be huge, and because they freeze well. I can only get them from The Cook's Garden (www.cooksgarden .com or 800-457-9703). And I have to get those radishes from Johnny's.

I like the prices at Fedco (www.fedcoseeds.com or 207-873-7333), a seed coop from Maine, and believe that coops are a good way to serve both producers and consumers, so I often order some things from them. And I like to buy from local seed companies that grow organic seeds, so I need to buy some from High Mowing Organic Seeds, of Vermont (www.highmowingseeds .com or 802-888-1800).

Starting seeds indoors is not for everyone. It requires that you take care of your seeds every day for weeks at a time. I love it. I feel it saves me money, allows me to start new varieties I couldn't find as plants, and it keeps me sane during the long winter and mud season.

Oaks

Looking out on a stark winter landscape one day, I spotted a squirrel digging in the semi-frozen soil. Before I could yell, "Not my tulips!" it unearthed an acorn, and scampered off. Although glad that my bulbs had been spared, I was struck by another notion: The world has now been deprived of a tree. Inside that acorn was the seed of a mighty oak, one that might have lived five hundred years.

Indeed, depending on snow cover, soil conditions, and the threat of seed snatchers, winter is a fine time to plant acorns. For hardcore gardeners with cabin fever, planting acorns in the dead of winter may be just what the doctor ordered.

The first thing to remember is that most oaks eventually get huge, many reaching eighty to one hundred feet tall and more than fifty feet across. Secondly, as relatively slow-growing trees, they should be given every encouragement possible, which means planting them in full sun and catering to their soil preferences.

Oaks generally fall into two categories. Those with rounded leaf edges and nuts that germinate in the fall are considered white oaks. Red oaks have leaves with pointed lobes and produce acorns that only germinate after a cold period of thirty to sixty days, in a process called stratification.

Any acorn—red or white—can be planted now or in the spring. Avoid any that are still wearing their caps, as they are wormy or otherwise not viable.

Planting acorns is easy. Using a dibble or trowel, dig a hole an inch and a half deep. Drop the acorn in, cover it with soil, pat it down, and wait.

If digging in frozen ground doesn't appeal to you or if the squirrels are watching your every move, acorns can be collected in winter, stratified in a refrigerator for thirty to sixty days, then planted in the spring. Store them in a paper bag in the vegetable drawer to keep them from drying out. By spring, the squirrels will have better fish to fry (like the tender shoots of my hostas).

White oak acorns should already show rootlets. Red oak nuts may need help opening their shells if they have been stratified, or preserved indoors, because they do not go through multiple freeze and thaw cycles. Simply score the acorn with a knife or rub it with 80-grit sandpaper until the kernel is exposed.

Not all acorns will germinate the first year, which makes sense from a Darwinian point of view: If a drought or a forest fire kills off some seedlings this year, others will be able to pop up the next.

Each season I get a little more like the squirrels, which—contrary to popular belief—never remember where they put things. They find acorns by smell, but I depend on white plastic markers, which I'll poke in the ground like little mouse tombstones. (It's probably only a matter of time, of course, before the squirrels figure out what is buried beneath.)

One of the best red oaks for suburban areas is the pin oak, *Quercus palustris*. It is smaller than many oaks (still, it grows to about sixty feet), with shallow fibrous roots that can thrive in the heavy clay often found in the disturbed soil of subdivisions. It prefers acidic soils, so it does well in the Northeast.

Pin oaks grow more quickly than many oaks, often adding two feet of height or more per year, and they have a profile that is handsome year-round. Like all the oaks discussed here, they are hardy in Zones 4 to 8 or 9.

For yards with sandy loam, another red oak, *Q. rubra*, is best. It, too, grows quickly, reaching perhaps sixty to seventy-five feet in thirty years and spreading nearly that wide. It tolerates less than ideal conditions, gamely breathing polluted air.

Q. alba, a white oak, is majestic and can live five hundred years or more, attaining heights of one hundred feet. It does best in deep, moist, well-drained soils. It is susceptible to anthracnose and other diseases, but thrives in the wild from Maine to Florida and as far west as Minnesota and Texas. It is worth planting where space permits.

The chestnut oak, *Q. prinus*, has been known to live twice as long as white oaks. It is handsome, with deeply furrowed bark and a nearly globe-shaped form that is striking in winter. It can survive in dry, rocky places that would be eschewed by other trees. My favorite example is a forty-year-old that sits on the Dartmouth College campus, is about thirty-five feet tall and wide, and inexplicably produces a heavy load of acorns only every five years.

Native Americans have eaten acorns for centuries, boiling or soaking them to get rid of a bitter tannic flavor and grinding them to make porridge. Sam Thayer, a wild-foods educator in Wisconsin, sent me some red oak grits, which I boiled briefly in milk. They were tasty: Nutty, and not at all bitter; even better with a little maple syrup.

If I plant some acorns this weekend, I may be able to harvest my own breakfast during some distant winter—in, say, fifteen to twenty years. More immediately, of course, I will have had a good excuse to get out of the house and poke around.

Postscript: Since this article appeared in *The New York Times* on Groundhog Day of 2003, Sam Thayer has published two fabulous books on food-worthy wild plants: *The Forager's Harvest* and *Nature's Garden* (http://foragersharvest.com/books/). Both are full of precise and useful information and hundreds of good photos. They are must-haves for anyone interested in harvesting edible wild plants.

Landscaping by Subtraction

It was a gray day in February, and I'd been slaving away all day on my computer. It had been raining all day, which made it easier to stay indoors—the snow had been ruined for cross-country skiing. Our dog Abigail, the intrepid explorer, slept soundly in her basket by the woodstove all day, and had not once begged for an adventure. Then in the late afternoon the rain stopped, the sun came out, and we fled the indoors.

There is a logging road going into a forest not a mile from home that I'd skied down, but never walked up. Abby and I followed it. Soon I noticed a small stream near the logging road, and we pushed our way though brambles and elderberries into the forest to get a better look. Lo and behold, we'd entered Narnia—or so it seemed. I haven't seen the Narnia movie, but I read *The Lion, The Witch and the Wardrobe* when my boy, Josh, was little. The forest I'd entered was most certainly the Narnia of that book. But this was no accident—someone had transformed a small bit of forest into a magical place. It made me realize how easy it would be to transform a bit of my own forest into such place—or how you could transform yours.

This bit of Narnia is a narrow strip of dense evergreen forest that borders a small stream. It is only about fifty feet wide and as long as a football field. It is dark inside, a sharp contrast to the bright open sky of the logging road, which immediately gives it the feeling of a cave, or perhaps a cathedral. Someone had cut off all the lower branches of the hemlocks and white pines up to a height of about fifteen feet, opening up the space like a church.

Someone cleaned up the forest floor. Not only were dead branches gone, the saplings and small trees had been removed, and the stumps were cut flush to the ground. I found myself wandering around looking up at the big trees, and surely would have tripped if any stumps had been left at the usual four to six inches height, as most people would have done.

After my visit I called the landowners, who live elsewhere in town, to find out more about this secret space. Kathleen Maslan explained that she, her husband, and two young sons have been using and improving this special place for a number of years, and that the previous owner had started the process of cleaning it up.

Several of the big trees have interesting aboveground roots and cavities, which the boys decided were perfect for fairies. They arranged twigs and bark to create little houses for them, and always brought cookies—some to eat, some to leave for the fairies. And when they returned, the cookies were always gone— proof that fairies do exist.

The landowners were careful not to disturb the native ferns and mosses, and their natural beauty was enhanced by the fact that they had not been planted or arranged in any way. It felt like a forest primeval even though someone had removed a fair amount of growth, so that one could see the stream, the three "sisters"—ancient, gnarly sugar maples—and the young yellow birch racing straight up for a bit of sunlight.

This was landscaping by subtraction, not addition. Over a

period of years a young family had cleared out the usual mess of the forest, grooming it, but in natural ways. They didn't leave brush piles in their special place; they lugged the brush away. And they kept the place secret by only creating one small path as an entrance, a path I'd skied past in previous years and never noticed.

Not everyone needs to have a cave to retreat to, but many of us do. In fact, I'd counted myself as one of those people who needs a promontory, not a cave. I love to look out on a landscape from above, and I even lugged an overstuffed chair up our spiral staircase to place it where I can see most of our gardens. It satisfied some primal urge. But this cave, this bit of Narnia, also made me feel relaxed, soothed, and happy. The flowing water and stones brought a sparkle to this cavelike place, and I was mesmerized.

So this winter I'll spend some time my own woods to see if there is a special place that I can clean up and turn into my own little Narnia. Someplace to retreat to in the heat of summer. Someplace my grandson George can enjoy, and where we can bring cookies for the fairies.

Starting Seeds in Soil Blocks

If you're tired of buying soilless potting mix and those little black plastic six-packs every year to start your vegetable and flower seedlings, there is an alternative. You can buy a tool to make freestanding soil blocks using peat, sand, compost, garden soil, and minerals.

We've all had it drummed into our heads (by the standard gardening texts) that we must use a sterile starting mix or we'll lose everything to a fungal disease known as "damping off." Most books tell gardeners to use sterile potting mix, or to bake soil in the oven to kill the fungi.

According to Elliot Coleman in his 1995 book, *The New Organic Grower*, damping off is more a result of overwatering, lack of air movement, not enough sun, and overfertilization. He states that in over twenty years of using unsterilized homemade starting mixes, he has never had a problem. Not only that, he believes that the good soil microorganisms in soil and compost help to produce better plants. I agree.

His technique employs a simple hand press that makes soil blocks, each roughly a two-inch cube. His recipe is such that the cubes don't disintegrate when kept moist, and they provide plants with good nutrition without chemical fertilizers. A friend gave me some seedlings that had been started in homemade soil blocks, and they performed beautifully. I've been making my own blocks ever since.

For me, the deterrent to making soil blocks was the cost. A simple machine that makes four planting blocks costs about $35 from Fedco Seeds in Maine (www.fedcoseeds.com or 207-873-7333). But I never thought to calculate the cost of the plastic six-packs or the potting soil I buy every year. I start about three hundred seedlings every year, so I spent about $15 per year on disposable stuff.

Before buying my own tool, I visited Jean and John Sibley in Etna, New Hampshire, who have been making soil blocks for years. They let me make some blocks, and I learned that it's easy. They lent me a block-maker and here is what I did once I got home:

I started by collecting the ingredients: Compost, garden soil, peat moss, peat humus, sand, and a variety of ingredients to provide nutrition. Digging up compost and soil was tough: The soil in winter was frozen down eight to twelve inches, though I got through it with a pickax. Wear safety glasses if you try it— or plan ahead next fall: Dig some, and save it in the basement. I sifted the compost and soil through screen (hardware cloth) with half-inch squares into a wheelbarrow.

The recipes that I got from the Sibleys, from Coleman's book, and from the Fedco catalog varied slightly. I made my own mix which included Azomite, a ground mineral mix sold and recommended in the Fedco catalog, and ground granite dust I use for energizing my soil. One friend uses no peat, substituting home-made compost. Another skips Azomite and sand.

Here is what I did: Using a two-quart plastic juice pitcher, I put into a wheelbarrow ten quarts of dry peat moss, and mixed in a quarter cup of limestone (to counteract the acidity) and one cup Azomite. I mixed it well. Then I added five quarts of coarse sand, ten quarts of peat humus, and one-half cup of each of the following: Colloidal phosphate (rock phosphate also works), greensand, granite powder, and organic blood meal (for nitrogen). I mixed well, then added six to eight quarts of compost and six quarts of garden soil. The other recipes suggested ten quarts of the last two, but the mix seemed right to me with a little less. The above quantities provided me with over ten gallons of mix, enough for three to four hundred blocks, I'd guess.

To make the blocks, I mixed four quarts of dry mix with one to two quarts of water in a recycling bin, stirring it with my hand (wearing a rubber glove). It was gooey, but firm, not watery. Then I made a pile of the gooey stuff four to five inches deep, and compressed it into blocks by pressing down on it with the block maker. The mix filled up the cavities of the blocker and I rotated the blocker, scraping it against the bottom of the bin to clear it of excess material. The tool ejects the blocks with the squeeze of a spring-equipped handle.

The Sibleys showed me how they devised a clever self-watering system that will wick up water to keep the blocks moist but not soggy. First, I made platforms for blocks by cutting half-inch plywood into nine- by nineteen-inch pieces, and scrap lumber into cubes for feet, which I attached with screws. I put the platforms in standard plastic flats, the kind I use for starting seeds in plastic six-packs. Then I cut polyester backing material—a fuzzy synthetic cloth—sized to fit over the platforms and dangle into the water on all four sides. The material wicks up the water, keeping the blocks evenly and consistently moist.

The soil blocks hold together well, and plant roots hold them together even better as time goes on. I found that the plants don't get root-bound in soil blocks as they do in plastic cells. The roots stop, poised for action, when they hit free air at the edge of their growing block. In plastic pots, roots often circle around and get entangled, but that doesn't happen with blocks. The blocks have lots of good nutrition, but later—when my plants get good-size—I add a little liquid fish fertilizer to their water. Most commercial organic growers I know now use soil blocks to start their plants.

This technique is a lot of work, but as an organic gardener, I think it makes sense to start plants in a living soil. In the long run it will save me money, and I like the idea of cutting down on the use of plastic. And it sure is fun to play with something that reminds me of mud.

Sustainable Stew

I love to cook, especially when the food is prepared using my own homegrown ingredients. Even in February I always have plenty of garden bounty to cook with. As you plan your garden for the year—which you should be doing now—think about growing food not only for eating fresh, but also for storing. Here is what I call my "Sustainable Stew," along with how I stored the ingredients.

Henry's Sustainable Stew
  2 large onions
  3 medium carrots, sliced into rounds
  3 cloves garlic, minced
  1 quart frozen kale, chopped
  6 whole frozen tomatoes
  3 ice cubes of tomato paste
  1 cup dried apple, chopped into ½-inch chunks
  2 cups apple cider

1 tablespoon fennel seeds
1 tablespoon dried parsley
3 small sprigs fresh thyme
1 sprig rosemary
1 butternut squash
1 cup celeriac root, chopped
1 to 2 tablespoon olive oil (not my own)

Sauté onions and garlic in olive oil. Take whole frozen tomatoes and run under hot water and rub off the skins. Let sit 5 minutes, core, and chop. Add to onions. Chop dehydrated apples and add to stew, along with apple cider. Cut celeriac root into half-inch slices and then peel with an ordinary potato peeler; Then chop into pieces and add to stew. Add spices and simmer for an hour.

About half an hour before serving, cut carrots into rounds and add to stew. Peel and chop squash into ³/₄-inch chunks and add to stew. Chop frozen kale and add to stew. Simmer 30 minutes and serve with bread. This stew has a sweet-sour quality that I found delectable.

Tomatoes, I freeze whole or make paste and freeze that, as described in the August chapter. I try to freeze fifteen one-gallon bags of whole tomatoes each summer, and fill four one-quart bags of frozen paste. I like to make at least a few jars of canned tomato sauce each summer for a quick supper. Peppers freeze well, and some years I buy half a bushel from a farm stand, slice, and freeze them—I don't grow many, and tend to eat all mine fresh.

All serious gardeners should have a good food dehydrator. I use a Nesco/American Harvest product called the Gardenmaster Pro. It allows me to dry cherry tomatoes, apples, hot peppers, and more. I like the fact that it has a thermostat, so I can dry parsley at a much lower temperature than tomatoes, for example.

And, of course, you need a big freezer—or three, as I do. I have apples pressed, and cider made each fall; I freeze eight gallons of fresh cider most years. I use it not only for drinking, but in cooking. You can use it just like white wine in most recipes. I also make hard cider, and with that, my own vinegar. I freeze blueberries and blackberries, too. I put them directly in freezer bags and into the freezer.

I keep my freezers in my basement, which is very cold in winter, thus reducing the amount of energy I use. If I had a garage, I would keep the freezers there. The tale that putting freezers out in the cold ruins them is a myth; the freezers just don't run all winter.

I also have a root cellar for storing things like celeriac, carrots, and potatoes. It is a simple rectangle made of cement blocks, two high, with an insulated plywood lid. But in very cold times I move the buckets of produce upstairs and store it in a pantry that stays about 45 to 50 degrees; they might freeze otherwise. Winter squash, garlic, and onions I store in a cool upstairs room that stays very dry and around 60 degrees.

I usually have rosemary and sometimes parsley growing in flower pots on windowsills all winter. This winter I forgot to dig up chives, but they do fine inside, too. Most herbs dehydrate well.

So plan your garden with the thought of eating out of it all winter. In this economy, you really can save a lot of money. It will take some investment—a freezer and a dehydrator—and lots of your time on summer evenings. And of course I will never become fully dependent on the garden for my food. But wow, what a treat it is to eat your own food when the snow is falling and the temperature hovers near zero.

Trees with Winter Interest

In winter, trees can really show their character. Without leaves to hide their form, or flowers to distract us, they stand out against the snow, showing off their bark and branching structure. Here are some favorites of a few serious gardeners from around New England (who are also all my friends).

Paperbark maple *(Acer griseum)*. Steve Sweedler, Horticulturist at Plymouth State College in Plymouth, New Hampshire, loves this tree. "It is far and away my favorite for bark and branch structure." He explained that the bark has a rich red-brown color and curls off the trunk, providing texture. "Even the feel of the bark is great," he said. Reliably hardy to minus 20, it suffers occasional winter dieback in Plymouth, but comes back well.

Threadleaf Japanese maple *(A. palmatum dissectum* var. "Crimson Queen"). Sydney Eddison of Newtown, Connecticut, is a garden designer and the author of *The Gardener's Palette* and many other great books. Her favorite Japanese maple is "nearly forty years old, and it is indeed a regal presence at the end of the long perennial border. The outline is low and broadly spreading, and the beautiful angular branches appear at their absolute best trimmed with snow or as both shadow and substance against the snow. Even in an open winter, the complex tracery of limbs and twigs gives us something lovely to look at." Reliably hardy to minus 10, it does well in protected areas farther north.

Horse chestnut *(Aesculus hippocastanum)*. According to Susan Pildner, a garden designer in Stratford, Connecticut, horse chestnuts are great because "they have a gruesome, nightmarish quality, particularly at night. They are lumpy, bumpy, and scary at night. They have a malevolence that I get a kick out of." Though the nuts are not fit for human consumption, the wildlife enjoys them. Hardy to minus 35.

White birch *(Betula papyrifera)*. Betty Smith Mastaler of Weathersfield, Vermont said, "I love this tree because of the play of black and white and texture. It's spare almost in the sense of Japanese haiku. I like the way it bends and bows, and bears the weight of the snow gracefully, with flexible strength." Hardy to minus 50, it is healthiest in northern New England.

American yellowwood *(Cladrastis kentukea)* is the favorite

of two Vermonters, both horticulture professors. Dr. Norman Pellet of UVM (retired) says, "I like the smooth gray bark which is similar to American beech. Yellowwood has a low, wide branching habit and rounded head which stands out against the winter sky and snow." Pamelia Smith, a landscape architect and teacher at Vermont Technical College, seconds his sentiments: "The color of the bark is wonderful in winter, and the living quality of the bark is like skin, complete with folds." Hardy to minus 25, and even more once established.

Red-twig (or Tartarian) dogwood *(Cornus alba)*. My sister, the late Ruth Anne Mitchell, a garden designer, commented that "the landscape in winter is essentially monochromatic, but the red stems of this tree just glow. I love the sight of the bark in a snowstorm. I look at it, and I know there is still warmth in the world." She also pointed out that cutting back a third of the stems to the ground each year will produce brighter colored bark. Hardy to minus 50.

American beech *(Fagus grandifolia)*. Doris LeVarn of Meriden, New Hampshire loves a thirty-plus-year-old American beech on her property. "Mine keeps its leaves in winter, and they shake, rattle, and roll. It has nice sound quality, and of course it has that simple, gray bark." The late Lewis Hill of Greensboro, Vermont (coauthor of the *Flower Gardeners Bible*) agrees, "The dry leaves make an interesting rattle in the wind, and their nuts furnish food for many kinds of wildlife. Its trunk has many limb crotches where collected snow contrasts nicely with its smooth, gray bark." Hardy to minus 35.

Alberta spruce *(Picea glauca* var. *albertiana)*. Denise Larson of Bath, Maine, has six-foot-tall Alberta spruces that line her driveway. "These Teletubby-shaped evergreens, chubby at the bottom, tapering quickly to the top, are wonderful. The deep gray-green color is luxurious to see during the bleakness of February. The slope of the tree allows snow to cling and linger, often creating a nature-made garland of snow." Hardy to minus 50.

Amur chokecherry *(Prunus maackii)*. Garden writer Barbara Damrosch (author of *The Garden Primer*), picked this little known native tree because of its "cinnamon-colored bark" and because it "has a nice shape, is fast growing, and is a healthy tree." She also noted that it's one of the first trees to leaf out in the spring, and one of the last to lose its leaves in the fall. Hardy to minus 50.

American elm *(Ulmus americana)*. Nicole Cormen, of Lebanon, New Hampshire selected this tree for its shape, despite its losing battle against the Dutch elm disease, "That grand vase, open to the sky carries our gaze to the heavens with it," she said. Disease-resistant varieties are now available, including Delaware #2, Liberty, and Washington, though even these may succumb. Hardy to minus 50.

So go outside and look at the trees. Visit an arboretum if you can, or knock on the door at a house with a splendid tree to learn more about it. We can't plant them just now, but we can enjoy them.

Winter Work: Reading About Gardening

I love old books about gardening. Each winter I try to set aside some time to read a few: There is always something to learn, tricks of the trade that have gotten lost over time. I like to climb the stairs to visit Left Bank Books on Main Street in Hanover, New Hampshire to see what oddities might be lurking on the shelves. I found a treasure: *Lois Burpee's Gardener's Companion and Cookbook* (HarperCollins, 1987). It's a gem.

I'm in love with Mrs. Lois Burpee. (Note to Mom: Don't worry, I won't be running off with her. She graduated from Wellesley in 1934, married David Burpee of Burpee Seeds in 1938, and is currently gardening in heaven.) Her delightful book that came out in 1983 is now out of print, but readily available in used bookstores.

Mrs. Burpee's book gives you not only useful information on

how to grow things (plant dill in clumps so the wind won't blow it over), she gives recipes for each of the dozens of vegetables she covers in the book. Other growing tips include these:

Beets: Soak seeds overnight before planting. She also hilled up soil over beets as they grew to keep the tops covered, thus avoiding loss of color and taste.

Broccoli: Mrs. B explains that they are shallow rooted, and suggests planting seedlings deep, covering part of the stem and the first two sets of leaves, but not the uppermost leaves.

Parsnips: Her husband's favorite side dish was candied parsnips, so she grew plenty (see recipe below). In order to get better germination she placed a board over the row of seeds, and kept it in place until they germinated—about two weeks for parsnips. That keeps the soil from drying out, which is fatal for them. She raised the board for a few days to provide shade before removing. I've done that with carrots in dry times.

Swiss chard: She liked to plant three seeds together in a bunch, then kept only the most vigorous when two inches tall. She harvested mature leaves individually with a knife, but always left the outer leaves and innermost leaves "to keep them healthy and growing." Fordhook chard, one of the better varieties available, was named after the farm she and her husband lived on in Pennsylvania for fifty years or more.

Tomatoes: Obviously, she had to promote Burpee brand tomatoes, but I believe her when she said that her two favorites were Burpee's Delicious and Golden Jubilee. I went to Burpee's Web site, and found neither still for sale. But a Google search sent me to R.H. Shumway's where both Golden Jubilee and Delicious seeds are available (www.rhshumway.com or 800-342-9461). Mrs. Burpee describes Golden Jubilee as "a large, beautiful golden-orange fruit with a flavor and texture different from red tomatoes." She adds that "there are times when I just don't want that red tomato color on the dish." I want to try it, in part because Mrs. Burpee has endeared herself to me through her writings—

and I trust her judgment. She must have been a great gardener. (P.S.—I did try it, and it is a nice tomato).

Another vegetable Mrs. Burpee liked—but I'd never even heard of—is celtuce (pronounced "sell-tuce"). Celtuce is an Asian vegetable that tastes much like celery, but has leaves like lettuce. Young leaves are good in a salad, while stalks are an inch thick and can be stir fried. Burpee Seeds no longer sells celtuce, so I Googled it and found a seed company that specializes in Asian vegetables, Kitazawa Seed Company of Oakland, CA (510-595-1188 or www.kitazawaseed.com).

Kitazawa Seed Company is the oldest Asian seed company in America, started in 1917. Aside from the shameful period during WWII when the owners were locked up in an internment camp, it has been in business ever since. If you like Asian foods, check out their Web site or call for a catalog—they have over 250 specialty items.

Since parsnip season is coming up soon—we leave them in the ground all winter, and harvest them early in the spring when the ground thaws—I'm sharing Mrs. Burpee's recipe.

1 pound parsnips
$^3/_4$ cup brown sugar
$^1/_4$ teaspoon nutmeg
$^1/_4$ teaspoon cinnamon
3 tablespoons butter

Boil parsnips in salted water until a fork goes through easily, about forty-five minutes. Drain and remove skin. Cut across into $^3/_4$-inch-thick slices.

Rub an ovenproof dish with butter. Mix sugar and spices, and layer over parsnips.

Cover with aluminum foil, and bake at 375 degrees for 30 minutes. Remove foil, baste the parsnips, and bake uncovered for 15 minutes more, basting twice.

Mrs. Burpee was born in Palestine and lived there as a girl—her father founded a medical mission—which may account for her interest in flavors that were not popular in America in her time. She was also clearly smart, and interested in everything. Her book is a delight: She prepared vegetarian meals, when America's idea of dinner was steak with baked potatoes as the vegetable. She gives recipes for celtuce and green tomato pie and carrot drop cookies. She shares her grandmother's apple dumpling recipe. And her own Borscht Concentrate for the freezer—for use now, when we are longing for fresh vegetables.

So go find a used bookstore and explore. You may not find Mrs. Burpee, but you'll find something worth reading, and we can't work in the garden now anyhow.

Talking Gardening with Ray Magliozzi, the *Car Talk* Guy

Anybody who has listened to National Public Radio's *Car Talk* program knows that Ray Magliozzi is not your average car mechanic. There is his quirky sense of humor, that outrageous laugh, and of course his knowledge of at least a little bit about almost anything. Some days he dispenses advice to the lovelorn, other days he analyzes the cost and benefits of a new transmission, and every week he makes Americans chuckle.

What listeners do not generally know is that Ray Magliozzi is a serious gardener. He lives in a modest ranch house on a large lot tucked away on a back street in a suburb of Boston, where he gardens for the sheer joy of it.

I first met Ray in a public garden in Washington, D.C. We were admiring plants and reading the labels of unusual things. Ray and I struck up a conversation and—after awhile—introductions were made. We talked plants, and went our separate ways. Later, I tracked him down and asked to talk plants some more.

Figuring out what makes a person turn to gardening has always been interesting to me. Ray has not always been a gardener. He grew up in Cambridge, Massachusetts, a "city kid," who knew next to nothing about growing things. The only gardener in his family was his grandmother, who had emigrated from Italy, and grew one much-pampered fig tree and lots of grapes. She had a huge grape press and made wine in the cellar. He figures that gardening is part of his heritage.

It's fun to talk plants with Ray Magliozzi because he has the same enthusiasm and excitement and wonder about growing things that eight-year-old boys have. When Ray and his wife, Monique, bought their first house he cut the grass, but only "grudgingly." He wasn't interested in growing things. But there was a bare spot where the previous owners had placed a swing set. Ray seeded it and watered—and the grass grew. "That hooked me. The fact that you could plant a seed and grow something . . . it's a miracle," he said.

As his children were growing up he didn't have much time for gardening, but one year Ray and his son planted some pumpkin seeds, and then forgot about them. While they were out in the Grand Canyon on a three-week vacation that summer, Ray called his Dad who was looking after the place. "There is something growing in your yard. It's huge. What should I do?" asked his father. Ray couldn't imagine what it was, but said to leave it. They came back to find a pumpkin vine had taken over the yard. "One day a pumpkin was the size of a golf ball, the next day it was a softball. You could hear it grow!"

Ray started getting serious about gardening in his early forties. They bought their current house partly because it had a huge yard, but also because they first saw it when all the rhododendrons were in bloom. It seemed like a little Eden to them.

In his early days of gardening, Ray had a golf course-perfect lawn. Now he is totally organic, partly due to his conviction that a beloved Border collie died after repeated exposure to lawn chemicals. He doesn't have time to deal with the lawn himself anymore, but he found a fellow who uses fish fertilizers and other natural products. "Everything I put on the lawn, you could eat," he explained. Might not be very tasty, and there are a few weeds, but it is no longer dependent on chemicals, which Ray feels is important.

Stepping out his back door, one is greeted by trumpets; Angel's Trumpet, or *Datura*, that is. An eight-foot bed of them. Ray encountered Angel's Trumpets outside a restaurant at the Cape. He liked them, so he got some little seedlings there the following year, but found they didn't transplant well. He persisted. He gathered seeds in March and planted them. "Before I knew it, I had a jungle." Now they reseed every year.

The Angel's Trumpets are typical of how Ray does things: He asks questions, he tries different approaches, he doesn't give up. And when he finally succeeds in growing something, he is pleased as punch. "I love to smell them at night," he said of his Angel's Trumpets with a grin. "I go from one to another like I'm the pollinator."

He planted a Southern magnolia *(Magnolia grandiflora)* eight years ago, which is doing quite well despite being at the northern edge of where they survive. After one tough winter, the tree appeared dead in the spring. It produced no leaves. But Ray does not give up easily, and had a hunch that it was down, but not out. His neighbor encouraged him to remove it, even offering to help. But Ray persisted. To everyone's surprise, the next spring it leafed out, and is doing well.

Ray's yard and gardens are fairly traditional, a lawn surrounded by flower beds and trees. He has executed some nice gentle curves with his flower beds, which are full of perennials.

Roses are one of Ray's pleasures, and he has figured out a way to help his hybrid tea roses survive Boston's winters. He knows that the drying winds are what kill roses most often, so he protects his by spraying them with an antidesiccant late each fall, usually waiting until December.

Ray has also been known to put up plywood barricades near his roses to break the wind in winter. He pointed out that planting stuff is always a "crapshoot," and he doesn't mind buying a few new roses to replace those that have been killed off by the weather.

I asked Ray if there was a common thread between his two passions, working on cars and growing things. Without missing a beat he said, "Dirt. But garden dirt washes off more easily." He laughed. "The reason I love gardening is that I love getting my hands dirty." He paused for a moment, and then added, "When we fix cars, it's not all science. There's an art to it, too." I saw art in Ray's gardens, and although they are not likely to appear on the pages of a glossy garden magazine, they give him great pleasure.

Postscript: I called Ray in September of 2010 to see what happened to his southern magnolia with a troubled past. He reported that he finally cut it down because "it was rather tormented." But he has had great luck with another one that he planted at their vacation home on Cape Cod. His magnolia is a variety called Edith Bogue, which is the hardiest of all Southern magnolias. It's now twenty-five feet tall and the flowers each year are large, beautiful, and fragrant. "The aroma is magnificent," he said. It flowers every day for six weeks in June and July, and sometimes even produces a few bonus blossoms in August, he told me.

What else is Ray growing now? "I've taken to growing a lot of annuals—especially giant dahlias. I love the colors," he said. "It's nice to have something that blooms all summer." Instead of digging the dahlia tubers each fall and replanting them in the spring, he buys new, full-size plants at the nursery each year. He figures that it's better to have someone else do the work of getting them to bloom size so that he can start enjoying them right away. And why not? Our summers are short enough that we deserve as many blooms as we can get.

INDEX